Silent
Heroes

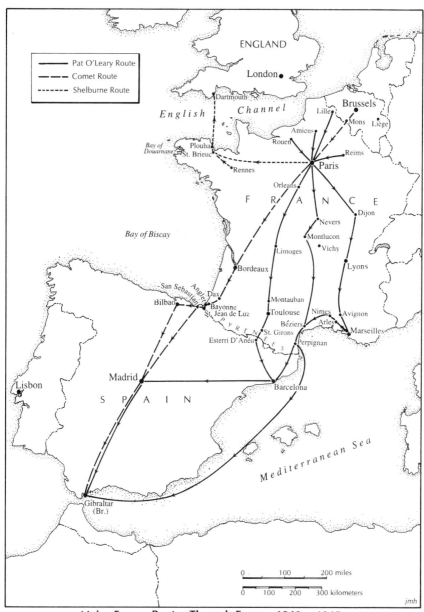

Major Escape Routes Through France, 1940 – 1945

Silent Heroes

Downed Airmen

and the

French Underground

SHERRI GREENE OTTIS

THE UNIVERSITY PRESS OF KENTUCKY

Scholarly publisher for the Commonwealth,
serving Bellarmine University, Berea College, Centre
College of Kentucky, Eastern Kentucky University,
The Filson Club Historical Society, Georgetown College,
Kentucky Historical Society, Kentucky State University,
Morehead State University, Murray State University,
Northern Kentucky University, Transylvania University,
University of Kentucky, University of Louisville,
and Western Kentucky University.
All rights reserved.

Editorial and Sales Offices: The University Press of Kentucky
663 South Limestone Street, Lexington, Kentucky 40508-4008

05 04 03 02 01   5 4 3 2 1

Frontispiece: Major Escape Routes Through France, 1940–1945.
Map designed by John Hollingsworth.

Library of Congress Cataloging-in-Publication Data

Ottis, Sherri Greene, 1964-
   Silent heroes : downed airmen and the French underground /
Sherri Greene Ottis.
      p. cm.
   Includes bibliographical references and index.
   ISBN 0-8131-2186-8 (alk. paper)
   1. Great Britain. MI9—History. 2. World War, 1939-1945—Secret
service—Great Britain. 3. World War, 1939-1945—Underground
movements—France. 4. World War, 1939-1945—Aerial operations,
British. 5. World War, 1939-1945—Aerial operations, American. 6. Air
pilots, Military—Europe. 7. Flight crews—Europe. 8. Excapes—France—
History—20th century. I. Title.
D810.S7 O75 2001
940.54'8641—dc21   00-012278

This book is printed on acid-free recycled paper meeting
the requirements of the American National Standard
for Permanence in Paper for Printed Library Materials.

Manufactured in the United States of America.

For my family,
Steve, Brian, and Catherine,
and my friend
Kirk Ford

Contents

Introduction

With a hurried but sincere expression of gratitude, Royal Air Force crewman John Brown took his leave of Georges Mandet, the Frenchman who had unselfishly extended to him the hospitality of his home and a meal. It was the early morning of July 19, 1944, and though not yet dawn, the day had already been far too long and eventful as far as Brown was concerned. He and his crew had taken off late the night before on a bombing mission to Revigny, a small town in northeastern France. Just after releasing its bomb load, his Lancaster bomber had been shot down by German fighters over the Revigny countryside. Brown did not know the status of his crew, but he had been fortunate enough to fall into the hands of Mandet, who had taken him into his home for a rest and directions. Brown knew he had to resist the temptation to remain in the comfort and relative security of his new surroundings, since German patrols were quite active in the area. Discovery would mean imprisonment for him and harsh retaliation against Mandet and his family. So, guided only by a map that his newfound benefactor had given him, Brown apprehensively set out on foot across the unfamiliar terrain of the French countryside, looking for a small church. On finding the church in Revigny, Brown entered and hid inside, waiting for daybreak, when he hoped to get his bearings from the map he had been given. As he studied the map, he realized that it included Mandet's name and address. Knowing what would happen if he were captured and the map were found in his possession, Brown concealed it beneath the baptismal font in the church and continued on his journey.

Brown was fortunate. He did not fall into German hands, but was able to make his way to the security of his own lines and ultimately back to England. Almost forty years later, in 1981, John Brown returned to France to renew his friendship with Mandet and to retrace the journey that had led him to safety. The trip took him back to the small church where he had rested briefly during that long and harrowing wait for dawn his first night in France. Curious but doubtful, Brown reached beneath the baptismal font. He was truly amazed when his fingers encountered the brittle and crumbling edges of the map. Later, in the midst of a joyous reunion, Brown was able to return the fragile document to its original owner. His journey was at last complete.[1]

Brown's determination to thank and to cherish the friendship of the family that placed themselves in danger to assist him is very typical. In the course of collecting information for this study, I have yet to encounter an airman who has not expressed great admiration for and appreciation of those in France who were willing to risk everything to help the airmen escape and return home. Although it is impossible to separate the stories of those in France who became known as "helpers" from those they helped, the focus of this work will be on the former. Their acts of quiet and unassuming courage were common throughout all of occupied France during the war, but for the many Allied airmen who escaped capture or perhaps worse at the hands of the Germans, these acts were never common and never forgotten.

John Brown was one of tens of thousands of Allied airmen shot down over Europe during World War II who received help from ordinary civilians in various countries, particularly Belgium, the Netherlands, and France. The work of these good Samaritans is not well known. In fact, when one thinks about France during the Second World War, the images that inevitably come to mind are those of the miraculous evacuation of Dunkirk in late May and early June of 1940, and of Allied forces storming ashore on the beaches of Normandy on June 6, 1944. Yet, during the four years that passed between these two events, many people in France waged a war of resistance in varying degrees against the Nazi occupiers and their Vichy collaborators. Some took up weapons and joined armed Resistance groups, while others engaged in more subtle forms of opposition. This book examines the efforts of those who struck back at the enemy by aiding the evasion and escape of Allied airmen who had been shot down over their country. With the creation of elaborate escape lines, organized in a fashion similar to that of the American Civil War's Underground Railroad, people—mostly civilians—rescued almost six thousand downed airmen by clever ingenuity and a willingness to sacrifice whatever they had, including their lives, to facilitate the men's escapes.

Allied intelligence services, which supported these escape efforts, distinguished between escapers and evaders. Escapers were men who had been in enemy hands—even if only for a few seconds—and had managed to free themselves, while evaders had never been in enemy hands and were attempting to avoid capture. Obviously, the courage, tenacity, and resourcefulness of the airmen themselves is part of this story, as is the work of the various Allied intelligence agencies that sought to facilitate the operations of the numerous escape lines that developed in France during the war. While all Resistance organizations required secrecy to protect their work and the people involved with carrying it out, the escape lines had an added element of danger due to the emotional attachments that developed between the helpers and evaders. All intelligence organizations struggled to protect themselves from penetration, and this problem was more difficult to overcome within the escape lines than in other areas of resistance. Those who directed the escape networks or worked in them knew that they could at any time fall victim to penetration operations conducted by German military intelligence, a turncoat within the network, or a simple human mistake. All of these possibilities became realities, producing devastating results for those involved in assisting both escapers and evaders.

This study focuses primarily on those in France who became known as helpers because of the assistance they gave to aid the evasion, and ultimately the evacuation, of allied personnel. Some became helpers by actively seeking participation in the escape lines; others did so when they unexpectedly found themselves confronted by a terrified young man whose eyes appealed for mercy. Regardless of their motivation, these men and women put their lives—as well as the lives of their families—at great risk. The fact that the helpers were willing to make such sacrifices to aid the airmen served to create bonds of friendship that have endured for more than fifty years.

In 1979, Keith Sutor, an American airman who had been shot down over France in 1944, returned to that country for a visit and was reunited with one of the helpers who had aided his escape more than thirty years earlier. Together they retraced the path to the evacuation site near the village of Plouha on the northwestern coast of France—a site known

during the war, and since then, as Bonaparte Beach. Several historic markers had been erected to commemorate the events that took place there
during the war. While reminiscing about those events, Sutor and his companion were approached by a young couple who asked if they could tell
them the meaning of the markers. The young couple were fortunate to
have had all their questions answered. Still, I cannot help wondering how
many others may have made their way to that spot or others like it with
a similar question without receiving an answer. The events described in
this study may one day serve to answer the questions of those who, like
the young couple at Bonaparte Beach, have the interest and curiosity to
ask, "What happened here?" More importantly, though, this book is meant
to be a tribute to the silent heroes who know.

The creation of this book has been one of my most rewarding un-
dertakings, in that it has enabled me to present this story of courage and
sacrifice to a new generation of students of the Second World War. To
those helpers and evaders who expressed their pleasure and honor that I
chose to write their history, I want them to know that the pleasure and
honor were indeed all mine.

1

Science Fiction
or Military Strategy

The Activities of MI9 and MIS-X

Against the noisy backdrop of an Italian air raid, Donald Darling, a member of British military intelligence stationed in Gibraltar and connected to Room 900, listened in silence as Frenchman André Postel-Vinay recounted his treatment at the hands of his German captors, an experience Darling had never expected him to survive. Postel-Vinay, a member of the Pat O'Leary escape line in France, had been arrested for his efforts to help downed Allied airmen and servicemen evade capture by the Germans. A series of almost miraculous events, including capture, interrogation, a nearly fatal suicide attempt, and his meeting a sympathetic German doctor, had led to his arrival at Darling's Gibraltar office in September 1942.[1]

It was the responsibility of Room 900, the executive branch of MI9, to organize and support such lines and to protect those who worked on them to the best of their ability. "To the best of their ability" was, to say the least, a frustrating position for the intelligence service, since Room 900 was headquartered in free England and the lines' activities took place in German-occupied northwestern Europe.

Escape and evasion took on a new meaning during World War II, but it by no means originated there. There have been many escapes and evasions throughout the course of history, one of the first and most well-known cases being that recorded in the Bible when Joseph took Mary and the child Jesus and escaped into Egypt. Historian M.R.D. Foot and former escaper James Langley suggest that perhaps Saint Joseph might be considered the patron saint of escapers. Other famous escapers and evaders include Louis XVI and Marie Antoinette, who attempted to avoid the violence of the French Revolution, and, not long afterward, Napoleon, who escaped from the island of Elba and returned to wreak havoc in Europe before his final defeat at the Battle of Waterloo.[2]

The escapes that were most fresh in the minds of the British people in 1940, however, were those of Allied servicemen, enacted with the help of a British nurse by the name of Edith Cavell in Brussels, Belgium, during World War I. Unfortunately, these same escapes were also fresh in the minds of British military intelligence services, and unpleasant memories associated with them had left a bitter taste in their mouths that would make things difficult for the evasion intelligence service, MI9, yet to be formed. Cavell had been employed by MI6, the intelligence service that focused on intelligence gathering, and when she was caught helping Allied servicemen escape, the Germans executed her. MI6 allowed this experience to color more than their view of escape and evasion as a form of intelligence. It prejudiced them against the use of women as intelligence agents in any manner.[3] Claude Dansey, assistant chief of MI6 and very powerful in the intelligence arena, was particularly opposed to women working in intelligence, claiming they were untrustworthy.[4] And yet, as the evasion networks developed throughout the course of the war, women proved repeatedly that they could function as intelligence agents and endure the physical, mental, and emotional demands of the job.

Escape and evasion was first studied as a separate intelligence service by two men, each associated with unrelated branches of the British War Office. A.R. Rawlinson, an intelligence officer in World War I, had had some experience in repatriating POWs, as well as in supporting escape efforts. During the interwar period he spent his time studying escape and evasion as a form of guerrilla warfare. But it was J.C.F. Holland who first addressed the need for an organization to assist escapers by providing them with escape aides of various kinds. He suggested that forcing the enemy to deal with escapers would divert valuable manpower from more productive areas of the enemy's war effort.[5]

Although the Joint Intelligence Committee (JIC) approved Holland's suggestions, some controversy arose over which military service should control the new organization. The Air Ministry favored a new organization to take care of all three military branches—army, navy, and air force—while Director of Military Intelligence Major General Beaumont-Nesbitt felt the Royal Air Force (RAF) should have its own organization. In the end, all three military branches were placed together in a separate agency. The Air Ministry later regretted this when it became obvious that most of the evaders were airmen shot down on bombing missions. It tried hard at that time to reverse the ruling, but was unsuccessful.[6]

Initially there was some question as to who should lead the new organization, MI9. JIC felt that an escaper from World War I should have the position since he had experience in the very activity the agency was to promote. But Holland argued that World War I evaders would be biased by experiences they had had that might interfere with their ability to do their job. Holland's argument won the day, and MI9 was officially created December 23, 1939, and placed under the leadership of Maj. Norman R. Crockatt (later Brigadier General). Crockatt was chosen on the merits of leadership, organization, quickness, and the ability to appreciate the antagonism that might arise between escaper/evaders and members of the staff of MI9. He gave Rawlinson a position within his staff and placed him in charge of the section dealing with German POWs. This department later became a separate division called MI19, but it remained under Crockatt.[7]

Though MI6 agreed to the formation of MI9, it was not compassion that influenced its cooperation. In fact, Dansey thought an escape organization was completely useless and a waste of good agents.[8] His willingness to cooperate was, rather, a fear that yet another independent intelligence agency like the recently created Special Operations Executive (SOE) might spring into being, further hindering the work of MI6. SOE had as its purpose the sabotage of Germany's war effort and as an organization was greatly resented by MI6.[9]

Regardless of the reason MI6 agreed to support MI9, Crockatt had little choice but to accept the agency's assistance.[10] Dansey suggested to Crockatt that MI6 help with agent recruitment, and not being in a position to get MI9 off the ground on its own at the time, Crockatt accepted his offer. As a result, Donald Darling, an MI6 agent, was attached to MI9 and proved to be a valuable asset to the agency.[11]

Dansey approached Darling in July 1940, asking him to go to Portugal and Spain, which were neutral, to reestablish communications between England and France for MI6, and to assist MI9 by setting up an escape line between France and Spain. Dansey later relieved him of the communication work, freeing him to focus on the escape lines—a position for which Darling was well qualified. He had a good knowledge of both French and Spanish and was familiar with both countries, having lived in each.[12]

Dansey's willingness to support MI9 did not go so far as embracing it as one of the "true" intelligence services. Military intelligence distinguished between espionage and sabotage activities and work on the escape lines. Escape organizations were considered humanitarian work. Dansey was often annoyed with the overlap that occurred within his intelligence services, but it was hard for an agent to resist aiding an airman trying to escape, particularly if it was one's own countryman.[13]

Crockatt later recruited two additional members to the MI9 team, James Langley and Airey Neave, both of whom played prominent roles in the operation of the escape lines. Both of these agents had the advantage of having been "in the field," as Neave called it.[14] Their experiences as escapers enabled them to better appreciate the problems associated with escaping as well as the risks taken by those who helped. Langley, a member of the Coldstream Guards, had been wounded in the arm and head. Transported by ambulance to the water's edge at Dunkirk, he was left behind because he could not get up from the stretcher on which he lay. The orders for the transporters had been that only those men who could sit or stand could be evacuated, and Langley could do neither. Four healthier men could sit in the place that his stretcher would have occupied.[15] This was probably quite difficult for Langley to accept at the time, but his experiences as an escaper over the next few weeks played an important role in his work throughout the rest of the war.

Langley's arm had been amputated and was still festering when, in October 1940, he escaped from a hospital in Lille and made his way into unoccupied France. On reaching the port city of Marseilles, he had to wait on the formation of a medical repatriation board, and it was only a matter of time before he met people such as Ian Garrow, Donald Caskie, and Louis Nouveau, who were taking early steps toward establishing an escape line.

In February 1941, the medical repatriation board, made up of French and German doctors, classified Langley unfit for military duty. When he subsequently returned to England, Dansey approached him about working with MI9 as a liaison between that agency and MI6. Dansey impressed upon the newly returned escapee that the men who had been left behind at Dunkirk and the new problem of downed airmen evading capture complicated matters for his intelligence agents in France. He suggested that Langley help resolve this problem by finding a way for the men to get out without interfering with the work of Dansey's agents. Langley agreed, and Dansey turned him over to Crockatt, who gave him an office on the second floor of the War Office. The small size of the room made it quite clear that Crockatt was not exaggerating when he said, "Evaders and escapers in the occupied countries are as yet very small beer."[16] It seems ironic that Langley was considered unfit for military duty and yet took a position in a military agency that over the course of the war facilitated the return of about five to six thousand downed Allied airmen. Perhaps the Germans would have rethought their definition of unfit had they been able to foresee the aggravation Langley would help cause.

Airey Neave also experienced escape and evasion firsthand before taking his position with MI9. He had been wounded at Calais in May 1940 and transported to a French hospital, from which he was eventually transferred to a POW camp in Germany. The Germans transferred Neave a second time in May 1941, after he tried to escape, hoping to quell his efforts by making conditions more difficult. They moved him to Colditz, a POW camp just southeast of Leipzig that had been created from a huge fortress and reserved for what the Germans referred to as "problem escapers." The Germans thought the protective walls of Colditz were impenetrable, but by placing all of the persistent escapers together in one camp, they almost guaranteed that someone would succeed. The determined escapers put their minds together and formed one escape plan after another. It was determined that up to the time of the Allied invasion half of the British officers who made successful escapes came from Colditz. Neave was the first. He escaped on a snowy night in January 1942 dressed as a German officer and arrived in neutral Switzerland just over three days later.[17]

By way of France, Neave evacuated to England by the Pat O'Leary line, an escape network formed from the small group of people Langley had met while waiting in Marseilles for repatriation. Within days of returning to England, Neave was recruited by Crockatt to work with Langley in the second-floor rooms of the War Office.

Early in his MI9 career, Neave received a briefing by a man he referred to as their chief at the War Office and whose description and conversation sound strongly like Dansey. The practiced intelligence agent stressed what was by then known to MI9 as the favorite War Office example of Edith Cavell. As Neave listened, he became aware of the negative attitude with which the escape lines were viewed. The War Office saw them only as a threat to other *more important* intelligence agencies. Neave found this view disheartening and wrote, "When one has been in the field with the workers of the escape lines, it is difficult to be anything less than enthusiastic about providing aid for them."[18]

It was from this low position on the intelligence totem pole that Langley and Neave began working together supporting the escape lines. Langley was assigned the code name "P15," though his agents knew him affectionately as "Jimmy," and Neave took the name "Saturday." Between the two of them, they squeezed a desk, table, and two large file cabinets into their office and began their careers as MI9 agents. Jimmy and Saturday, and their four walls, were the executive office of MI9, charged with the operation of the escape lines throughout northwestern Europe, including France, Belgium, and the Netherlands. Their mailing address was c/o Box 900, War Office, and from this came the name by which their office was known, Room 900.[19]

After December 1941 and the bombing of Pearl Harbor, British and American military agencies began working together. Under the circumstances, England was delighted to have a new ally in her fight against Hitler and welcomed the greater American contribution that would be forthcoming now that the United States was in the war. It took time, however, for the American people to mobilize industrially for the war effort, and it was February 1942 before U.S. Maj. Gen. Carl Spaatz went to England to make arrangements for the U.S. Eighth Army Air Force to transfer its headquarters there. He met with Crockatt, who briefed Spaatz on the efforts of MI9 to help POWs escape as well as to aid downed airmen in evading capture. Amazed at what the agency had been able to do, Spaatz requested that a member of British military intelligence travel to the United States to explain the agency to the American General Staff. He also asked that an American be attached to MI9 so that he could learn how to provide similar services for American airmen.[20]

The kind of work done by MI9 appealed to Spaatz's staff officer Robley Winfrey, a former civil engineer who was sent to Crockatt for training. MI9 had by this time created numerous imaginative means of smuggling escape aids into prisoner-of-war camps and had developed special aids for aircrews in case they found themselves in the position of having to evade capture. Winfrey remembered that he was "elated to participate in such shenanigans upon a foreign government."[21]

Unfortunately, convincing the U.S. General Staff was not an easy task. Even after reviewing the work and results of MI9, U.S. Secretary of War Henry Stimson remained unimpressed, his opinion of the matter being not so very different from Dansey's. He could not fathom the idea that such an agency could possibly be successful. The whole concept, so far as he was concerned, seemed "more appropriate to the art of science fiction than the science of military strategy."[22] Stimson's determination forced Spaatz to enlist the help of Chief of Staff George C. Marshall and Dwight Eisenhower's Chief of Intelligence, Maj. Gen. George V. Strong, to finally persuade the Secretary of War of the effort's merit.

It was some time before the American equivalent to MI9 became active. The first Eighth Air Force squadrons transferred to England in May 1942, and in August of the same year Americans began operating independently of the RAF, increasing the Allied assault against the Germans by carrying out daytime operations, while the RAF continued its night missions.[23] Not until October 1942 was the American escape agency, MIS-X, officially created under the command of POW Branch commander Catesby Jones. He assigned Lt. Col. W. Stull Holt to England's MI9 to serve as a liaison between the American and British agencies, while Winfrey, recalled to the States, put into practice the techniques he had learned from MI9's agents. He headed the MIS-X operations at Fort Hunt under the direct leadership of Col. J. Edward Johnston.[24]

Like MI9, the MIS-X headquarters was top secret and given a number designation in order to make it less conspicuous. Located about twenty miles south of Washington, D.C., at Fort Hunt, MIS-X was housed in a World War I coastal artillery bunker in Alexandria, Virginia. Its post office box address was 1142, and it was this number by which it was known.[25]

From the beginning, the relationship between MI9 and MIS-X was amicable. When the Americans entered the war, they were determined to set up their own organizations equal to those already in action under the British agencies. As a result, many of the mistakes the British agencies had made early on were repeated by the American intelligence services. This was not the case with MI9 and its American counterpart, MIS-X. Where escape and evasion were concerned, the Americans gladly joined into an already successfully functioning organization. Though British intelligence had done the initial groundwork and organization, the Americans proved to be every bit as imaginative and hardworking as their British partners. Langley wrote that the Americans were extremely helpful with regard to providing material needs. MI9 agents liked to use .32 Colt automatics, which were difficult to find in England, so an American liaison agent agreed to get some from the United States. Within a month he delivered twenty of them into Langley's hands, with a promise for up to three hundred more, if needed. Thrilled with this windfall, Langley asked how the agent had managed such a feat. The agent nonchalantly replied that he had sent a cable to the U.S. War Department requesting that the mayor of Chicago make an appeal to the city's gangsters, asking them to help with the war effort.[26]

Crockatt met with Strong, Jones, and Johnston in early 1943, at which time they decided that they would geographically divide the world so that each agency had a sphere in which it was the leader, while acting as a second in the other sphere.[27] Great Britain's sphere included Europe, North Africa, the Middle East, India, and Burma, while the American sphere contained North and South Americas, the Pacific, and China. Even so, the two agencies continued to work well together in both spheres, often assigning equally ranked officers from each agency to work cooperatively together. Langley recalled that the main sources of strife between the British and American agents had to do with the Americans' higher rate of pay and their habit of starting the day earlier and so wanting to have their meals earlier. Langley and his American co-commander, Col. Richard Nelson, finally had to agree to separate mealtimes for the two groups.[28]

The cordial relationship between MI9 and MIS-X extended beyond the agents' abilities to work together, to include the goals that were set by each organization. At its creation, MI9 developed a series of objectives by which it planned to carry out its work with the escape lines. These objectives included facilitating the escape of POWs and their return to England, collecting information from the escapers and exchanging it with the appropriate agencies, and serving as a means of moral support to those still held in POW camps.

It was not long before MI9 realized its error in concentrating so heavily on escape to the exclusion of evasion. Aircrews were being shot down on a regular basis and were trying to evade capture by the Germans rather than trying to escape from them after having been captured. After discovering the omission, MI9 changed course in the flexible manner that Crockatt maintained for his agency, keeping the escape instruction, but including evasion training as well.[29] MIS-X incorporated these changes into its list of objectives from the beginning. Along with the goals first established by MI9, MIS-X added instruction for aircrews on how to evade capture and provided escape aids to assist them along the way.[30] In effect, MI9 and MIS-X were concerned with four main principles: they worked to give assistance to escapers trying to free themselves from enemy hands by (1) providing them with escape aids; (2) training would-be evaders and escapers; (3) creating and supporting escape lines on which both of these could travel; and (4) accessing intelligence from those being held in POW camps.

One of the important tasks of the evasion intelligence agencies, both British and American, was providing escape aids for the aircrews who went on bombing operations over occupied Europe. C. Clayton Hutton was one of MI9's original team of workers and is best remembered for the amazing variety of escape aids he developed. Though he had some ingenious creations, he also had a knack for getting into trouble, often as a result of his efforts to get materials for his inventions. Foot and Langley wrote that at one time or another Hutton was in trouble with "all three services, MI5, MI6, Scotland Yard, the Customs authorities, the Bank of England, the ministries of food and production, and several local police forces."[31] In an effort to defend Hutton's propensity for trouble and retain one of his most creative workers, Crockatt wrote a letter to an army provost marshal that said, "This officer is eccentric. He cannot be expected to comply with ordinary service discipline, but he is far too valuable for his services to be lost to this department."[32] Hutton truly was an invaluable member of the MI9 team. He asked the British Museum to track down and purchase actual World War I escape stories from secondhand bookshops, then used them to determine what aids would be most useful to escapers and evaders. From these he developed silk maps, which were used by aircrew members to determine their locations after bailing out of their airplanes. By using fabric he eliminated the problems associated with a map being folded and unfolded too many times. Another advantage was that in the event the airmen landed in water or were forced to spend time in the elements, the fabric dried to its original state, unlike paper maps, which tended to disintegrate. Compasses were important, and with the help of an English firm that specialized in precise instruments he created compasses in a variety of forms and sizes.[33]

Though he was responsible for the creation of many helpful aids, the escape kit is the one for which Hutton is best known. The escape kit was a rectangular box with enough provisions for a man to survive two to three days on his own.[34] The men were instructed to carry the box throughout every mission and, more specifically, to carry it inside their flying suits, where their parachute harnesses could hold it in place. About eighty percent of all evaders used their escape kits in one way or another, either for themselves or to repay a civilian for his help. Many an evader had reason to regret the loss of his kit when he set it on a seat in the plane and left it behind or put it into an unfastened pocket on his flying suit and lost it on bailing out.[35] This happened to Wesley Coss, an airman with the USAAF, who left his escape kit on the plane and wished later that he had been more conscientious about keeping up with it. He landed in an area where there were no farms in sight and, having alternately walked and run to put distance between himself and his landing site, became very thirsty. He thought often about the water bag and purifying tablets in his escape kit and how much help they would have been.[36] An amusing example of an airman who realized his mistake before he hit the ground is that of Roland Barlow (USAAF) who, watching his escape kit tumble toward the earth, made a mental note to button his flight suit pockets the next time.[37]

Besides the water bag and Halazone tablets for purifying the water, the kit had a number of other items that were useful to a man on the run. It contained a tube of condensed milk or candy bars, which provided energy, as did the Horlicks malted milk tablets also included. Benzadrine tablets in the kits helped combat fatigue. In many cases the men had been up since before dawn preparing for their mission, and these tablets counteracted the shock and exhaustion that resulted from the combination of a long waking period and the experience of being shot down in enemy territory. Instructed to take no more than one at a time, since the drug could have a stronger effect on some than on others, some men claimed it had no effect at all. Others, such as USAAF copilot David Turner, said it made him so alert that he kept hearing imaginary dogs barking after him.[38] Other practical supplies in the kit included matches, a sewing kit and adhesive tape—both useful for mending clothes torn while bailing out—and chewing gum for promoting the production of saliva. A compass, included in every kit, enabled the evaders to keep up with the direction in which they traveled.[39] Other items sometimes included in

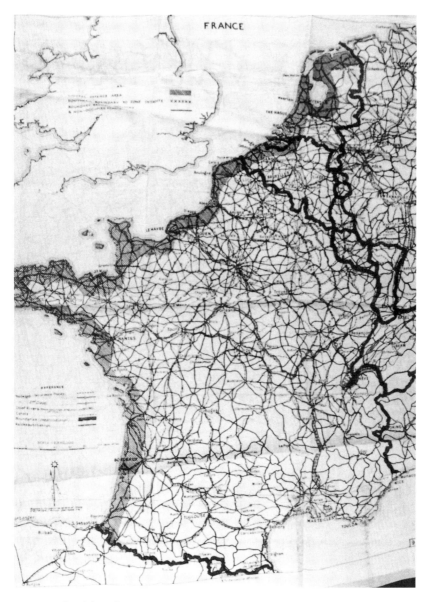

An example of the silk maps issued to airmen in their escape kits. This particular map was given to Burgundy guide Georges Guillemin by one of the evaders he assisted.

the kit were fishing line and a hook or a razor and soap, since European men were usually clean-shaven.

One escape aid issued to the men going on bombing operations proved especially useful, the language phrase card. The card helped the airmen communicate with civilians they encountered on the ground by providing English, French, Dutch, and German translations for numbers to twenty by ones, and then through one hundred by tens. Also included on the card were the days of the week and a series of phrases that could be used to request aid in the form of civilian clothes, food, shelter, directions, or railroad tickets. Identification phrases were given so that a man could tell the helpers that he was an airman of a specific nationality. Most of the American, English, and Australian airmen had no understanding of the French language, but some of the Canadian airmen spoke it well. Though pronunciation remained a challenge, when all else failed, an evader could hand the card to his helper and point to the phrase he wanted to say. While some historians have claimed that few evaders used the language card, many of the flyers have said it was one of their most useful items.[40]

Another escape aid used by many of the airmen was the escape purse, which carried currency of the occupied countries over which the airmen were assigned to fly. On the morning of the operation (or night if one was part of a RAF aircrew), each member of the aircrew was issued his escape kit and purse. The purses were color-coded depending on the country the crew would be flying over. Red purses contained 2,000 French francs, while yellow purses held 1,000 French francs, 350 Belgian francs, and 20 Dutch guilders. In addition to the money, each purse also had a silk map and a compass. The money was especially useful for purchasing food and railroad tickets.[41] Roland Barlow, a young gunner from Mississippi who served aboard a B-24 bomber, had volunteered for the Army Air Force in 1942, thinking it would be better to sign up for the service that most appealed to him than to be drafted into the infantry. He developed a method of making purchases that he thought would prevent anyone from knowing that he had no idea how to use the foreign currency in his pockets. He wrote, "Regardless of what I was buying, I simply gave the largest denomination bill I had. Usually that was satisfactory, and I received some change back."[42]

The money was often used to pay helpers for food they provided to the evaders, though many helpers refused such payment. Sometimes

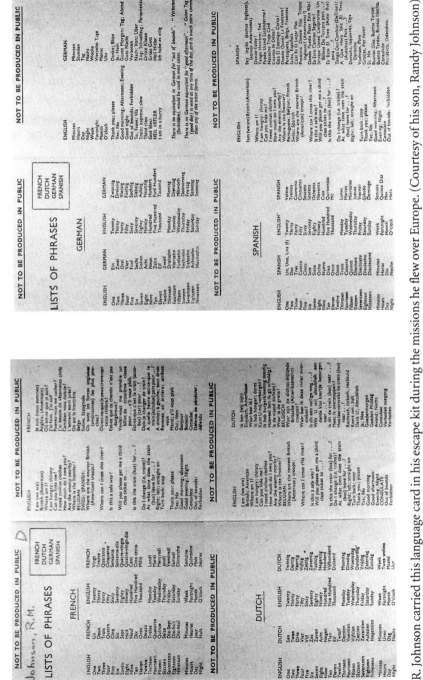

R. Johnson carried this language card in his escape kit during the missions he flew over Europe. (Courtesy of his son, Randy Johnson)

money was the only means of thanking helpers for aid they were not aware they had given. John McGlynn was a pilot for the USAAF 7th Photography Reconnaissance Group who landed in a town when he bailed out of his plane. After walking several blocks, he entered an open cellar door. Upon finding two bottles of wine inside, he took one and climbed to the top storage shelf to hide while he watched for German patrols. McGlynn stated, "The wine steadied my nerves. I lay there holding the bottle like a club for anyone who walked in."[43] When he left, McGlynn poured the remainder of the wine into the water bottle from his escape kit and put two hundred francs into the empty wine bottle to repay the owner.

Though the escape kit and purse were the most popular of the escape aids developed for evaders, others also proved useful. The RAF issued to some of its airmen a pair of flying boots that could be cut down to serve as a pair of shoes. It was important that the men had good, sturdy shoes if they were shot down, because evasion usually entailed a great deal of walking. Ken Skidmore, engineer on a RAF Halifax bomber, was wearing a pair of these boots when he was shot down on November 11, 1943. Within the collar of the boot was a penknife, which he used to cut off the top part of the boot, leaving himself with sturdy walking shoes. He used the fur-lined tops of the boots to wrap around his chest and back for added warmth in the cool fall air.[44] John Brown was another RAF evader who was able to make use of the shoes he had left after cutting away the boot portion. Brown wrote that he took his "flying boots" home and used them as work shoes for years after the war was over.[45]

Adding to the gathered escape stories from World War I, the escapers and evaders of World War II soon began arriving home with suggestions of their own. In conversations with the staffs of MI9 and MIS-X, the airmen told which aids were most useful and which needed to be changed or adjusted. However, interviews with the evaders were useful for more than just identifying the best escape aids. Each airman who returned to neutral or free territory was interrogated so that the agencies could find out as much as possible about the men's experiences and the conditions in the occupied territories. In this way, agents like Langley and Neave could also keep up with the status of the escape lines they were responsible for sustaining. Barney Rawlings, a B-17 copilot, commented on the number of times he was questioned about his experience as an evader, parodying a well-known speech of Winston Churchill's,

"Never before in the history of human conflict had so many debriefed, so often, so few who knew so little."[46]

Evaders arriving in neutral territory were debriefed by military intelligence and then returned to England, where they were debriefed again. A repatriated airman was first assigned an Escape and Evasion number (E and E) and asked a number of questions aimed at acquiring pertinent information with regard to his personal statistics and service record. The E and E number was an identification number assigned to repatriated airmen in the order in which they returned to England. The airman listed the members of his crew, the events surrounding the plane's destruction, and any information he might have concerning the current condition or whereabouts of the other crew members. A series of appendices was then attached to the report, each designed to give information relating to certain specific areas of the evader's experience.[47]

Appendix B was of great interest to those departments that determined which areas should be targeted for bombing. It contained military information the evader may have seen or about which he was told by the people who helped him. Local civilians often had extensive information concerning the locations of ammunition dumps, airfields, factories, troop encampments, or, equally important, reports regarding the morale of the civilians or enemy troops stationed in the areas in which the evader had traveled. Copies of Appendix B were sent by MI9 and MIS-X to those agencies that could best determine what should be done with the information.[48]

Appendices C and D, the attachments most useful to MI9 and MIS-X, were quite detailed, depending on how long an airman may have stayed with a given helper. Appendix C included descriptions of the helpers, such as name or pseudonym, age, appearance, occupation, family situation, location, and kind of home in which they lived. Military intelligence provided interrogators with guide sheets to assist them in prompting the airmen about certain kinds of information. The questions were geared toward learning the best areas for getting in contact with the Resistance, hiding places for evaders, travel conditions—in essence, anything that might help the agents learn as much as possible about the areas and people who associated themselves with escape and evasion.[49]

The detailed information contained in Appendix C served a number of purposes. Darling, the interrogator for MI9 in Gibraltar, was able to make mental notes of people and places as he questioned evader after evader. He became familiar with the helpers' families, pets, homes, furnishings, gardens, and other bits of knowledge that were valuable for identification purposes. In some cases, he claimed he could tell an evader where he had been by a description of the skyline outside the window of the evader's hiding place.

Darling also became familiar with the pseudonyms used by the helpers, which was useful in determining the escape line down which the evader had traveled. He kept up with who worked for which lines, which helpers were new to the networks, rendezvous points for the various lines, and even which helpers might actually be German infiltrators sent in to penetrate the escape lines. All of this caused Darling a number of sleepless nights, particularly when he realized that two different lines were using the same Paris rendezvous points, but each without the other's knowledge.[50]

The "C" reports were also valuable at the end of the war when the evasion intelligence agencies tried to help the civilians in the formerly occupied countries. After the war, there were severe shortages of clothes, food, and money, and the agencies tried to relieve the suffering of those who had risked so much by helping the evaders. The E and E reports identified the helpers and often authenticated their stories about the airmen who had stayed with them or to whom they had given some form of assistance. In some cases, helpers did not appear on the E and E reports for various reasons. Either they had maintained such good security that no evader was ever able to identify them properly, or they had been in the position of offering incidental help and so were not acknowledged in the report. In these instances, the U.S. War Department sent letters to the former American evaders asking them for more detailed information about their helpers.[51]

Appendix C held great importance with regard to studying the possible infiltration of traitors into the lines or unusual circumstances involving arrests of large numbers of airmen. In January 1944, a betrayal in the Liberation Vengeance escape line resulted in the arrests of two airmen and several helpers, one of whom was executed when he tried to escape. By studying the E and E reports of those airmen aided by Liberation Vengeance, MIS-X made deductions concerning where responsibility lay for the betrayal. In so doing, they could determine means of avoiding a similar betrayal in the future.[52]

The last attachment in the E and E reports was Appendix D, a questionnaire pertaining to the usefulness of the escape aids. Often these questionnaires were filled out by the airmen themselves rather than by the agent conducting the interrogation. On seeing his full report for the first time in 1997, David Turner recognized his handwriting but did not remember filling out the form.[53] The form helped the agents determine whether the escape kit and purse were used, and if not, why not. It also helped intelligence agents determine which items were the most or least useful and allowed the airmen to comment on the usefulness of evasion lectures they had received prior to their evasion experiences.[54] Two USAAF evaders, George Jasman and Hobart C. Trigg, made important comments concerning the American slang word "yeah." Both suggested that American evaders should avoid using the word because it sounded too much like the German word "Ja."[55]

Probably the most important use of the E and E reports during the war was in teaching other airmen how to evade capture should they be shot down. Instructors used the reports to pinpoint errors in airmen's evasions which future evaders could possibly avoid repeating. Because they had the documents to look at, those giving the lectures could use actual experiences to illustrate lessons they wanted the airmen to learn and remember.

The lectures taught the potential evaders how to conduct themselves in enemy-occupied territory, told them what they should look for, and helped them to understand how they should handle some of the varied situations in which they might find themselves. The lectures were initially given by agents of MI9 and MIS-X who had studied evasion, though as the war continued and men began successfully evading and returning to England, these repatriated airmen often replaced the agents, since they had firsthand experience.

Intelligence agencies taught the men in the Allied forces that it was their duty to evade capture or escape from German hands if they were caught.[56] These instructions were not lost on the Germans, who were in fact well aware of the efforts that the Allied intelligence services put into getting their aircrews back safely. During the war, the Germans developed a pamphlet entitled "Means of Escape of the Anglo-American Flying Personnel." Based on material and information they collected from airmen they captured, they pieced together a large amount of information about Allied escape and evasion and put it together for distribution to relevant agencies. The copy that exists in the National Archives belonged to the Office of Strategic Services (OSS) in London and was valuable for counterintelligence purposes on the part of the Allies. The Germans wrote in the booklet that the 305th Squadron had made it the duty of their men to escape, translating the order as "Every member of the United States' army is obliged to avoid capture by the enemy, or if captured he must escape. The same applies to members of the RAF."[57] The German writer went on to note, "It is supposed that the enemy works hard to produce constantly new means for flight and new ways of hiding them [the aircrew]."[58] The OSS agent assigned to study the German booklet apparently maintained his sense of humor as he read through the information the Germans had gleaned about escape and evasion. He underlined the phrase "the enemy works hard" and wrote in the margin "and how?"[59]

The lecturers were extremely thorough about explaining to the flyers the things they might encounter on landing in enemy-occupied Europe. They were also quite clear on what the men would probably experience if they were captured. One instructor told the men that the only weapons they would have to depend on were "what brains the good Lord gave you and what guts you can dig up from time to time. You'll need plenty of both, and there is no substitute for either one."[60]

In some cases, however, the airmen had other means of assistance. In the event that they were injured and unable to drum up reserves in brains and guts, many of them were fortunate enough to find an alternative. It was this alternative aid, the helpers and the escape lines, that Langley and Neave spent so much time and effort nurturing. The escape lines of northwestern Europe, established and/or supported by MI9 and MIS-X throughout the war, can legitimately claim responsibility for rescuing about two to three thousand British and Commonwealth airmen and three thousand American airmen.[61] Though it would appear that the lines and the airmen were dependent on the evasion intelligence agencies to carry out their work, in fact, the people who dedicated themselves to working on the escape lines carried a great deal of the responsibility for the lines' success. In addition, the airmen played a large role in the continued existence and work of the escape lines. Both airmen and helpers were responsible to, and dependent on, the other to keep the escape organizations running smoothly. Their efforts allowed the lines to function like a great mechanized engine, enabling the Allies to carry on with the war effort and permitting the people of the occupied countries to contribute what they could to the Allied effort so that they might reclaim their countries for themselves.

2

It Was Raining Aviators

The Evaders

All the effort put into rescuing downed Allied airmen carried with it the understanding that they were a valuable part of the fighting forces. Though escape lines initially evacuated any servicemen, the Air Ministry soon requested that airmen be given priority.[1] Donald Caskie, a Presbyterian minister and keeper of the Seamen's Mission, a vital point of entry for the Pat O'Leary line, said the other servicemen found it difficult to accept the order from British intelligence that flyers receive first priority in escaping, and he often regretted having to follow the directive.[2] Considering the amount of manpower necessary to defeat the Germans, it is fair to question why aircrew should have received priority status in escape and evasion.

Aircrew were expensive to train, with figures ranging from $40,000 to $60,000 for a bomber pilot and $60,000 to $90,000 for a fighter pilot. Their costly instruction made them extremely valuable members of the fighting forces—a fact that was not lost on the Germans, who called them "the best qualified forces of the English and American nations."[3] In addition to the high-priced training, it took many months to prepare a crew for action, and since there was not an abundant supply, their loss was troublesome. Within the British and Commonwealth forces, repatriated airmen played a valuable role in replenishing the bomber squadrons in the air, but this was not the case with the American airmen, who were usually sent home. On arriving in the United States, they were granted a short leave, after which they either taught in USAAF training schools or worked for MIS-X, using their evasion experiences as teaching tools.[4] USAAF leaders enacted this policy as a protective measure for the Europeans who helped the evaders. It was too much to hope that an airman shot down on a subsequent mission would be lucky enough to evade capture a second time, and any information the Germans persuaded him to tell was potentially fatal to his former helpers.

The return of more and more escapers and evaders to England had another unforeseen advantage, which took both the British Air Ministry and military intelligence by surprise but made the Air Ministry take more notice of MI9's work. The morale of airmen on bases rose considerably when they saw their buddies miraculously reappear after having been shot down over occupied Europe, particularly during those periods when losses were extremely high. At one point in October 1943, known as Black Week, B-17 losses were so high that the USAAF considered abandoning its daylight bombing strategy and adopting the night bombing techniques associated with the RAF. October 14, 1943, is well remembered by many as the day when the Eighth Air Force lost eighty-two bombers, carrying about eight hundred men, over occupied Europe.[5] Leslie Atkinson, a Frenchman who aided airmen in their run for freedom, said that in the most difficult period of the air war, "It was raining aviators."[6] For off-duty airmen remaining on base, it was difficult to watch the decimated squadrons return day after day, but according to S.Sgt. George Buckner, a young American airman who later evaded capture in France, "Nobody, it seemed, could bring themselves to admit to even a closest friend their fears. The result was that we were left to wrestle alone with our personal demons as best we could."[7] The repatriation of downed airmen eased those fears.

With greater numbers of escapers and evaders returning to their bases, the Air Ministry began to demand more respect for MI9's efforts. As a result, financial assistance improved, as did the availability of agents and wireless radios. Even so, though MI9's contributions were valuable, the agency did not carry the clout that some of the other intelligence services did, and its work remained a low priority throughout the war.[8] Thankfully, MI9's achievements were better received by the airmen. Aircrew members paid closer attention to evasion training lectures when they understood they might actually have the opportunity to use these tactics to save themselves from capture or worse. The Germans realized this as well and concluded:

> Considering the escape assistance measures from the
> psychological point of view, it can not be denied that they

have likewise a certain morale value. Young flyers, and even more experienced ones, sometimes feel a certain awkwardness before a raid, especially if heavy losses had occurred. But if they are constantly reminded that in case of emergency they can parachute and that they have numerous chances to escape and safely reach their units, their fighting force is strengthened. The flyer has more self-confidence and starts easily on a raid. Considered from this point of view, the well-prepared measures for escape assistance are of real value.[9]

It was an amazing feat for an evader to return in 1941–1942, but by 1943 Allied airmen knew that should they be shot down over occupied territory, they had a 50 percent chance of successfully evading and returning home.[10] David Goldberg, a former evader from the Royal Canadian Air Force (RCAF), wrote that "the greatest asset for an evading airman is to be positive about evading capture. It is easy to be overwhelmed by the idea that one is all alone in a foreign land and hunted by hostile forces."[11] The high percentage of repatriated airmen made it much easier to think positively about evading capture.

Thinking positively was not the only factor that determined whether or not one would successfully evade. The time of year also played a role. Winter snow made it difficult for airmen to hide their tracks. Rain and mud left the men looking like tramps, increasing their awkwardness when asking for help, but also leaving them subject to questioning by the police. Late spring to early fall was the best time for evading, owing in part to the better weather conditions and also because of the growing season. Men traveling alone could find fruits, vegetables, and nuts during this period, and a full stomach meant they would not risk capture by shopping in towns and villages. It followed that men whose basic needs were satisfied were less likely to surrender to Germans in desperation.[12]

The area in which an airman was shot down also figured heavily into his evasion efforts. Men downed in Germany found themselves in territory where there were no organized escape lines and few, if any, civilians who supported the Allied cause. Eluding capture in the heartland of Germany was certainly difficult, but not impossible, and a large number of men managed to work their way across Germany, Belgium, and France before returning home via Spain. Because of the existing escape lines, landing in Belgium or Holland was less hazardous than landing in Germany, but it was still more of a challenge than landing in France due to distance. This is not to suggest that evasion in France was easy. Evasion was fraught with uncertainty, danger, and countless unexpected challenges no matter where one was shot down, and the escape lines extending into southern France ultimately had to contend with the Pyrenees Mountains.[13]

In the months immediately following German occupation of Belgium, the Netherlands, and France, the evaders' status was unclear. Unlike escapers, they were not mentioned in the Geneva Convention (1929). However, from the beginning, men who were caught evading—in uniform or civilian clothes—were treated as POWs and moved to prisoner-of-war camps.[14] During the latter half of 1940—referred to as the romantic period of escape and evasion—avoiding capture was not as difficult as it became later in the war. French civilians who had fled the occupation flooded the roads trying to return home, allowing the evaders to blend in easily with the crowds. Surprised by their unexpectedly quick victory, the Germans were unorganized and confused, which enabled the evaders to bluff their way through rough spots with less difficulty.[15] Once the Germans established occupation offices in the various regions of France, and the French Milice[16] was organized, evasion became much more of a challenge.

The very nature of evasion lent itself to the idea that airmen should disguise themselves in order to keep from looking obviously out of place. The most common way for an evader to do this was to dress in civilian clothing. This was sometimes easier said than done, and even if one was able to get civilian clothing, it did not necessarily mean the clothes would fit. Since American men were generally taller than most Frenchmen, any clothes the French had to offer were likely to be too short. Quite often the airmen got articles of clothing from several different helpers, so they looked a bit mismatched. Even the helpers were occasionally amused at the attire worn by the men who arrived at their homes—for example, outdated formal wear left over from celebrations long past.[17] Some disguises were quite creative, though William Howell (USAAF) might possibly have been insulted that his youthful appearance and small stature allowed his helpers to dress him in a Boy Scout uniform and hide him in the woods temporarily with a tent and sleeping bag.[18]

Oddly enough, while the French people were usually able to recognize an evader as he made his way through their town or village, the Germans often could not. Most of the time, evaders tried to avoid walking through towns, doing so as a last resort or because they were completely lost. The latter was true of Bernard Rawlings, who had joined the USAAF as a twenty-one-year-old from Kansas City. He wanted to be a pilot, and volunteering had seemed a good way of going about it. Rawlings wandered into a village and found that "everybody in the village watched me as if they knew exactly who I was, in spite of my civilian clothes, but the Germans did not seem to catch on."[19]

Shoes were more difficult to find than clothing. It was not uncommon for airmen's shoes to be thrown off by the force of their parachutes opening, and great numbers of men found themselves barefoot on reaching the ground. Those who managed to keep their shoes on often had only their flight boots, which were very heavy and uncomfortable for walking long distances. The French people tried to provide shoes for those who needed them, but once again the difference in size between Americans and Frenchmen was a problem. More often than not, the shoes were too small, and within a few hours the evaders' feet were blistered and sore. Quite a number of airmen told of blistered, bleeding feet aggravated by the dust of the roads leaving them in too much pain to walk. For some, only the presence of fellow evaders kept them moving. Others claimed that they were in so much pain that they did not care if they were picked up by the Germans, and even welcomed it as the lesser of two evils. Colin Bayliss (RAAF) found himself in this miserable position. Sitting in the kitchen of a young French woman, he was sure she and her friend had called the Germans to come pick him up, but he did not care. As far as he was concerned at that point, imprisonment was preferable to the pain and discomfort to his feet from the small shoes.[20]

When they shed their flight uniforms in exchange for civilian clothes, airmen rid themselves of the danger of being identified as evaders by their clothing, but were left vulnerable to charges of spying for the Allies. Pre-capture training instructors pointed out that it was only reasonable to expect airmen to dress in civilian clothes while evading, and it took more than clothing to determine spy status. They encouraged men to keep their dog tags or identification tags with them at all times as a means of proving their identities. Roland Barlow placed his tags in his coat pocket, but took the coat off during the flight and left it behind when he bailed out. Fearing he might be picked up as a spy, he "borrowed" a set of tags left with his first helper by a previous evader.[21] Others had their helpers sew their tags into the seams or lapels of their civilian clothing or carried them in their shoes to keep them safe and out of sight.[22]

One way to decrease the chance of being arrested as a spy was to avoid evading near airfields or defense installations, where, if caught, it might look as if one were searching for military information. But this was not always easy. The men focused so much of their efforts on evading that they sometimes found themselves accidentally in places they should not be. Walking in the early morning darkness, evader Paul Kenney and his pilot found what appeared to be a large, open highway. They were glad to exchange the swampy fields and rough country roads for the level, concrete walking surface and thought the lack of nearby houses an additional advantage. Their spirits were high as they made their way south toward Spain, and it was a terrible blow to their morale when the highway ended and they faced a long string of lights that told them they had been walking along a German airstrip. A hasty retreat spared them the difficult task of convincing German interrogators that they truly were lost airmen and not spies.[23]

Some airmen were slower to realize when they wandered into dangerous areas. One evader, thinking he had found a good hiding place in a bombed-out house, was unpleasantly surprised a few hours later to discover that what he thought was a safe, secluded spot was actually attached to a busy German barracks.[24]

Airmen were prohibited from carrying firearms or civilian clothes on operations, as those traveling with these items appeared to be planning aggressive or secret actions and were immediately suspected of undercover work. For the same reason, taking notes on military information found in the areas through which they traveled was forbidden. USAAF Wayne Eveland's evasion brought him into contact with a number of people involved in other means of resistance besides their work on the escape lines. As he moved from place to place, his helpers gave him information regarding underground Maquis units,[25] parachute drops, and other related intelligence. Fearing he would forget what he was told, Eveland got a map and made pinholes on the numerous places about which he had information, thinking that if he held it up to the light at a future date it would jog his memory about what the French people had told him. Unfortunately, when he reached England, Eveland's "good idea" earned him a fierce tongue lashing from a British intelligence officer who pointed out that "any German intelligence idiot would know enough to hold it up to the light and discover the pinpoints."[26] Such a discovery would have confirmed any suspicions that Eveland was a spy and led the Germans to punish him as they saw fit.[27]

Military intelligence discouraged evading airmen from committing sabotage on enemy communications or installments. Airmen caught engaging in such activity could not claim POW status and were more likely to be arrested as saboteurs and shot. Evaders who found themselves in the hands of particularly active elements of the Maquis were especially vulnerable in this regard. While in the care of Maquis units, some airmen participated in sabotage work, but, knowing the danger involved, did so with some reluctance. Others, like carpetbagger John Meade,[28] embraced the work of the SOE-controlled Maquis group in whose hands his French helpers placed him. He told the British intelligence agent John Coleman that he much preferred to work with the group than spend his time hiding in an attic, so Coleman contacted London, and Meade was attached to SOE for the remainder of the war.[29]

On rare occasions, an outside intelligence agency actively used evading airmen to pass intelligence documents to Allied intelligence. Hélène De Champlain, a young French woman working for the OSS, arranged for a guide to take a pair of American airmen across the Pyrenees Mountains. Before turning them over to their mountain guide, she gave them a set of maps and sketches for delivery to Allied intelligence services in North Africa. In this case, De Champlain was assigned the job by her OSS liaison, so the crossing of the intelligence agencies was intentional. However, this was the exception, not the rule.[30]

The possibility of capture created a great deal of turmoil for evaders. The men needed help but were aware of the consequences to French helpers for giving aid to downed airmen and felt responsible for protecting them. According to the Geneva Convention, all that was required of a captured airman was his name, rank, and serial number. Not surprisingly, the Germans often demanded much more information and were quite willing to resort to violent physical, mental, and emotional mistreatment to compel cooperation. USAAF evader Doane Hage's story is particularly tragic, considering the ramifications of his experience in German hands. Hage was shot down on a bombing mission to St. Nazaire and received help from the Angulo family, which consisted of a married middle-aged couple, their four daughters, a four-year-old French orphan, and two Spanish refugees, one of whom was their intended future son-in-law. Hage wrote, "All of these people treated me as though I were one of their family during my stay and took care of me in every way possible to the best of their ability in sickness and in health and shared their all with me."[31] M. Angulo tried to take Hage across the Spanish border himself, but it was too heavily guarded, so he took him back to the Angulo home and acquired for him an ID card as a Spanish refugee. He bought Hage a railroad ticket to Bordeaux, where there was a rail connection to the French–Spanish border. Unfortunately, Hage's papers were different from those of other people around him, so when the Germans checked ID cards near Bordeaux, he did not show his. They arrested him and turned him over to the Gestapo headquarters, where he was interrogated and beaten for four hours. Hage lied about his experiences to protect the Angulos, and his captors sentenced him to death as a saboteur, despite the fact that he had his dog tags with him when he was arrested. The Gestapo moved Hage to Fresnes prison in Paris and kept him in solitary confinement for almost two months, after which they removed him, ostensibly for trial. But instead of a trial, five members of the Gestapo took Hage to a private home and placed him in a cellar room with standing water and no light. He stood there for several hours, a difficult task considering his legs were infected from the filthy conditions he had endured at Fresnes. After some time, they interrogated him again, brutally mistreating him and threatening to kill him for lying to them. Hage felt he could no longer hold out against the beatings and the solitary confinement. He wrote, "I had left the Angulo family in February and it was then April so that I felt that perhaps the Angulo family had enough time to escape so I told them eventually a portion of the truth."[32] Less than two weeks later, the Germans transferred Hage to the first in a series of POW camps. He was liberated by American troops in May 1945. Hage wrote that he worried about the Angulo family throughout his two and a half years as a POW—and with good reason. On May 8, 1943, the entire family was arrested. M. Angulo was executed the following October, and the rest of his household members received prison sentences of varying lengths or were deported to concentration camps until the liberation.[33]

Hage's experience was not an isolated incident. When German soldiers arrested Wilf Gorman (RCAF) during his second attempt to cross the Pyrenees, they took him to a small hotel, where he thought he would be fed. Instead, the soldiers pushed him down a flight of stairs into a cellar. The next day they launched the first of many interrogations, punctuating their questions with beatings. Gorman wrote, "I told them I had been shot down from a bomber and parachuted out. I gave them my name, rank, and serial number, but they wouldn't pay any attention to that. They always referred to me as a spy. They thought if they beat me hard enough, I would eventually break down. But I didn't break down. I'd taken great care to avoid knowing the names of my helpers so I couldn't betray them, regardless how punishing and painful my interrogation."[34]

Unlike Hage, Gorman's life was never threatened, but he was imprisoned in Fresnes prison for an extended period of time in poor, crowded conditions. The only break in the monotony of his existence was the periodic interrogations and beatings the Germans continued to perform, though at greater intervals than before. Eventually they transported him to a POW camp, from which, toward the end of the war, he marched 240 kilometers on foot to another camp farther into Germany and away from possible liberation forces.[35]

Capture was the greatest threat to evaders, and all the other hazards they faced arose out of their efforts to avoid it, but much of the time successful evasion was no more than good luck, as David Goldberg (RCAF) pointed out when he wrote, "In my case, and certainly in the case of all those who had shared my type of experience, the fact that we were not caught was due to sheer happenstance and good luck. Realistically it was just so often a mere fluke that I or a member of our group was not apprehended in so many different circumstances. All of us are completely aware and thankful for the part played by good fortune, luck or whatever you seek to call it."[36]

There are countless examples of lucky breaks for evaders, some of which came about due to chance decisions concerning whom to ask for help. American evader Frank Hines had two houses to choose from and selected the one on his right. He knocked on the door, only to find himself immediately dragged into the house by the homeowner, who explained that the family next door was pro-German.[37]

Inattentiveness on the part of the Germans resulted in good fortune for many evaders. Newly downed evader William Hawkins (USAAF) crossed the road in front of a carload of Germans on their way to examine the wreckage of his plane, but they completely ignored him despite the fact that he was fully dressed in his flight clothes. The same lack of attention that allowed Hawkins to escape also permitted airmen to drink at bars and dine at restaurants among Germans—even, on some occasions, at the voluntary expense of the Germans. In an effort to improve relations with the French people, German soldiers occasionally bought meals or drinks for men in bars and cafés. Unknown to them, their guests were sometimes evaders.[38]

While luck played a significant role in an evader's successful repatriation, evasion training was invaluable to those who, in a few terrifying minutes, found themselves removed from the company of comrades and delivered to the lonely existence of an evader in enemy-occupied territory. Some airmen claimed their evasion experience was very much like the simulated training they received before participating in operations, while others said they felt that nothing could have prepared them for such an experience.[39] Though not everyone felt that the training took care of all the questions and predicaments that arose from evading, it is obvious from examining the E and E records that most of the men did profit from their training.

Airmen learned, for example, that evasion did not begin on the ground, as there were several factors associated with evacuating from a disabled plane that could improve their chances of avoiding capture. With regard to bailing out, the most important factor was to get to the ground quickly.[40]

Delaying a jump was important, and sometimes made the difference between evasion and capture.[41] Though it sounds contradictory, delaying a jump simply meant to delay opening one's chute until near to the ground. One reason for doing this was that there was less physical strain on the body from a physics standpoint. But another, more important reason was that bodies falling through the air were not as visible from the ground as those swinging from large parachutes, and since German ground forces sometimes shot at men in parachutes, it was a good idea to wait as long as possible before giving them such sport. A number of airmen found themselves the objects of target practice, and others watched helplessly while fellow airmen were victimized by German ground troops. Such was the case when evader Richard Reid watched from his hiding place as a parachutist was attacked by a German fighter. USAAF evader William Koger commented that the ground troops "missed me completely, but as I had nothing else to do while I was floating down, I counted eight holes they put through my chute." Lt. Harry Robley (sometimes spelled Robey), a USAAF pilot, was not so lucky. He was shot and killed while parachuting from his crippled plane. His was not an isolated incident, as another airman had his chute shot from over him, causing him to die in a free fall.[42]

In some cases airmen were treated in a friendly manner by German fighters. Dick Smith was one of a few airmen who received good wishes from the pilot of the German fighter that shot him down. As he parachuted, the German ME 109 flew near enough to him that Smith saw the pilot wave a hand at him. Smith wrote in his memoir, "He tipped his wing and waved, so I figured if he wasn't mad, I wasn't mad either, so I waved back."[43]

Another good reason for delaying a jump was to give the Germans as little time as possible to organize a landing party. Richard Faulkner (USAAF) was told by his helpers that several other parachutes besides his were seen when he bailed out, but it took them such a long time to get down that the Germans were waiting on the ground when they landed. The airmen captured were not members of Faulkner's crew, but of another that had been shot down at about the same time. Faulkner was the only survivor of his crew; the other nine died in the plane.[44]

Though they realized the importance of delaying their jumps, many airmen found it hard to resist opening their chutes early out of a fear that they might not open at all. Scores of men voiced surprise and relief at the sight of the white canopy unfolding in the sky over their heads. Unfortunately, their fear was not completely unwarranted, as there were instances when parachutes did not work properly. John Reitmeier (USAAF) pulled his ripcord to no avail and resorted to desperate jerking on various strings to get his chute open. He was fortunate to escape the fate of other men who died of injuries sustained when their parachutes did not open completely. James Mayfield was a ball turret gunner on his first mission with the USAAF when he was forced to bail out of his B-17. He sustained serious injuries when his parachute did not open properly. Over three months later, his wife was still expecting word from him any day. She understood that he had been taken as a POW but was unaware that he had later died in a German war hospital in France.[45]

Time and again, men were injured either in the act of bailing out or on landing. Injuries resulted from loose plane parts flying around the aircraft, bailing out too close to the ground, or not having one's chute straps fastened tightly. Oftentimes the men simply had the wind knocked out of them and needed time to collect their wits.[46] Considering all of the hazards associated with bailing out, it is not difficult to understand how the men may have been a bit bewildered when they reached the ground. Still, it was important that they gather their wits quickly, because they did not have much time to get away from their landing sites before the Germans arrived to search for them. Interrogations of repatriated airmen revealed that many of their crewmates were picked up in the first few hours as a result of remaining near their crash sites.[47] Brambles or gullies served as good hiding places in the first minutes or hours after landing, and if they were in the country, the airmen could usually find wooded areas in which to hide. Robert Horsley, a wireless operator in the Royal Australian Air Force, climbed an oak tree to avoid a German search party. He lay among the branches, watching a large search patrol walk just underneath and hoping that none of its members would think to look up. Fortunately for Horsley, his hiding place was just enough out of the ordinary that the troops did not discover him. Germans were sticklers for method, and men who did the unexpected had a better chance of evading successfully.[48]

Until 1943, most airmen landed unnoticed by local civilians. In many cases they literally hit the ground running, pausing only long enough to hide their parachutes and flying equipment and then heading for the nearest woods or field to hide from the search parties they expected to arrive at any moment. It was a frightening time for the airmen, most of whom were little more than boys when they found themselves alone and hunted in occupied territory. The majority of evaders were on the low end of the nineteen- to twenty-five-year-old bracket. A very young Harold Brennan of the RCAF remembered well his feelings of being "confused and somewhat terrified. I really didn't have a clue what I should do other than hide."[49] Jack Stead felt the same fear as he lay under a pile of tree branches watching Germans search for him. He recalled that "the day was indeed long and I was frightened and hungry and wanted to be just about anywhere but there."[50] Like many other airmen during this period, Stead found help from local French people right away. He remembered thinking how odd it was that even though the Germans could not seem to see him in his pile of branches, the French knew exactly where he was. At one point a Frenchman walked past and told him to stay where he was, then returned for him after dark.[51]

USAAF evader Joseph Lilly ran about three-fourths of a mile away from his aircraft before he started looking for a place to hide. A Frenchman spotted him and ran to help him. He gave Lilly his coat, beret, and watch and told him he would be back later. Lilly lay hiding in mud and water for over six hours while he watched the Germans search for him. One walked within ten feet of his hiding place.[52]

Quite often men landed near homes or farms and were promptly seen by family members or farmers in the fields. One of the more unusual experiences was that of USAAF evader Richard Weiss, who landed in the yard of a farmhouse and was whisked into the home, where he was named honorary godfather to a baby born at almost the same instant as his entrance. Weiss was not alone in such an experience. The helper to gunner Robert Vandergriff (USAAF) gave birth in the bed in which he and his fellow evaders had been spending their nights. Vandergriff wrote that they all felt like godfathers to the child and were saddened to learn fifty years later that the baby had died of meningitis a month after it was born.[53]

It was not uncommon for airmen to be assisted right away by local patriots. Often German troops extended their search for airmen to houses that lay in the vicinity of a downed aircraft. To protect themselves, the French commonly hid the men in woods, fields, haystacks, or ditches until the search had been called off, then moved the men to more comfortable quarters or at least provided them with a meal and perhaps some civilian clothing before sending them on their way.

Men were occasionally taken into homes just after landing in spite of the search parties, particularly if they needed medical attention. In such cases, a watchman was assigned to keep an eye out for Germans. One French couple posted their child at the door while they attended to USAAF evader Michael Negro's wounds and helped him to change into civilian clothing. When the child warned of the Germans' approach, Negro was able to safely get away.[54]

Another American evader, William Olsen, had a close call when German troops arrived moments after he entered the home of his helpers. Olsen had just enough time to race out the back door and into a clump of tall grass in the backyard before the Germans entered the house and questioned the couple at gunpoint. Though the couple misdirected the Germans by claiming Olsen had run down a side road, the troops remained nearby for most of the day. Watching the search from his hiding place, Olsen feared for the people who had tried to assist him as much as he feared his own capture.[55]

French civilians sometimes joined German search parties but had a secret motive in aiding with the search. If the French people found an airman, they instructed him to stay where he was and returned later to move him to a safer, more comfortable shelter. In the meantime, they directed the Germans' search away from the evader's location. On one occasion, while helping the Germans search, a gendarme stepped carefully over an airman, pretended to look around, then led the Germans in another direction, turning their focus away from the area in which the man was hidden.[56] Archibald Robinson watched French peasants search for him while hiding in a thicket, but had contradictory thoughts about the wisdom of exposing himself to them. They might help him to evade, but then again they might turn him over to the Germans. Rather than reveal his presence, Robinson chose to remain hidden, and as a result he managed to avoid being captured. On the other hand, he may have missed his chance at being picked up by an escape organization, which would have saved him from having to arrange his evasion alone.[57]

As the air war intensified during 1943–1944 in preparation for the European invasion, increasing numbers of evaders found themselves traveling and hiding in occupied Europe. When bomber formations flew overhead, French civilians watched for parachutes and met the airmen at their landing spots in large groups. Some took spare clothes to help the airmen disguise themselves quickly, and when possible they provided hiding places in the woods or in barns. Often, however, heavy German presence in the area or recent helper arrests made people reluctant to take the airmen into their homes. Nevertheless, even in these circumstances they were able to help by hiding the men's equipment and telling them which direction to take in order to avoid German patrols.[58] Tail gunner Keith Sutor (USAAF) was met on the ground by a group of about fifty people, some of whom took his equipment from him then pointed in the direction of the woods about half a mile away and told him to "scram." Sutor did just that, leaving his equipment behind to be disposed of by the French.[59]

The creation of a number of smaller escape lines, either through military intelligence or among individual groups, meant more experienced people were available to provide assistance to downed airmen. Helpers grew quite adept at finding innovative hiding places. USAAF flyer John Dutka's helpers found an ideal place for him to hide while waiting for German forces to call off their search. The family patriarch had died and his funeral was scheduled for the afternoon, but until then they hid Dutka under a sheet with the coffin. After the German troops called off their search, he was safely moved elsewhere.[60]

Unfortunately, the RAF, RCAF, and RAAF did not receive the advantage of landing parties, since most of their operations were flown at night. American airmen on their own also searched for assistance among the civilian population, but the landing parties sometimes connected them with help more quickly.[61]

The best way to contact a helper was to approach a single person or a lone farmhouse, identify oneself as an Allied aviator, and use the language phrase card to communicate the need for food, clothing, or a hiding place, or to find out the whereabouts of the Germans. Usually approaching the French people directly resulted in one of three responses. First, those who were afraid to help slammed the door in the airmen's faces (or if out in the open shook their heads and continued on their way). Webber Mason (USAAF) stopped a girl on a bicycle to tell her he was an American airman who had been shot down, but was only able to get out the word American before she jumped back on her bicycle with wild, frightened eyes, told him goodbye, and left.[62]

Second, though a large number of French people were willing to help, there was always a risk involved in approaching complete strangers and asking them for assistance. Some airmen received a terrible shock when they found themselves betrayed to the Germans by civilians who they thought were going to help them. Paul Kenney was arrested when the "helper" transporting him by car delivered him to German police at a roadblock. Faced with the realization that his evasion had ended in capture, Kenney "felt shock, anger, and hatred for the Nazis, fear of the unknown which lay ahead, and remorse for the brave people who were being betrayed." Other evaders, such as Leo Arlin, had the opposite problem. He approached a woman working in a field and offered her some Dutch money from his escape kit in exchange for food. Thinking he was a German, she sent for a man to kill him, but on arriving the man realized Arlin was an Allied airmen and took him home instead.[63]

Airmen who never connected with an escape line were still indebted to individual people and families who fed, clothed, and sheltered them throughout their evasion. This was particularly true after the D-Day invasion in June 1944, when Allied destruction of French railway lines forced the escape lines to stop moving men toward Spain. Both David Chapple and Charles Kroschel were RAAF evaders who conducted their evasions without the assistance of organized escape lines, but who could not have succeeded without the individual help provided by so many of the French people. Chapple wrote that about twenty families were responsible for his success in evading until he could join the Allied forces. Kroschel also had the assistance of many spur-of-the-moment helpers, who fed and sheltered him on various occasions, enabling him to evade successfully even though he was not attached to an organized network.[64]

The third reaction airmen might expect—and the one which was most hoped for—was one in which the French took the men into their homes and cared for them until they could filter them into an escape organization. Evasion training instructors lectured, "In such a case you have hit the jackpot—Stick around and do as you are told."[65] It was important that the airmen not ask to be connected with an organization, as airmen who asked specifically about organized help were immediately suspected of being German infiltrators. The men knew the organizations existed and resisted with some difficulty the natural tendency to ask about circumstances that directly affected their safety.

Reactions from airmen regarding their feelings of security while in the hands of escape networks vary. Bombardier Paul Kenney never felt completely safe and wrote, "Although we had some pleasant times with the people who sheltered us, I never had the feeling of being safe and I'm sure they didn't either. Betrayal could come at any time."[66]

For the most part, once an evader was picked up by an escape organization, his life became somewhat easier. He still had difficult moments ahead, but unlike the evaders on their own who had to forage for food, his meals, meager though they may have been at times, were provided by his helpers, who often went far out of their way to care for their evaders' needs. Usually he had the advantage of sleeping in a bedroom or attic room, where he was protected from the elements, rather than having to resort to haystacks or pine boughs in the woods. Evaders who had been picked up by an organization no longer had to worry about how they were going to get back to England, since the escape lines existed for that purpose. This was difficult in its own way, however, because of the time required to arrange a successful evasion. Airmen had to be patient while false ID cards were made and guides were found to move them along the escape line.

Airmen passed the time away by playing cards, reading, and visiting with other evaders or helpers when possible. Some evaders helped with chores around the house or in the fields, which not only helped break the monotony of the day but also enabled them to repay their helpers for the sacrifices made to protect them. RAAF evader Neil Roggenkamp helped in the fields picking potatoes and harvesting wheat when there were no Germans around.[67] Some evaders helped with apple harvests, cider making, coffee grinding, or fieldwork, while others tutored schoolchildren or assisted with child care. The time spent assisting a helper held special meaning for some like engineer/gunner Gus Bubenzer, who had a newborn son at home with whom he had spent only a brief twenty days before leaving for England. His helpers' baby was a surrogate for his own child, and he spent his mornings rocking the infant while her mother did her daily housecleaning. Bubenzer was sorry to learn many years later that the infant was killed in a bicycling accident a few years after the war ended.[68]

The frustration of having to wait indefinitely for his evacuation to be arranged was a problem for almost every evader. Airey Neave, British evader and intelligence agent, wrote that the feeling "was something one would never mention to those who risked their lives to get you back. But it was there all the same. I heard it from hundreds of others."[69] Boredom was alleviated somewhat by the presence of another crewmember. Having someone to talk to who spoke English helped considerably, and in cases when there were several airmen hidden nearby, the helpers tried to get them together as often as possible for socializing. George Bennett was hidden in an area relatively free of German patrols, which enabled him to visit a crew member at a neighboring farm with little worry about capture.[70] But for the many evaders who hid alone in attic rooms, it was a lonely existence. Keith Sutor passed much of his time staring out the window at German troops doing calisthenics in distant fields.[71]

When in the care of an escape organization, it was crucial that evaders follow their helpers' directions to the letter. In many cases, the helpers had been doing their jobs long enough to know the hazards involved in caring for evaders. An airman who did not do as he was told ran the risk of endangering his helpers as well as other airmen who were evading with him. Unfortunately, such lapses arose more often than one might think—sometimes with tragic results. In April 1941, Zoe Evans and two other women were convoying twenty-one British airmen to Paris. They and the men had hidden in a cargo car, but just before the train left, a German sentry noticed smoke coming from the car and called for a search. An airman had lit a cigarette, and the smoke had called attention to their presence, resulting in the entire group being arrested. Mme Evans was beaten, tortured, and condemned to fifteen years of forced labor, but still refused to give the Germans any information about the escape organization with which she was working.[72] Another failure to follow his helper's instructions led to the arrest of Robert McGee (USAAF), who had false papers stating that he was a farmer but who refused to dirty his hands to go along with his feigned occupation. When alert Germans checked his ID on a train, they noticed McGee's clean hands and questioned him. They discovered very quickly that he was not a farmer, but an evader.[73]

Most of the time the airmen tried hard to adhere to the helpers' instructions, but automatic reactions could be a problem. Helpers warned their evaders never to speak while riding on trains, but an English evader unintentionally let good manners get the best of him one day when he accidentally trod on a woman's foot and in a very distinct English accent said, "I beg your pardon." Fortunately, though the lady smiled, she and other travelers who overheard the apology made no comment. The evader and his helper most likely passed some uncomfortable moments as they anticipated possible consequences from the inadvertent remark.[74]

Though the arrangements for their evasions were in the hands of the escape organizations, the men were not relieved of the responsibility of trying to fit in with the civilian community while being moved from place to place. Trying to appear casual while standing still for a paper check was a nerve-wracking experience for airmen who never felt completely sure of their false papers. When American evaders Milton Mills and Ken Morrison exited the train in Toulouse, they and the other passengers lined up on the station platform for an ID check. One of the British evaders traveling with them was arrested, which added to their anxiety over having their false papers scrutinized by the Germans. Mills later wrote that his stomach turned over with fear when his and Morrison's papers were checked, and it was a great relief to see the Germans move on to the next person.[75]

Being in the care of an organization did not mean that an airman's evasion was going to be a simple experience, only less frustrating than it might have been trying to arrange such a journey alone. Crossing the Pyrenees Mountains was a major obstacle for evaders. Toward the end of the war a naval escape route was established, as was a holding camp in the forest, when pre-invasion bombing rendered the railroads unusable. But for the majority of evaders, their only means of repatriation was to cross the Pyrenees.[76]

There were a number of hazards involved with crossing the Pyrenees, especially in the winter. However, one of the problems associated with the trip was troublesome no matter what the season. In most cases, the airmen had been shut away for weeks or months in small bedrooms and attics where silence was mandatory and room to exercise was nonexistent. In addition, food shortages in France were severe, and though the French did their best, often offering the choicest portions to their evading guests, it was difficult to feed young men with voracious appetites. As a result, most of the men had lost a fair amount of weight by the time they crossed the mountains. They were already weak and often received little food during the mountain trek, which made for a grueling trip. Roland Barlow ran into difficulty due to weakness and illness, which finally resulted in his being left behind in a mountain cabin in blizzardlike conditions. The guides believed his inability to keep up was a hazard to the rest of the group, so he was ordered to stay in the cabin long enough to let the rest of the group get safely into Spain. Only then was he to try to travel back down the mountain on his own.[77]

Illness and injury were major problems for men crossing the mountains. Ralph McKee developed dysentery from drinking water out of the mountain streams, which left him very weak.[78] John Katsaros, one of the men crossing with Jack Stead, had been badly wounded in the arm when he was shot down. Katsaros never complained, though Stead knew the effort must have been both difficult and painful since he, himself, was relatively healthy and yet still struggled through the four-day crossing.[79]

The lack of proper attire was a dilemma for evaders, particularly those crossing in the winter months. Footwear continued to be a problem for many evaders; Roland Barlow was troubled by shoes that were not only too small, but had nails poking into his feet from the wooden soles. Wilf Gorman had to turn back toward France when his shoes fell apart on his first evasion attempt, leaving him with no protection against the snow.[80]

One of the most difficult crossings was that of Wayne Eveland's group, which ran into a blizzard a few hours into the trip. Eveland claimed the next three days were probably the most dangerous he ever lived through. None of the men had clothing suitable for the conditions they faced—there simply were no clothes for them. The French did what they could, but after so many years of war they had little clothing to give away.[81]

In addition to the lack of warm clothing, the men were quickly exhausted from walking through deep snow, and it became difficult to stay awake during the frequent, needed breaks. Several men developed severe frostbite and one became delirious with exhaustion and snow blindness. Rather than leave men behind to die in the snow, the stronger members of the group took turns carrying those who were too weak to continue on their own. Though two men and a guide had to be left in a deserted mountain cabin, the majority of the group finally made it into Spain.[82]

Eveland's group was not the only one to experience such weather crossing the Pyrenees. Both of Barlow's and Gorman's evasions were beset with difficulties aggravated by winter weather, as was USAAF evader Fred Glover's. Glover's better physical health, however, allowed him to cross with fewer complications and enabled him to help his guides with those who were suffering.[83]

Many of the airmen who crossed the Pyrenees remember it as being one of the toughest things they ever did. Fifty years after the experience, Angus MacLean wrote that after the first twelve hours of the trip, he had "never been so tired in my life, before or since."[84] Though large numbers crossed the mountains without major complications, many men felt that they would never get across this final stumbling block to freedom. It is likely that at no other time in their lives was a destination so happily reached as that of Spain, which marked the end of their evasion experience.

The countless examples of men continuing on in the face of extreme difficulty is a great testimony to the tenacity of the human spirit. The stubborn determination of the airmen to avoid capture and return to England played a large part in their success. However, the perseverance they showed in the face of adversity, admirable though it was, is secondary to that of the French helpers who risked all that was most precious to them in order to give the evaders their freedom. The helpers gambled their homes—even the lives of their families—to help the airmen escape, and many of them lost. Realizing all of their efforts to rescue the airmen, it is not difficult to understand that over fifty years later tributes are still paid to the World War II helpers, and enormous gratitude still remains with each of the airmen saved by these heroic people.

3

My Brother's Keeper

The Helpers

In a farmhouse in France, a woman worriedly looked at her husband over the sleeping airman whose head she held cradled in her lap. Her nightgown was torn where she had ripped away some of the cloth to use as a rag to clean shrapnel wounds on his face and leg.[1] Her feelings of sympathy for the young man, who was little more than a boy, were tempered with fear for herself, her husband, and their three young daughters, because she understood the possible consequences of their act of humanity. If she had had any doubts, the decrees of German general Otto von Stülpnagel would have reminded her. The decrees were tacked on posts and buildings in villages and towns throughout France to remind the citizens what would happen should they get involved with aiding downed airmen: "All men who aid directly or indirectly the crews of enemy aircraft coming down by parachute or having made a forced landing will be shot in the field. Women who render the same type aid will be sent to concentration camps in Germany. People who capture crews who are forced to land or parachutists, or who contribute, by their actions, to their capture will receive up to 10,000 francs. In certain particular cases this compensation will be increased."[2]

In posting the decree, the Germans sought to discourage the people of occupied France from aiding downed Allied airmen. In case the fear of death or deportation was not enough to elicit cooperation, they offered large amounts of money to people willing to betray those of their countrymen who helped evaders. Fear of these traitors, described by one evader as "a slimy breed of dog whom I hope will roast in hell over a low and smoky fire for eternity," was as bad or worse than fear of the Gestapo.[3]

In spite of these threats, many people stepped forward to aid the young men who had been forced out of their aircraft and into the strange and frightening world of occupied Europe. Those who have not experienced the brutality that Hitler brought to France and all of Europe during World War II have had difficulty understanding the enthusiasm and persistence with which the helpers carried out their tasks. The survivors did not publicize their acts, as they were merely reacting to their hatred of Nazism, love of humanity, and the desire to restore liberty to their country. Helping airmen was their way of taking part in the struggle to free their homeland.[4] The general public has become much more aware of the significance of the helpers' actions over the last twenty years, due to the declassification of intelligence documents related to escape and evasion and the creation of organizations to honor the memory of those associated with this form of resistance.[5] Sadly, a lack of understanding still exists among many of the young people of France. Reine Mocaer, a former helper, recently wrote a memoir of her family's work with the escape lines for her grandchildren, but was surprised by her daughter's comment that the war was over so why talk about it. Mocaer responded, "Thank God she never had to go through it. Things like that you don't and can't forget . . . I assure you that as long as I live, I will remember those horrible years."[6]

According to Airey Neave, an estimated twelve thousand people worked with the escape lines. In fact, the true number of helpers is unknown,[7] since it is impossible to know how many French men and women helped with incidentals as the airmen evaded. Even recognizing a man as an evader and keeping quiet or steering the Germans away from an evader were means of aid, of which the airmen may have been unaware and thus unable to report during later debriefings. In the case of American evader Charles Adcock, several French laborers caused a distraction so that he could pass through town unnoticed. Because Adcock did not learn their names and never saw them again, he could not identify them in his report to military intelligence. But the fact that he could not give their names or tell anything else about them did not take away from their efforts to help him, since had they been caught the consequences would have been no different than had they hidden him in their homes.[8]

A more sobering figure is the number of helpers who were shot or died under torture or in concentration camps as a result of helping evaders. James Langley of MI9 believed it was far more than the five hundred names that were recorded. Like the number of helpers in general, the number of those who died for the evaders' cause will remain forever unknown, but Langley felt it would be accurate to say that for every man who successfully evaded, a French, Dutch, or Belgian helper lost his or her life. If in addition to those who died at the immediate hands of the Germans one considers the number of helpers who succumbed after the war to the ill treatment received while imprisoned in concentration camps, this may very well be true.[9]

Among those who study escape and evasion, as well as the former evaders who experienced the humanity of the French people, the question remains as to whether they, themselves, would have acted in a similar fashion under the same circumstances. All would like to say without hesitation that they would have overcome their fears and done what was right, but most realize that the answer is not that simple. Australian evader Stan Jolly recently wrote, "When my family was young I would ask myself would I be prepared to risk my life and the lives of my children and wife to help a complete stranger, and I am afraid to say, I still don't know the answer."[10]

Helpers assisted evaders for a number of reasons, but primarily out of a sense of duty. It was the one way most French patriots could strike back at the German occupiers. Alain Camard was only thirteen years old when his father and brother became active in the Resistance, hiding airmen and obtaining false IDs for them. He wrote, "It was a war, we had to help our Allies. We were fighting for liberty."[11] Many were simply angry that France had been invaded yet again by the Germans and were determined to fight the enemy in any way they could. For men who were veterans of World War I but were too old to assume combat duty in World War II, helping airmen was a means of fighting back.[12] As Reine Mocaer wrote about her father, "Do you think a man who suffered so much in the trenches, wounded at Verdun, could accept to see our France occupied by the Germans?"[13]

Not all those who took part in evasion work in France were French citizens. Greek, American, Polish, Russian, and British civilians who remained in France during the war also became involved in helping the Allies fight the Germans by aiding evaders. Englishman Benjamin Leech worked for the British War Graves Commission as caretaker of a World War I cemetery in the Somme region. He and his oldest son, Maurice, hid evaders in the cemetery tool shed while they arranged for the men's

Georges Broussine escaped to England on the Pat O'Leary line, joined the BCRA, and returned to France to organize the Burgundy escape line. (Courtesy of Georges Broussine)

transfer to the next safe house on the line. Maurice wrote that duty and anger were two of the reasons his family became involved with the escape line, but they were also influenced by the horrible sight of large numbers of women, children, and elderly people massacred by German fighter planes while fleeing the invasion.[14]

There were also some Germans who worked on the escape lines. Two German women held prominent positions in the Pat O'Leary line. One was the secretary to the line's chief. While in hiding, Neave was embarrassed when he commented to some of his helpers that only those who had endured imprisonment by the Germans could understand "what swine they could be."[15] He was corrected by one of the helpers who told him she was German, and while she hated Nazism, she loved her country. The incident helped Neave to understand that the escape organizations were a form of humanitarian warfare within which there were no nationalistic barriers.[16]

For young people involved with the Resistance, the danger of helping evaders was not always as readily apparent as it was to more mature adults. Teenagers, who tended to be adventurous even in the most settled environments, found that helping the evaders was like having a license to play tricks on the German authorities. One teenage girl who played a very active role in the Comet line claimed, "It was great fun" to be able to take part in defending her country by resisting the Germans.[17] Georges Broussine, chief of the Burgundy escape line, stated, "We were all young, and clandestine life was very exciting."[18] Broussine also found a great sense of moral satisfaction in helping evaders because it was a means of conducting the war with Germany without killing others.

The feeling of compassion that arises in most people confronted by someone lost and alone, wounded, or frightened compelled the people of France to help airmen. For parents with sons who were fighting or imprisoned, and for women with young husbands, empathy for the airmen's families often influenced their willingness to help. Such feelings inspired helper Denise Bacchi to write to her evader, "Seeing you so young and so far away from your wife who was the mother of your month-old baby that you had never seen so filled our hearts with hurt because of the enormous joys of which the war was depriving you."[19] Denise buried the letter in a can in her backyard with some other mementos so the Germans would not find them. The American evader, Paul Clark, did not receive the letter until October 1997, by which time both Denise and her husband Felix had passed away. Clark now keeps up correspondence with their son Claude, who was thirteen years old at the time Clark hid with the family.[20] Langley believed the kind of compassion shown by the helpers was part of a value system from that period that is absent in today's society. The people who helped the airmen did not do so for recognition, but out of a desire to help those in need. In so doing, they contributed much to their country's fight for liberty.[21]

Personal experiences moved Bertranne Auvert to aid airmen. A young medical student and the widow of a French pilot killed by German forces in 1939, she lodged airmen in her Paris apartment despite the disapproval of her in-laws. In defending her actions, she told them, "I am an aviator's wife. Shouldn't it be a normal thing for me to help Allied aviators?"[22]

Though whole families were usually drawn into aiding evaders, individuals sometimes kept their activities secret for various reasons. Teenagers often feared their parents would stop them if their activities were known and so kept quiet about them. But when Peggy van Lier (Langley), a young Belgian girl who worked for the Comet line, felt she could not lie to her parents any longer and told them about her work, she was pleasantly surprised at their offer of support.[23]

In some instances, however, divisions of loyalty created the necessity for secrecy within families about escape work. This situation was complicated when the division occurred between generations that shared

Former evader Paul Clark with his wife Bettye at their home in 1998. Although Clarke was never able to reunite with his helpers, he maintains a close relationship with their son, Claude. (Courtesy of Paul and Bettye Clark)

the same home, as was the case with a pro-Allied farmer and his wife
who lived with his pro-German parents. Because the house was divided
into separate living areas for the two couples, the farmer was able to hide
airmen without his parents' knowledge, but it was a worrisome situation
for both the young couple and the evaders they sheltered. Divisions even
occurred between husbands and wives. One woman deliberately ignored
her husband's order not to help evaders, concealing them in the hayloft
of their barn. What she did not know was that her husband was working
for Allied military intelligence, and his instructions were issued out of
fear that the airmen's presence might destroy his cover.[24]

The people who worked on the escape lines were determined to
carry out their work regardless of the cost. Even when whole sections of
the lines were broken due to mass arrests by the Germans, the workers
that remained replaced those who had been executed or deported, piec-
ing together the ends of the line so that the work of aiding evaders could
continue. Helpers reconstructed the Comet line at least three times, in
both its Belgian and French headquarters, when its chiefs and top organizers were arrested. Those helpers' efforts allowed the line to continue
its work, evacuating airmen throughout the duration of the war.[25] The
determination that motivated the helpers is apparent in a letter written
by Denise Bacchi to evader Paul Clark: "In spite of their [the Germans']
threats, their tortures and their firing squads, the invaders will never make
us surrender. We will fight them, some with the arms your side has parachuted to us, others who have no arms will rebel against them by hiding
others like yourself. . . . We were happy to face the threat of death from
the German authorities in order to preserve your liberty. Four years of
misery, deprivation and suffering. Far from considering your actions as
piracy . . . for the clan of patriots you were our liberators."[26]

Many helpers, even those who were arrested and deported to German concentration camps, felt it had been a privilege to help downed
airmen. Sisters Valeria and Esther Fosset were sent to Mauthausen concentration camp for aiding evaders, but after their liberation wrote to a
friend, "We have been so happy to have had under the German occupation the privilege of being able to show our liberators fallen from the sky
all our gratitude. How magnificent they were! . . . We loved them spontaneously. They were so different from the German brutes who surrounded
us."[27] For these women and many other people like them, their suffering
was worth having been able to help the airmen continue the fight.

French patriot Denise Bacchi with her mother-in-law, Mme Bacchi, and evader Paul Clark in 1944. After Clark left their home, Denise wrote him a letter and buried it in a can in her yard. Clark did not receive it until 1997, several years after Denise's death. (Courtesy of Paul and Bettye Clark)

The successful work of the escape lines depended on the unheralded yet extraordinary courage of many ordinary people. Donald Darling found it amazing that people who had never been involved in any form of clandestine activity seemed to adjust so quickly and easily to secret lives as helpers.[28] Men, women, and children of all ages took part in helping airmen. Women were invaluable in the escape lines. They ran safe houses where men could hide, provided meals, and nursed injured airmen. Teenagers, particularly girls, were useful for convoying men on trains and around cities. Because they were nearly the same age as the evaders, the boys passed as comrades, but the girls could tuck their arms into those of the airmen and gaze adoringly at them, suggesting a more intimate relationship. This was evader Paul Kenney's experience when he stepped from a train, unsure of what to expect since he had been left by his previous helper one stop earlier. To his surprise, a young girl ran to him, threw her arms around his neck, and gave him a big kiss. Kenney had never seen her before, but found it was very easy to join in the act, since he "was genuinely very happy and relieved to see her."[29]

Some have criticized the Resistance in France for being fraught with political infighting, each section working to advance a private agenda for the postwar period.[30] Escape lines were different, however, in that people of many different political ideologies worked together for the common purpose of helping evaders. The same was true of religion, according to the Burgundy line's Genevieve Soulié (Camus), who stated, "In our network, there were Catholics, atheists, Protestants, Jews and people of different political parties and social classes. Our view was that we were still at war against the enemy occupying our country, and that was the important thing."[31] Jean François Nothomb, an agent for the Comet line, remembered having some animated conversations with his chief, Andrée "Dédée" de Jongh, whose liberal religious and political beliefs contrasted with his more conservative ones. Still, he said, these differences did not affect their work together helping evaders. His claims are confirmed by the great success Comet had in evacuating airmen to Spain.[32]

While most of the people who helped evaders were farmers or café workers, the range of occupations was quite wide and included mayors, doctors, nurses, clergy, teachers, laborers, artists, housewives, and students.[33] Some occupations made people better suited for certain kinds of work. Farmers were most likely to make early contact with airmen, because evaders felt more secure about approaching isolated farmhouses or men in the fields. Priests were good initial contacts, because they often knew what was happening within their communities and could connect the airmen with people who might be associated with an escape line. One helper was an insurance agent, whose work required that he visit from house to house on a routine basis. Consequently, he was able to travel throughout the region collecting airmen without looking suspicious.[34] Doctors, nurses, and veterinarians were valuable to the escape lines, since they provided medical assistance to wounded evaders. In some instances, gendarmes were also eager to help, but could only risk doing so when they were alone or with known patriots. RAF evader Alfred Martin had a close call when he was captured by two gendarmes suspicious of his unkempt appearance. After finding Flight Lieutenant Martin had no identification papers and observing his pretense at being a deaf-mute, one of the gendarmes finally asked him if he was English. Martin admitted that he was, and after a brief consultation with his partner, the gendarme told him to go quickly on his way.[35]

While helpers were a diverse group of people, they all carried certain personality characteristics that made them successful at their work. Hatred of the Germans and a strong sense of patriotism might inspire one to become a helper, but survival depended on a steady nerve and a quick wit. On more than one occasion, a woman guide pretended to have an epileptic seizure when she noticed that the evaders traveling with her were being closely watched. Another helper gave an amusing explanation for the large numbers of evaders living in his apartment, one that was sure to discourage further examination. The helper, known to the men as Fouquerel, told his concierge that he was a specialist in the treatment of venereal disease and that his patients needed extended personal care. Fouquerel was later arrested and shot for his work with the escape lines.[36]

Successful helpers exhibited qualities of leadership, the ability to serve as an inspiration for others, and stamina for enduring mental or physical stress for prolonged periods of time. The helpers' constant worry about the men under their care and the risks to themselves and their families was mentally exhausting. Guides leading men long distances on the railway system and accompanying them across the Pyrenees were additionally affected by physical exhaustion. The best helpers were courageous, original, and flexible—both physically and mentally—and, when needed, able to engage all of these qualities at the same time.[37]

Though there was no organized system of grouping helpers based on their work, a natural division evolved separating the helpers into four different groups. A large number of helpers fell into the category known as "chance helpers." These were helpers who, though not necessarily part of an escape line, found themselves confronted with an evader and did their best to provide for him while searching for an organization to take control of his evacuation. Once he or she either arranged the airman's delivery into an escape line or sent him on his way after exhausting all efforts to find a line, the chance helper returned to his or her daily routine.[38]

The second category consisted of people who helped airmen on a regular basis. These helpers collected airmen from various places and hid them for indefinite periods of time until false papers could be ob-

tained and the men could be moved further down the line.[39] These
shelterers were sometimes assisted by other helpers who provided food,
clothing, medical attention, and even entertainment on occasion. Several evaders debriefed by Donald Darling in Gibraltar had with them a
photograph of a cabaret dancer, wearing only a pearl necklace and high-
heeled shoes, who had performed for them while they were in hiding.
Her contribution earned her the nickname "The Fair Charmer" by MI9
interrogators.[40]

The last two categories of helpers, agents and chiefs, were closely
related in that both held a great deal of responsibility for keeping the
escape lines functioning smoothly. Agents lived a nomadic lifestyle, always moving from place to place, making sure the airmen's needs were
being met and that the helpers were receiving the necessary assistance to
allow them to meet those needs. They worked under the guidance of a
chief, with whom they maintained close, regular contact, and served as a
middleman between the chief and the workers on the line. The chief
acted as the line's overseer, in addition to working as an agent. Often,
though not always, he was trained for his job by military intelligence,
though this was more true of later lines, such as Burgundy or Shelburne,
than earlier ones whose creation was spontaneously inspired by sympathetic bystanders. Lt. Comdr. Pat O'Leary and Dédée de Jongh, two of
the most successful chiefs, whose lines were established in the early period, had no training at all in escape and evasion.

In many cases, agents took over leadership of their line if their chief
was arrested. O'Leary was an agent who became a chief, and de Jongh's
father, Fréderic, an agent in her line, replaced her after she was arrested.
Strong leadership abilities were necessary for both chiefs and agents, since
they were responsible for all of those working under them and largely
influenced the success of the line's operations.[41]

The responsibilities associated with being a helper were many, varied, and often more complicated than those related to sabotage or intelligence gathering. Saboteurs could set their explosives to detonate and
then disappear, putting distance between themselves and their work. In
much the same way, intelligence operatives could dispose of written evidence by some prearranged method and could relocate when their positions were compromised. But people hiding evaders did not have the
luxury of moving their families from place to place at a moment's notice,
and they could hardly tuck the airmen into books or behind doors for

safekeeping if the Germans decided to search their homes. The nature of helpers' work made it very difficult for them to dispose of their "evidence" in an efficient or timely fashion.[42]

The services provided by helpers can be divided into two categories: basic needs and evasion needs. Basic needs included such things as shelter, food, clothing, and medical care, while evasion needs consisted of verifying the evaders' authenticity, obtaining false papers, and organizing guides to accompany the men as they moved from place to place. Though both sets of needs had to be met, there was a hierarchical framework in that the basic needs of the evaders had to be met before helpers could engage in the more complicated work of arranging their evacuation.

The importance of finding shelter depended on the time of year an airman was shot down. During the winter, men looked for lodging as soon as possible. One American airman remembered hiding in an open barn the first night after he parachuted into France, wrapped in blankets provided by his helpers. Every two hours a girl carried coffee out to him to help him stay warm. When he awoke at one point, there were three inches of snow covering the blankets, but his discomfort was greatly eased by the helpers' efforts.[43]

Helpers often hid airmen in a barn or some other temporary place while they waited for the Germans to finish their initial search through the area. This allowed them to look for more permanent shelter for the airman but still claim he had hidden on their property without their knowledge if the Germans found the evader. A variety of hiding places was used, though one of the more interesting locations was a manure pile. A farmer hid five Americans under the pile, and when the Germans searched the farm, they fired into the grain pile and haystacks but did not give the manure pile a second look. After the Germans left, the evaders were dug out, given a good shower, and hidden in a room in the farmer's house. The farmer, M. Leger, was later denounced, arrested, and deported to Büchenwald. He returned home after the liberation weighing only eighty-four pounds.[44]

Those who hid airmen in their homes tried to keep the men's presence a secret, since it was impossible to know which of their neighbors might be collaborating with the Germans. During the war, Maryse de la Marnierre (McKeon) was a fifteen-year-old schoolgirl whose parents sheltered airmen in their home. To her family's knowledge, no one was aware that they were hiding airmen. Obviously, they were shocked to find a note in their mailbox one day that asked if the Americans ate a lot of bread. Nothing came of the note, but Maryse later claimed it was a miracle that they were not caught. The de la Marnierre family was eventually forced to go into hiding, spending the last six months of the war in a cottage in the woods with no electricity and no means of providing food for themselves. They were cared for by other Resistance members in the area until the liberation.[45]

Helpers sacrificed what few comforts they had to shelter airmen, but they did so without complaining or letting the airmen know the inconvenience or risk their presence produced. One helper slept in her winter coat because she had given all of her blankets to the evaders staying in her apartment; another family slept four in a room after giving an evader the daughters' bed. Sometimes the helpers were forced to provide services to the Germans while they were hiding airmen in their homes. A woman living on a heavily traveled road always fed the Germans who stopped for food, even though she had men hiding upstairs. She felt that if she gave the Germans what they wanted, they would be less inclined to search her house.[46]

Jean Crouet took two airmen to his home and put them to bed in an upstairs room, in spite of the fact that the Germans were conducting a thorough search for them throughout the countryside. He wrote at the time, "They [the airmen] don't know, but my wife and I know that Germans are patrolling in the village. We are on hotspots, but the men are tired and they do need bed. We give them a bed upstairs."[47] It was not unusual for the airmen to be exhausted by the time they found shelter, particularly if they had had a difficult experience bailing out or landing, as was the case with RCAF evader Donald Cheney. He landed in the Bay of Douarnenez, off the southwestern coast of France, where he floated in the chilly water for several hours before being picked up by resisters in a small boat. He received a spirited welcome by the villagers on shore, but when offered food, the smell caused his stomach to react to the large amounts of salt water he had ingested, and he vomited. Though he felt embarrassed, the incident alerted the rescuers to his poor condition, and they set about finding shelter for him. Cheney was turned over to the Québriac family, who provided him with a bedroom, clean clothing, and a place to wash, but his exhaustion was such that he could not do more than wipe his face with the damp cloth. Seeing him sitting on the edge of

RAF evader Donald Cheney bailed out of his plane over the Bay of Douarnenez, off the southwestern coast of France. He floated in the bay for several hours before being picked up by French resistance workers. (Courtesy of Donald Cheney)

the bed in this state, Mme Québriac pushed the fresh clothing aside and settled Cheney into bed, with instructions to get some rest.[48]

Their willingness to hide the airmen did not mean the helpers had no fear about what they were doing. There were always things that could go wrong in sheltering airmen, even when plans had been carefully laid. The Le Cren family transported five airmen into the village to be distributed among four other families and themselves. During the transfer, however, German troops had congregated in the village for an indefinite period of time, and some of the helpers refused to shelter the men for fear of retaliation. Faced with a house full of evaders, Mme Le Cren told her family, "Well, if we could be shot for hiding one airmen, what more can they do to us if they find five?"[49] All of the men stayed at the Le Crens' temporarily until they could be moved to a new location.

Quite often, the Germans suspected airmen were being hidden by the local people, but they could not very easily conduct widespread executions of everyone in the village. Instead, they conducted periodic searches for airmen, but even then sometimes missed them. A Canadian evader pressed himself flat against a bedroom wall during a house search, escaping undetected when the soldier carelessly glanced into the darkened room without entering.[50] On occasion, Germans found themselves in the presence of airmen but were not astute enough to notice. American Paul Clark, taken by surprise when a German soldier entered the living room of his helper's home, jumped up and returned the soldier's

"Heil Hitler" with a sharp American salute. Luckily, the German did not notice the discrepancy.[51] A similar situation at Maurice Bidaud's home could have had tragic results except for the Germans' single-minded focus on their own needs. Bidaud had several evaders staying with him when, at the evening meal, an evader pointed toward the door and told him there were Germans behind him. Bidaud was a mechanic, and his workplace was attached to his home. The German troops had come to find out whether his shop was large enough to suit their needs. Because their visit was unrelated to evasion, they paid no attention to the large group of men sitting around the table.[52]

Safe houses were found in isolated countrysides and villages as well as in busy towns and cities. Dwellings of all kinds were incorporated into sheltering airmen. Farmhouses and apartments were most commonly used, but offices, warehouses, and hotels also sheltered men on a regular basis. Even brothels were popular due to their low cost and the nature of the activity that took place there, which discouraged police from performing regular raids.[53] Helpers hid men in remote places where Germans seldom roamed and in places that were overrun with Germans. One of the latter was Napoleon's tomb—a safe house for the Burgundy escape line—which was constantly surrounded by enemy soldiers sightseeing in Paris. They were hidden across the street from and next door to German military headquarters and sometimes in apartment buildings, where they were literally under the feet or over the heads of German officers. Australian evader Tony D'Arcey actually spent the day sleeping in a living room that adjoined a kitchen shared with a German officer billeted in an upstairs room. When the officer entered the kitchen at lunchtime, he commented on the living room's closed door but did not attempt to investigate.[54]

Once they settled the evaders in a safe place, the helpers turned their attention to the airmen's other needs. One of the more serious needs of many evaders was medical care. As the air war intensified, increasing numbers of airmen were shot down over France, about one-third of whom needed medical care. Many men developed common colds or respiratory ailments while in hiding. Paul Kenney and Merrill Caldwell both suffered from bad colds during their evasions, and their helpers called doctors to attend them. A bad cough was a problem for those who were trying to remain quiet, and the helpers worried about severe respiratory infections turning into pneumonia. Caldwell remembered his helper, Mme Bredin, making herb teas and soups to nurse him when he was ill.[55]

Helpers often went to great measures to acquire medical attention for evaders, even playing the parts of nurses and assistants themselves in very crude conditions. American Jerry Eshuis, a ball turret gunner, was severely injured during an air battle and bailed out of his plane with shrapnel embedded in his thigh and groin. Though three of his crew members were too badly wounded to be cared for in hiding, Eshuis was carried away by French people, who quickly determined that the shrapnel needed to be removed since infection was setting in. A French doctor examined his wounds and on New Year's Eve 1943 removed the shrapnel through a nine-inch incision in Eshuis' thigh. Because the Germans kept close inventory on medicines in hospitals and doctors' offices, the operation had to be done without anesthesia. During the operation, helpers held Eshuis' arms and legs so that he could not move and stuffed cloths into his mouth to muffle his screams. American evader Robert Lorenzi also had surgery under primitive conditions, when he landed with shrapnel in his foot. Helpers arranged for the surgery within a few hours of his rescue.[56]

Men with severe injuries presented a particularly difficult problem, as they could not be moved for long periods of time. Seventeen-year-old Monique Fillerin faced a serious dilemma when villagers delivered Canadian evader Keith Patrick to her home with a broken collarbone and fractured skull. Her parents had already been arrested, and her house was frequently raided by the Gestapo. The doctor who examined Patrick explained the severity of the injuries, leaving Monique with little hope for the airman's survival: "You can do nothing for him. We have nothing to help him . . . if you put him outside on this cold night, he will be dead by tomorrow night. If you keep him in bed, keeping him warm without help, he will last three days. If you feed him hot meals, take care of him, he may come out of it, but you will have an invalid. . . . But the first thing to do, if you keep him, is to know where to bury him. If he does not die, let me know."[57] Monique chose to help Patrick, but she followed the doctor's directions, and without delay she and her fifteen-year-old brother dug a grave in which to bury the airman should he die.[58] Patrick survived both his injuries and several raids by Germans thanks to the dedication of these teenagers who, with the help of their sister Genevieve, risked everything to help him live.

Having suffered severe burns when their planes caught on fire, many men needed extended care from their helpers, particularly if their eyes had been damaged. Manuel Rogoff, temporarily blinded by his burns, found himself "under the constant care of physicians to whose skill I probably owe my sight. In spite of my conspicuous injuries, my helpers did not relax their care and successfully arranged my journey as soon as I was able to see."[59]

Helpers took great risks finding medical care for wounded airmen and protecting them until they regained their health and strength. When Germans conducted an intense search for an evader with a broken ankle, six Frenchmen placed him on an improvised stretcher and carried him across country for five hours. When they reached their destination, the men were exhausted and their hands blistered and bleeding, but they succeeded in protecting him from the Germans. After finding a doctor to set his ankle, they hid the evader until the liberation.[60]

Caring for wounded evaders was difficult for more than just logistical reasons. Doctors accustomed to providing care to those in pain found it frustrating to perform operations and procedures under primitive conditions, with limited medicines and supplies, and without trained personnel. Australian Alan Monaghan recalled an airman hidden with him who was so badly burned over much of his body that his ears were gone. A doctor came daily to scrape away the dead flesh, but his limited supply of ether was not enough to render the man unconscious, and Monaghan and the other evaders had to hold the burned man down while the doctor worked.[61]

While many airmen needed medical care, most were relatively healthy, with only minor cuts, bruises, or burns. But being young men, they had voracious appetites, and this caused an entirely new problem for the helpers. Food was available in varying quantities depending on where the helpers lived. It was more difficult to obtain food in the cities, and women housing evaders had to be careful when they shopped, because it looked odd for them to suddenly start buying food in greater quantities than usual. They often shopped in several different areas of town in order to purchase enough for their families and their evaders. Some helpers bartered for food, trading tobacco or sugar for meat or dairy products. Since money was scarce, doctors often received farm products as payment for their services. In many cases, though, there simply was not enough food for everyone. Tony D'Arcey remembered thinking that he had probably eaten not only his share of dinner, but his helper's share as well, though she claimed to be on a special diet and not hungry.[62]

It was much less difficult to feed airmen staying in the country, because people kept gardens and raised poultry, rabbits, and piglets. Those who had orchards put away fruit and cider for the winter months. The helpers were quite creative in cooking meals using the internal organs of animals to make soups or stews enhanced with vegetables. They also tried to please the evaders they sheltered by cooking foods that were familiar to them, such as corn on the cob, even though the French viewed corn as barnyard feed and refused to eat it themselves.[63]

Clothing the airmen was almost as great a challenge as feeding them, partly because the evaders were bigger than the Frenchmen, but also because clothing was scarce, especially during the latter years of the war. Yvonne Kervarec and her mother clothed a number of airmen from the large stock of unused attire left behind when Yvonne's husband was imprisoned and her father and brother went to England to fight with the Free French Forces of the Interior (FFI). Women whose husbands were deceased also supplied evaders with clothing. Quite often, however, helpers took the clothes from their backs to help the evaders disguise themselves quickly.[64]

René Le Cren and his brother Desiré went to great measures to provide shoes for an unusually large airman hiding at their house. The intelligence officer who delivered him to the Le Cren family asked that they find the evader a pair of suitable shoes to replace the air force boots he wore. A local tanner agreed to make a pair of size twelve shoes for four shoe tickets, but since few families had shoe tickets to spare, the brothers, along with three friends, robbed the town hall in a neighboring village to get them. René served as lookout while the other boys, wearing masks to cover their identities, stole a large quantity of ration tickets and, like wartime Robin Hoods, distributed them among the people on the streets before returning home with the needed shoe tickets.[65]

While large numbers of helpers attended to the basic needs of the evaders, others turned their attention to planning the men's evacuations from occupied territory. Before they began organizing in earnest, however, the helpers tried to establish the authenticity of the airmen. Whole sections of lines had been wiped out by German infiltration of fake airmen, so MI9 and MIS-X developed questionnaires that enabled helpers to establish the true identity of the airmen. The questionnaires, both British and American versions, were changed every four months, and the airmen had to answer seven out of ten questions correctly.[66] Some escape lines had radio operators who could radio to London for verification of an airman's identity. Jack Stead remembered being told he would be eliminated if London did not verify the information he had given to his interrogator. Hearing that, his only thought was, "Please God, don't let them foul up this time."[67]

Agents and chiefs sometimes found themselves in a dilemma when they could not positively identify an evader as authentic. There were instances when another evader was given the job of verifying someone's identity, with instructions to eliminate him if he proved to be a phony.[68] Pat O'Leary encountered a young German who initially claimed to be an evader, then later admitted he had been sent to infiltrate the line. On his knees, between two agents from another organization, the young man begged to be released, promising to work for O'Leary as a double agent. Though Pat's first inclination was to let the man go, he remembered a past experience when he and other leaders of the Pat line, not wanting to kill a deceitful worker, had shut him in a bathroom while they discussed their options. The worker escaped and turned in about one hundred of his fellow workers to the Gestapo, with tragic results. Many of the helpers were deported or executed. Standing in the foothills of the Pyrenees Mountains, O'Leary wrestled with his memory and indecision while, in the absence of orders to the contrary, the agents killed the German infiltrator.[69]

Before evaders could travel in the open, they had to have papers establishing their identity as Frenchmen. Blank ID cards, rubber stamps, and other materials necessary for making false papers were stolen from town halls by civilians involved with the escape lines who worked for the local government or in German offices. The escape lines issued each man an identity card, a work permit, and, if traveling in coastal or frontier zones, permits that allowed entrance to these special areas.[70] Military intelligence issued passport photos for some of the escape kits, which the helpers used to make the ID cards, assigning the men false names and occupations. When there were no photos included in the escape kits, helpers took the airmen to photo booths or photography shops to have pictures made. It was an unpleasant experience for the evaders who, alongside German soldiers, had to pretend to shop while waiting for the photos to develop.[71]

American airman Paul Clarke carried these photographs in his escape kit for use in making a false identification card. He gave them to his helpers Felix and Denise Bacchi when he left their home to continue his evasion. (Courtesy of Paul and Bettye Clark)

Those who created false papers tried to make them as authentic as possible so that the evaders could go through ID checkpoints without being detained for questioning. Guides kept up with changes to IDs or work permits to reduce the risks of being stopped while transporting airmen from one place to another. They obtained information concerning these changes from newspaper boys or railroad workers, some of whom were unaware of the service they were providing. Train conductors and station managers also helped the guides, warning them about German ID checks and providing security within the station as well as information about railroad traffic and station controls.[72]

All aspects of aiding evaders were dangerous, but unlike safe house keepers who worked behind closed doors, the helpers who guided men through city streets and helped them master the intricacies of the French railroad system worked in the public view. The nature of their work made it doubly important that they be able to think quickly, since unforeseen problems arose no matter how much care they put into their preparations.

Guides tried to decrease the risks involved by giving the men detailed instructions on how they should behave in public. Train travel was difficult, because the men had to sit in small compartments that they shared with French civilians and German servicemen. They could not talk, since their English conversation would alert everyone on the train to their identities, so they passed the time by pretending to sleep or read a newspaper. Both of these were useful activities in that they discouraged conversation from other travelers. During a particularly long journey by train, Australian evader Robert Horsley and a fellow evader seated close by communicated by means of tapping Morse code on the back of each other's arms.[73]

There were also cultural snares in which the airmen could get caught, and the guides tried to avoid these by training the evaders to engage in European mannerisms; for example, grasping their cigarettes from the burning end using their fingertips and thumbs and letting the butts dangle from their lips, rather than holding the cigarettes between their fingers and throwing the butts away. They also reminded the airmen not to jingle the change in their pockets, since this was a uniquely American trait. It was often small inconsistencies of this nature that caused airmen to be arrested by German soldiers, who had been taught to watch for unusual behaviors.[74]

To overcome the language barrier, guides taught the airmen to pretend they were deaf and dumb, but there was soon an overflow of "deaf" men in Europe. It is odd that the Germans did not wonder about the large numbers of deaf-mutes and half-wits running around France, since anytime a helper got caught with an evader, he or she usually claimed the evader was a mute or an idiot. British evader Taffy Higginson was greatly impressed with the cool demeanor of his guide when they were stopped by a German patrol just after crossing the demarcation line into unoccupied France. The guide told the Germans Higginson was crazy, but the patrol insisted on examining the small suitcase the airman carried. Inside, they found dirty socks smeared with melted chocolate, which inspired the guide to suggest Higginson had defecated in his suitcase. The Germans were convinced that the man was indeed crazy and allowed them to continue on their way.[75]

For most of the airmen, evasion through France was their first experience with a foreign country, and in spite of the guides' instructions, it was difficult to resist staring at the famous historical sites surrounding them. According to Comet line guide Micheline Dumon—better known in evasion literature as "Michou"—the airmen reacted in different ways to the sights around them. "The Americans were like children exclaiming over seeing new things,"[76] while the British airmen were more disciplined about expressing their impressions.

Because of the human element involved in convoying airmen, even the most organized plans sometimes went awry. Guides might be detained for unexpected reasons, and breaks in the escape lines due to helpers' arrests occasionally left men temporarily stranded in train stations, cafés, or on the streets while helpers tried to make alternate plans. Guides were very flexible, however, and could change strategies at a moment's notice when circumstances demanded, depositing airmen in a safe house or taking them to their own homes until new arrangements could be made.

Moving around in public with the airmen meant the guides had periodic encounters with Germans. While none of these experiences was pleasant, some were quite amusing in hindsight. Pat O'Leary was convoying two RAF evaders to Paris, and as none of them had eaten in about twenty-four hours, he took them into the restaurant car for a meal. The only seats available were at a table with two German soldiers, so Pat led the airmen to the table and ordered beers for each of them. One of the men was extremely nervous in the soldiers' presence and within seconds of receiving his beer knocked his glass over. Pat watched panic-stricken as the beer poured into the Germans' laps and they leaped up cursing and wiping up the mess. But the worst was yet to come. In his terror and embarrassment, the airman began to laugh, and Pat turned cold with fear. He began to apologize for the evader's behavior, but before he could speak, the Germans began laughing, too. Soon Pat, the waiter, and other diners were laughing as well. The Germans and the evaders could not speak to each other, but throughout the meal they exchanged smiles. Although things turned out well, Pat was relieved when he and his charges finished their meals and returned to their seats on the train.[77]

Unfortunately, not all encounters ended so well. One German policeman stopped an evader on a train and indicated that the airman should follow him. Seeing one of his party being led away, a second airman followed, as did four others. Amazingly, all six left with the German policeman of their own volition. The guide watched the chain of events helplessly, knowing it was too dangerous to intervene. All of the airmen had their dog tags, which allowed them to claim POW status, while the guide, if caught, could only look forward to deportation or death.[78]

Another unfortunate incident occurred when Raymond Itterbeek, a twenty-year-old Belgian guide for the Comet line, was stopped with two evaders at the Lille train station in northern France for an ID check. Itterbeek indicated from behind a newspaper that the men were to hand over their false ID cards, but the first evader carelessly handed the Gestapo officer his train ticket instead. The second evader had checked his papers before the Gestapo reached him and was ready with the correct documents, but his English accent was so strong that the Gestapo immediately identified him as an evader. Because Itterbeek was standing in between the two men, the Gestapo correctly assumed he was with them. The evaders were turned over to the German Luftwaffe, while Itterbeek was arrested, interrogated, and brutally beaten before being sent to Loos Prison. Itterbeek used a false ID card for his escape work, and it was two days before the Gestapo learned his true identity. As a result, the other workers on the line were able to ward off any immediate collapse of the line. However, several months later a careless American evader brought about a series of arrests that included Itterbeek's parents and sixteen others when German police caught him with a forbidden list of addresses for the people who had helped him.[79]

It is difficult to believe that despite the helpers' many warnings about the importance of following the guides' directions, there were still instances when airmen disregarded the rules. Pierre Moreau, a teenage

(Above left) Raymond Itterbeek is an active member of the Comet post war organization. He participates in yearly reunions and keeps in regular contact with former members of the line. (Courtesy of Raymond Itterbeek) *(Above right)* Wartime photograph of Comet guide Raymond Itterbeek. (Courtesy of Raymond Itterbeek)

Comet guide Raymond Itterbeek carried this false identification card at the time of his arrest while convoying two evaders through Belgium. Several years after the war, a friend recognized his picture while examining old Gestapo files and returned the card to Itterbeek. (Courtesy of Raymond Itterbeek)

guide, was escorting several airmen in the coastal region when he realized one of his group was missing. He left the men in a safe place and went to search for the missing evader, finding him examining German tanks on the main street. Recognizing the danger involved in approaching him, Moreau left the airman behind and returned to the group. He wrote that it was difficult not to overreact when the wandering evader later rejoined the party. But considering the possible repercussions of his actions, it is a wonder the helpers agreed to continue assisting him rather than leave him to the mercies of the German soldiers in whose tanks he had been so interested.[80]

Each escape line worker was one small link in a very big chain, but without the strength of each individual component the evasion networks could not have functioned. While the workers concentrated on doing their jobs to the best of their ability, they did so without knowledge of the results of their efforts. For their own protection and that of the airmen, escape line workers knew very little about the mechanics of the line's operation. René Charpentier claimed he knew the men were being taken to Spain, but that his part ended when he delivered the men to a guide in a neighboring town. It was not until after the war that he learned where the men had gone from there. Maurice Leech still does not know the details surrounding his involvement with the escape line. His father maintained communication with the escape organization, and Maurice simply followed his father's directions, escorting the evaders when and where he was told.[81]

The guides frequently worked on a relay system and had no time to develop any kind of relationship with the evaders. Much of the time they did not even know the names of the men they escorted. According to Pierre Moreau, guides and evaders "were sometimes just faces passing each other with no other contact than a silent handshake, but you could always read their thanks and gratitude in their eyes in the last gaze exchanged before they left."[82]

Many helpers went above and beyond the call of duty to make the evaders' forced confinement as bearable as possible. They took them sightseeing at various historical sites, though this brought them into close contact with Germans, which could be very unnerving.[83] English-speaking people visited safe houses, giving the men an opportunity to converse in their own language, and Maryse de la Marnierre (McKeon) remembered that she and her sisters used to dance with the evaders hiding at their house. She had three sisters, ranging in age from eleven to nineteen years. After the war, when asked why he hid airmen, her father responded that his daughters needed dance partners.[84] One woman decorated the inside of her house with British, American, and French flags and threw a party for the thirty-four evaders hiding in her chateau. Joining in the celebratory spirit, the evaders spent the evening paying tribute to the helpers for their assistance.[85]

Maurice Bidaud planned a unique excursion for the airmen he was sheltering. He took them to the local swimming pool, but ran into trouble when one of the airmen completed such a beautiful jump off the high dive that a member of the area swim team asked Bidaud if his friend might be interested in joining the team. Bidaud lost no time in explaining that this was impossible, as his friend was going away soon, and immediately left with his group.[86]

A few helpers tried to provide entertainment of a more intimate nature, as Jack Stead found out when his helper delivered him to a woman named Louise for the day. As Louise followed him around the room trying to be accommodating, Stead contemplated his options. Thinking his whole evasion situation suggested he was in enough trouble already, he convinced her that he was in no mood for amorous activity, and all he really wanted was a cup of coffee. Louise was surprised, but set about making a pot of coffee, and the two of them spent the day talking and becoming acquainted with each other in spite of the language barrier. In later years, Stead remembered that Louise was a "great gal." Her husband had been sent to Germany as forced labor. Stead never found out whether he survived to return to her after the war.[87]

Although the airmen appreciated the entertainment and have fond memories of the activities, they appreciated even more the way the helpers handled their comrades who died when their planes crashed. The French people made coffins and held funeral ceremonies for them. Disturbed by the anti-German sentiment that presented itself during these ceremonies, German patrols tried to collect the bodies first, often burying them in shallow graves nearby, but the French people dug up the bodies and reburied them in churchyards and local cemeteries. After the war, some of the airmen's bodies were moved to their own countries, but many were left in the small cemeteries where the French helpers had buried them. Even today, the graves are regularly cared for and annual ceremonies held to commemorate the sacrifices of airmen who died during the war.[88]

Whether helpers based their decision to aid airmen on duty, patriotism, or humanity, they all faced the same complications in carrying out their work. For most of the helpers, aiding airmen was a great financial burden. A few of the safe house keepers were able to cover the expenses involved, but most were not. Some sold their jewelry and household items to fund their escape work. Georges Rodocanachi, a safe house keeper for the Pat O'Leary line, spent almost his entire life savings helping people escape.[89]

Though Allied military intelligence gave considerable amounts of money to the leaders of some of the larger escape lines, it seldom filtered down to the majority of those hiding airmen. Obviously the money included in the escape kits was hardly enough to make a difference to those who housed airmen for indefinite periods of time. For the most part, helpers received no financial assistance for their work, and many have claimed that they would not have accepted it even had it been offered.[90] When former helper François Moal read that some American and British writers claimed the French had helped the airmen for money, he vehemently denied these claims, writing, "I am absolutely shocked . . . that these lies are believed. It is hurtful and an insult to the French Resistance. Let it be known that we freely and patriotically assumed these risks."[91] Considering the documentation and personal testimony of those who experienced the loss of family members to execution by the Germans, brutal torture by German officials, and the deprivation and misery of the concentration camps, it is difficult to imagine how the helpers could be accused of acting for financial gain. Besides the aforementioned documentation, the helpers' denials are supported by a large number of evaders like George Buckner, who vowed that the French people who helped him and other evaders "did so for a far higher purpose than mere money. Only fools would risk their lives and the welfare of their children and all else they held dear for money."[92]

While finances were a problem for helpers, children were even more problematic because of their contradictory role in evasion. They were useful for aiding airmen and carrying messages or serving as lookouts, because the Germans paid them little mind, but their youth also made it difficult for them to keep secrets, which increased the risks of hiding airmen with helpers who had children. Claude Bacchi, a young teenager during the war, served as lookout for his family while the evaders had their meals, but his parents took measures to protect him, and he recalled being sent to his room or to the garden whenever something important took place. He also remembered being evicted from his bed in the middle of the night on a few occasions so that a tired evader could rest in comfort.[93]

Alain Sibiril was only ten years old when the war broke out, but he remembers his father explaining to him about the people who were hiding in their house and the need to be quiet about it. Sibiril recalled, "I kept my promise. But with this secret I became a man in the body of a boy. At school I was not young like the others. From age eleven, I had my place in my father's network."[94] Sibiril worked as a lookout during the naval evacuations conducted by his father; he also served as a liaison, collecting and transporting intelligence papers concerning German defenses in the area. Though proud to have had a part in his father's work, Sibiril admitted that some events were traumatic. He never forgot the terror he felt when he arrived home one day to find an agent in the family kitchen who, concerned about Sibiril's youth, waved a gun at him and threatened to shoot him if he talked about the escape activity.[95]

Many children proved as quick thinking as their parents with respect to hiding the airmen. A seven-year-old girl hid two airmen in a pile of hay, then denied knowing anything about the flyers while the Germans searched for them. A group of airmen hiding among the tombstones was seen by two little girls who had gone to the cemetery to pray with their nanny. The girls indicated that the men should stay hidden and sent two older boys back with food and a message to remain hidden. The boys returned later that night and took the men to their home.[96]

Though many parents enlisted their children's aid in helping the airmen, it was not uncommon for flyers to be relocated because of the presence of young children in the home. The couple that sheltered Colin Bayliss wanted him to stay with them throughout the remainder of the war, but they were forced to move him into an escape line after finding out that their six-year-old daughter had told her school friends she had an uncle visiting her who spoke English.[97] This was not an isolated incident, and it was fortunate for Serge and Henriette van Nieuwenhuysse that the teacher who overheard their daughter's report was not a collaborator.

There are countless stories to corroborate the bravery of the helpers and their willingness to sacrifice their most precious possessions to help the evaders, even if that meant their lives or those of their families.

Some had to swallow the bitterness of lost loved ones even as they continued helping those who caused the loss. A Frenchman named Jacques gave up his job as a policeman to devote himself full time to aiding evaders. While traveling to Paris to meet a group of airmen, he was killed by American fighters who attacked the train on which he rode. The irony of his death at the hands of the very people he was trying to protect made his wife's grief even more difficult to bear. Less than an hour after hearing of her husband's death, another member of the escape organization, unaware of the recent events, arrived at Jacques' home and asked his wife Marie to hide five American airmen. Though she realized that she might be sheltering the men responsible for Jacques' death, Marie agreed to hide the evaders and carried out her husband's legacy of resistance by continuing his work with the escape line.[98]

Though death by Allied bombers forced to unload their bombs early was always a possibility, brutal treatment and torture by the Germans was by far the greatest threat to the helpers. German officials engaged in cruel tactics to compel resisters to give information about others involved in aiding evaders. When helper Raymond Lefevre refused to talk, the Germans tortured him so severely that his arms were torn from their sockets, leaving them completely useless after the war. Lefevre was a section chief and therefore in a position to betray the location of about fifty French helpers, but despite the vicious torture he gave no one away.[99]

Physical abuse was not the only form of torture used by the Germans. If they thought mental or emotional anguish might be rewarding to them, they employed those methods as well. Eleanor Cheramy, code-named "Pat," sheltered airmen for the Pat O'Leary line and provided a home base for O'Leary's radio operator. When they arrested her in July 1943, German officers also took her eighteen-month-old son Michel into custody. They took her to an interrogation room with her son, who giggled and reached for her, but when Eleanor reached out for him, a German officer hit her hands hard enough to make her withdraw. For one week the Germans taunted her with the presence of her small child, but each time she tried to touch him their response was the same, a painful blow to her hands and a demand for the truth. It is impossible to imagine the frustration of such a young child held in the same room as the mother he cherished but unable to go to her—held instead by men with rough voices who showed no kindness. It is also impossible to conceive of the pain Eleanor must have felt in being helpless to comfort her child and fearful of what might become of him in German hands. After a week of such emotional torture, Michel was taken away. The German police turned him over to the French Red Cross, which located Eleanor's housekeeper and gave him to her. The housekeeper took Michel to his paternal grandmother in Paris, who cared for him until the war's end. Eleanor did not see him again until he was almost four years old. She was sent to Fresnes prison, then deported to Ravensbrük and Mauthausen concentration camps. When she was liberated by American troops in spring 1945, she was barely alive as a result of poor conditions and a severe blow to her head by a German soldier. Though she weighed only forty-nine pounds when released from the camp, Eleanor lived—but she suffered permanent injuries that interfered with her activities for the rest of her life.[100]

Though the old adage "war is hell" is still used to explain away sensitive wartime events, for most people it is beyond understanding that humans could treat other humans as cruelly as the Germans treated those who resisted enemy occupation. Georges "Geo" Jouanjean was the chief of the Brittany sector of the Pat O'Leary line until its collapse, after which he went to work for the Oaktree escape organization. He evaded capture a number of times, but was finally arrested while trying to determine the safety of another helper's home. Jouanjean was brutally interrogated on numerous occasions by Germans, who beat him or held his head underwater until he lost consciousness. After transferring him to a

Georges Jouanjean led the Brittany section of the Pat O'Leary line and played an active role in the Oaktree organization until his arrest in 1943. (Courtesy of Gordon and Janine Carter)

prison, German officials locked him into a cage about four feet square and handcuffed him to the bars at the top of the cage. From his handcuffed position, Jouanjean was unable to sit down, and the small size of the cage made standing impossible. He wrote about his thoughts during this period more than fifty years after the war, but his sentiments seem as real as if the events had occurred only yesterday: "How long I stayed in that cage is impossible to tell. The seconds were like hours, the hours like days, the days like months. Time did not exist. Always nightmares, yet time passes. Then you get scared. Scared to die, scared of shaky legs, scared to be a coward. I know the end is coming. The bullets, they pierce you. They burn. They tear up your body. I can feel them and imagine them. When the door to this cell opens, it will be death."[101] After incarceration in Birkenau-Auschwitz, Büchenwald, and Flossenbürg concentration camps, Jouanjean was repatriated in early summer 1945. In spite of his horrific experiences, he was more fortunate than some of the concentration camp inmates who survived their imprisonment only to succumb later to the poor treatment they had received.

The bitterness of many helpers over their experiences as German prisoners was increased by the knowledge that they were betrayed by their own or Allied countrymen. Mme Leroy, a guide and safe house keeper for the Comet line, was arrested and tortured by Frenchmen employed by Germans. Rather than cower before their cruelty, she told them, "If you had defended France as stubbornly in 1940 as you are now interrogating me, my country should not have been beaten."[102] Mme Leroy was deported to a concentration camp and shot a few days before the liberation.

Hundreds of helpers were killed or deported to concentration camps when they were betrayed. In some cases those arrested were innocent family members of helpers, people who had no involvement in the lines. One of the Comet line's agents escaped when he was betrayed, but the Germans retaliated by arresting his wife and daughter instead.[103] Gabrielle Buffet Picabia and her younger daughter, both of whom were involved with the Resistance, escaped German capture after they were betrayed, but Gabrielle's older daughter, who had no Resistance connections, was arrested. Gabrielle recalled, "That was a hard blow for me. She had two children, and her husband was not in France at that time."[104] Still, Gabrielle continued with her escape work while trying to provide for her grandchildren, who had been left alone.

Knowledge of the responsibilities and risks involved with aiding downed Allied airmen did not necessarily carry with it an understanding of the mechanics of the escape lines. Because each helper had knowledge of only his or her part in carrying out the airmen's evasions, there had to be a hierarchy of chiefs and agents to organize the helpers and serve as liaisons between them and the military intelligence who worked to protect them. Some of the escape lines were created by MI9 and had trained agents. However, two of the three most successful lines were formed under the leadership of ordinary people moved by compassion for the servicemen left behind after the Dunkirk evacuation. While all three lines worked toward the same end, each was unique in the way it functioned. The successful efforts of the first two lines—Pat O'Leary and Comet—established a framework for military intelligence to follow in future attempts to develop escape lines, culminating in the triumphant Shelburne line, established in the last months of the war in Europe.

4

Adolph Should Stay

The Pat O'Leary Line, 1940–1941

Ian Garrow, member of the 51st Highland Division of the Seaforth High-landers, wandered through the crowded streets of Marseilles, a port city located on the Mediterranean coast of France. He had been left behind when German troops overpowered the Allied defenses near Dunkirk, ending the miraculous operation that evacuated about 340,000 British and French forces during late May and early June 1940.[1] Ironically, Garrow's abandonment was to prove a godsend for hundreds of service-men and airmen who had also been left behind or were subsequently shot down over enemy territory as the war progressed.

As he walked along the city streets, Garrow noticed large numbers of ill-clad, hungry men loitering in doorways and on street corners. They were British and Commonwealth servicemen who had managed to avoid being placed in a prison camp but upon reaching Marseilles had no place to go for shelter and provisions. Their situation was serious, and Garrow began to wonder whether there was some way he could help these men return to England, where they could continue the war effort. He had anticipated finding passage on a freighter bound for England, where he could rejoin his division, but thought he might be able to serve the mili-tary better if he remained in France to establish a means of helping other servicemen evacuate. Without some form of assistance, these men could expect arrest and incarceration in a POW camp, in which case their con-tribution to the fighting forces would be over.[2] This fact, combined with humanitarian concern for his fellow man, prompted Garrow to lay the foundation for the Pat O'Leary line—one of the most successful escape lines of World War II.

On Garrow's arrival in Marseilles, Vichy authorities had interned him in Fort Saint-Jean, a former Foreign Legion depot that had been transformed into a type of holding camp. Camp regulations were very flexible, and enlisted men were granted periodic paroles, during which they were free to explore as long as they returned to the fort at nightfall. Officers had the freedom to live outside the camp and often bartered their weekly rations for money, which they used to pay for lodging elsewhere. Garrow rented a room by this method and spent much time roaming the streets of Marseilles, developing his plans and meeting people, many of whom he recruited to work in his escape line.[3]

Initially evaders arranged their own evasions with the assistance of individual helpers in the towns and villages through which they passed. As the Germans established themselves more firmly in France in the months following the armistice, those who helped evaders began to organize themselves into groups in order to work more effectively. Anticipating the possibility that French civilians might try to aid Allied evaders, the Germans posted warning signs outlining the consequences of such activities.[4]

Apart from having to contend with the Germans and their French collaborators, Garrow faced other obstacles, not least among them his own personal appearance. He was very tall—in a country where most of the men were quite short—and he looked conspicuously Scottish. Though his French was improving, he spoke it with a terrible accent and was so out of place that his successor, Pat O'Leary, commented that Garrow met "all the conditions to be immediately arrested when met on the streets of Marseilles."[5] O'Leary, endearingly known to the evasion world as "Pat," was not the only one to voice surprise at Garrow's success as an organizer. James Langley of MI9, one of Garrow's early evaders, concluded that Garrow would not last long as a chief because of his conspicuous appearance and poor French. He wrote: "That my assessments of Ian Garrow's chances of survival and potential to achieve success were entirely wrong was due to failure to appreciate what he had to offer and complete ignorance of the attitudes to our activities of the Vichy Government police force and security services."[6]

British intelligence remained perplexed as to why Garrow was able to operate his line for so long in the face of these apparent shortcomings. The answer came in 1942 when the head of a French security department escaped to England and told them that both the French and German authorities were aware of Garrow's activity but found it unbelievable that the English would make such an outlandishly obvious choice for an agent. As a result, Garrow was left to his work while authorities tried to determine the real mastermind behind the network.[7]

Garrow received very little help from either the British government or military intelligence while the line was being formed. After June 1940, when British naval forces attacked the French fleet at Mers el Kebir in North Africa, relations between the two countries deteriorated, and the Vichy government refused to allow Britain to reopen its consular offices. The U.S. government continued to maintain diplomatic relations with Vichy France and attempted to represent British interests through its consular offices.[8] British major Hugh Dodds and his assistant Arthur Dean headed the British section of the American Consulate in Marseilles, overseeing the conditions at Fort Saint-Jean, as well as caring for the needs of British civilians. Providing assistance to Garrow, however, was another matter since the U.S. State Department prohibited its consular offices from aiding the escape or evasion of British military personnel.[9] Still, individual consuls tried to help where they could, by providing forms and stamps for use in preparing false identification papers for the evaders. In some instances they directed evaders who approached their offices to people who worked on Garrow's line, ensuring them the assistance they needed.

The lack of aid from military intelligence arose in large part from communication problems. MI9 was in its infancy as an organization, and both Airey Neave and James Langley, the future executive officers of MI9, were themselves still evading or imprisoned in Europe. Donald Darling, British vice consul in Gibraltar in charge of repatriation, eventually opened communications with Garrow by means of couriers traveling over the Pyrenees. Nubar Gulbenkian, son of a wealthy Armenian oil tycoon, served as one of the couriers, since his neutral passport allowed him to move easily between Spain and France. His father's business interests in France gave him a reason for being there and quieted any suspicion about his presence. Through Gulbenkian, Darling established a connection with Garrow and arranged for evaders to be collected at an automotive garage in Perpignan and subsequently led over the mountains on foot by paid guides. This system worked well until the owner of the garage, Michael Pareyre ("Parker") fell under the scrutiny of Vichy police, forcing Garrow to look for new guides.[10] Pyrenees guides were a vital link in the escape line. Most of them had made their living as smugglers during the prewar years. Their knowledge of the mountains and experience in crossing them on a regular basis made them invaluable for transporting evaders across the range while avoiding the German patrols that kept watch along the borders.[11]

Once a line of communication was established between Garrow and Darling, intelligence offices in London received a briefing on the line's activity and began sending money to pay the mountain guides and meet the needs of the line. Even so, the courier system, though helpful, was rather inefficient. In order to get a message to London, Garrow either had to find a trustworthy person who was traveling to Spain legitimately to smuggle a letter in for him, or he had to send someone on a specific trip over the mountains to deliver the message personally. He would then have to wait an indefinite period of time before receiving a response, which often came by way of the nightly broadcasts of the BBC. Buried within a litany of seemingly innocuous statements, such as "The carrots are cooked" or "John has a long moustache," would be the prearranged message confirming the arrival of Garrow's messenger. A radio operator would have allowed him to work more effectively, but the few French-speaking operators available were quickly enlisted by Secret Intelligence Services (SIS) or SOE.[12]

Garrow's limited knowledge of French hindered his work significantly, but his quiet determination and pleasant personality attracted many willing helpers. Though desperate for assistance, Garrow realized the importance of having trustworthy people to help him, and he personally checked the credentials of each person who volunteered his or her help. In time, he organized a group of people who served as some of the line's staunchest and most dependable workers throughout its existence.[13] Because of its status as a port city, Marseilles's citizens came from many different nations. The diversity of backgrounds was well illustrated in the make-up of Garrow's line. Unlike other escape lines which were organized and run predominantly by people of French, Belgian, or Dutch nationality, the Pat line (the more common name for the Pat O'Leary line) had workers from varied backgrounds, including Greek, English, French, Australian, Scottish, Belgian, and German.[14]

One serious problem in running the escape line was that of finances. It cost a great deal of money to arrange for the transport of evaders from one place to another, as well as to feed and clothe them while they were in hiding. Louis Nouveau, one of Garrow's earliest contacts, was indispensable in helping finance the line. Nouveau was an entrepreneur and commodities trader who had a large number of contacts and took advantage of them to help Garrow in his work. Though only in his forties, Nouveau's lungs had been badly damaged when he was gassed as a soldier in World War I. He was already searching for a way to get involved in the war effort when he met Garrow at an afternoon tea given by some friends. After learning of the effort to help evaders, Nouveau offered his services, and though disappointed when Garrow initially turned him down, the financial situation of the line eventually became such that Garrow agreed to accept Nouveau's help.[15] The men Nouveau sheltered had much for which to thank him, such as instructions on how to fit in among the French civilians, guidance and transport to safe houses, and the procurement of ID cards. Albert Leslie Wright was one of six evaders hiding at the Nouveau home at one time. He remembered Nouveau as a "slightly austere, no-nonsense person, brave and dedicated to working for the reseau."[16]

Nouveau kept a list of names and information about the men he hid in his apartment. He owned the complete set of Voltaire's works and wrote the information on the inside margins of volume forty-four. In volume one, he recorded the various trips he made to conduct the business of the line. Ultimately, Nouveau, with the help of his contacts, provided about 450,000 francs for the line. In addition to caring for the line's finances, he also sheltered about 156 evaders in his home between May 1941 and February 1942 and established new connections for the line in Brittany.[17]

Another staunchly pro-British couple, Dr. Georges Rodocanachi and his wife Fanny, entertained British servicemen stranded in Marseilles on a regular basis. Rodocanachi had been a British citizen, but renounced his citizenship to fight with the French during World War I.[18] His health and age had kept him from combat during the recent German invasion, but he too found ways to assist the British allies. By serving on the Franco-German Armistice Commission, which determined the medical fitness of servicemen, Rodocanachi tried to label as many men as possible medically unfit to return to service. This kept them from being transferred to POW camps and allowed them to return to England instead, where they rejoined the war effort.[19]

Garrow was familiar with the Rodocanachis, having been a dinner guest in their home on several occasions, but it was a young woman,

Elizabeth Hayden-Guest, who was responsible for incorporating them into the line. Elizabeth managed her work on the line while at the same time raising a young son. When her son became ill, the American consul directed her to Dr. Rodocanachi, to whom she explained Garrow's activity and then suggested that the doctor would be a great help to them in assisting evaders. As was the case with Nouveau and his wife Renée, the Rodocanachis provided an indispensable service to the line. Because his office was located in his home, it did not seem unusual for large numbers of people to go in and out at odd hours. This made it ideal as a safe house for evaders and a headquarters for the line. Garrow, and later O'Leary, had permanent rooms at the Rodocanachi home, enabling key agents to contact them more readily. The Rodocanachis offered Garrow and Pat a key to their house but both refused, fearing the repercussions if they were arrested and tortured into revealing where the key had come from.[20]

For the most part, the airmen who stayed with the Rodocanachis were respectful of the house rules and the need for silence, since the Rodocanachis had neighbors living above and below them. However, the first American pilot to hide with them caused a great deal of apprehension when he returned late one night inebriated and loudly singing patriotic songs while being led up to their home. Luckily, none of the neighbors seemed to be bothered, and they were able to get him inside the house with no further complications.[21]

Donald Caskie of the Seamen's Mission in Marseilles was another valuable link in Garrow's line. A Presbyterian minister who left Paris when the Germans occupied France, Caskie was also Scottish, which, in relation to Garrow, caused even more confusion among the Vichy authorities. Caskie went to the American Consulate to offer assistance to servicemen stranded in Marseilles and agreed to set up a refuge for escapers and evaders. Caskie's awareness that Vichy collaborators had infiltrated every level of French society even in the unoccupied zone led him to warily approach the Marseilles police department. Luckily, he met with a special-forces detective who guided him to the Seamen's Mission building. The detective was kind and helpful, but suspecting Caskie's real intentions, warned, "Let no soldier be found hiding there. And trust no man, m'sieur. You will be watched. I know it. You must beware of paid agents, and of sudden raids."[22] Offering his best wishes for success, the detective departed.

Scottish Presbyterian minister Donald Caskie ran the Seamen's Mission for the Pat O'Leary escape line in Marseilles. Though under constant vigilance by Vichy authorities, he was able to feed, clothe, and house large numbers of evaders on their final stop before crossing the Pyrenees Mountains. (Courtesy of Jenny and Ian Johnston)

Caskie searched the building for hiding places that might be used to shelter the men in the event of a raid. Discovering spaces beneath the floorboards, he pried up boards all over the building and refitted them so that they slid in and out of position easily. He disguised entrances to hiding places created behind cupboards and spaces under the roof so searchers would be unable to find them. These hiding places were important since French authorities had agreed that the mission could shelter only British civilians.[23]

The first task on taking in new arrivals was to hide them until Caskie could obtain civilian clothes for them. This was a continuing problem until Caskie discovered the Arab quarter in Marseilles. After dark, he took groups of five or six men at a time to this quarter and completely outfitted them in civilian clothing at the large bazaar held there daily. On the way back to the mission, they dropped their bundles of military clothing into the Mediterranean Sea.[24]

Supplying food for the evaders was also a difficult problem for Caskie, as none of the men hiding in the mission had ration cards. Sometimes it seemed that divine providence intervened in the events surrounding the mission. On one occasion an evader found six ration cards on the side of the road and happily turned them over to Caskie. As tempting as it was to keep them, Caskie returned them to the owner, a widow with six children, who he found kneeling beside her bed crying over the loss of her cards. His ensuing visit with the woman led her to introduce him to her minister, whose parish became a regular supplier of large amounts of food for the mission.[25]

Though Caskie intended from the beginning to aid escapers and evaders, he worked as an individual rather than as part of an organization. Garrow had stayed at the mission temporarily and, when developing his escape line, had asked Caskie to provide a last link before the Pyrenees crossing. The American Consul helped considerably, taking great pleasure in providing funds as well as papers, complete with the American seal, for the men Caskie was hiding.[26] On the advice of the consul, Caskie contacted Rodocanachi, who provided medical attention for the men. Rodocanachi knew that the men were evaders and passed on information about planned departures.[27] Caskie claimed Vichy police suspected that the Seamen's Mission was aiding in the escape of British soldiers and airmen, but could not prove it in spite of numerous raids. At any rate, the conversation at the mission was a good source of information concerning British clandestine activity, and the authorities kept it open for that reason.[28]

Caskie continued his ministerial duties as well by visiting prisons and delivering care packages to the inmates, though the contents of his packages were not what one might expect from a minister. He delivered ID cards, passes, information from the escape line, and sometimes small hacksaws to aid in breakouts.[29] On one occasion Caskie even delivered some pills designed to make the prisoners sick enough to require a trip to the hospital, where they encountered a young doctor who worked for the line. The scheme, hatched by Pat O'Leary, was successful. Caskie wrote, "I confess my hair was standing to attention on my scalp as he unfolded his scheme. He, I am sure, was very gleeful. It was characteristic of O'Leary."[30]

The physician who cared for the sick prisoners insisted that they were suffering from poor food and lack of exercise. He gave them a harmless prescription and ordered that they be taken for a daily walk. To Caskie's surprise, the fifteen men with four prison guards arrived at the mission for tea the following day. Shortly afterward, O'Leary arrived as well, armed with bottles of "fiery spirits." While Caskie served the prisoners, O'Leary gave generous attention to the entertainment of the guards, sharing his bottles freely. Caskie expressed the feeling that he thought it was probably "disgraceful for a man of my cloth to stand by and watch this alcoholic jamboree,"[31] but that he was under O'Leary's orders and could do nothing more than watch. When the celebration was over, the guards stumbled out, aided by their prisoners, oblivious to the fact that they were returning to the prison with fewer men than when they started. The "missing" prisoners were picked up by the line and escorted over the mountains.

Of all those known for aiding evaders, few are as highly revered as Patrick Albert O'Leary (Pat). The descriptions of him, both by workers on the line and members of military intelligence, instill a feeling of regret in those deprived of the honor of knowing him. It is interesting to consider that, technically, "Pat" was not an actual person. He had no birth or death certificate, he never married, and his house and phone number were never found in a directory. Patrick O'Leary was in fact the *nom de guerre* for Albert Marie Edmond Guerisse, a Belgian doctor who joined a cavalry regiment when the Germans invaded Belgium and France. He was evacuated at Dunkirk and on arrival in England joined the British Royal Navy, serving on the HMS *Fidelity* as Lt. Comdr. Patrick O'Leary.[32] While trying to rescue a group of Polish officers off the coast of southern France, he and four crewmen were arrested by the Vichy French coastguard and sent to a camp for British military prisoners at St. Hippolyte du Fort near Nîmes. His strong personality was quickly apparent, and within a short period the escape committee within the prison chose him as its leader. Feeling he could not leave his companions in

Maj. Gen. Albert Marie Edmond Guerisse, better known as Patrick O'Leary, served as chief of the Pat O'Leary escape line. He is remembered for his compassion, courage, and leadership. (Courtesy of Alex Wattebled)

prison while he escaped, O'Leary helped free them before considering his own escape efforts. When he earned ten days in solitary confinement for boosting one of his crewmembers over the courtyard wall, he used the time alone to perfect his own escape plan.[33]

While fellow prisoners caused a distraction in the prison's courtyard, O'Leary broke out of a cell, the restraining bar of which had been sawed apart over several days. Though chased by guards, he entered a hospice and was helped by the Mother Superior, who hid him in an old chest of clothes in the attic until dark. Guards, suspecting the nun was lying when she claimed O'Leary had run out another door, surrounded the building and hoped to catch him when he left. Fortunately, they were unaware of an underground tunnel that led into the vineyard. The tunnel had been used in years past to help harvesters transport the grapes into cool shelter more quickly. The Mother Superior led O'Leary through the tunnel and to the edge of the vineyard, where he escaped undetected.[34]

O'Leary was already familiar with Garrow's name, as it had been passed about in the prison. The men knew he had organized a system of guides to help evaders cross the mountains into Spain. Accordingly, following his escape, O'Leary set out for Marseilles. He arrived the next day, determined to return to England, rejoin the navy, and continue fighting the war. However, Garrow had other ideas and persuaded O'Leary to continue fighting the war in the shadowy world of the Resistance, in the very presence of the enemy from whom he had just escaped. Well aware of his own limitations, Garrow needed someone to help him with the growing line, someone who could compensate for his shortcomings. O'Leary's personality and excellent bilingual abilities made him ideal for the job, but these were not his only talents.[35] Most people who had dealings with Pat were drawn to his quiet ways and protective nature. Donald Caskie wrote: "Patrick O'Leary, RN, was one of the bravest men I have ever known. Gay and fearless, his sense of humour led him to enjoy situations so nerve-wracking they might have stopped the stoutest heart. But he was strict, kindly and protective to those under his command. Fighting the enemy he was entirely ruthless. . . . He was a man born with all the characteristics of a romantic hero."[36] People were naturally attracted to O'Leary's strength and kindness. One of O'Leary's chief agents, Alex Wattebled, described him as an angel.[37] Many airmen knew that Pat made the difference between repatriation and a POW camp, and helpers on the line saw him as the embodiment of reason in a world where reason had ceased to exist. Georges Zarifi, nephew of Dr. Rodocanachi and courier and guide for the line, wrote, "He was a most engaging man, extraordinary charm with a great simplicity of manner and calm. Never, in my hearing at least, did he raise his voice or brag. His authority was innate and his serenity in all circumstances was an example to us all."[38] MI9's James M. Langley wrote, "His modesty, shyness and delightful sense of humor effectively masked a first-class calculating brain and the indomitable courage he was to show in the future."[39] Even in the limited time evaders spent with him, his engaging personality, qualities of leadership, and extreme intelligence did not pass unnoticed. Escaper Taffy Higginson (RAF) recalls O'Leary as one who could "raise people's morale in any circumstances."[40]

In view of all this, it is not surprising that Garrow wanted O'Leary to stay in France as his assistant. Though willing to stay, O'Leary felt that as a military officer he could not make such a decision without the agreement of his commanding officers. Garrow sent a message to London asking that O'Leary be released from the navy and allowed to remain in France as an agent for the line. The understanding was that the BBC message "Adolph doit rester" meant he should stay.[41] Perhaps Garrow's wording of the message to Darling describing his new helper as a "blessing from heaven" convinced naval authorities to free O'Leary from his responsibilities.[42] Authorization for O'Leary's new position came about two weeks later. Donald Darling, who was dining with friends when he heard the BBC message, emptied his glass of wine in a silent toast as his hostess commented, "What rubbish these messages are!"[43]

Once given permission to become an active member of the escape line, O'Leary threw all of his energies into evacuating as many evaders as possible. His favorite operations were mass prison breakouts. Within a four-month period in 1942, O'Leary, aided by agents and accomplices, helped about fifty men escape from prison, then moved them down the line and out of France.[44]

Not all of these escapes went exactly according to plan. At the request of the RAF, arrangements were made for RAF Squadron Leader Taffy Higginson, Pat Hicton, and three other prisoners to break out of the Fort de la Revère by sliding down a coal chute, swimming across the moat that surrounded the fort, and crawling through a sewer.[45] The remaining prisoners planned a party to cause a diversion. Higginson and his comrades successfully escaped, though on occasion they were doubt-

Fort De La Revére prison, from which Taffy Higginson and Pat Hicton escaped by crawling through the sewage pipe and across the moat. They were collected by the Pat O'Leary line and evacuated to England. (Courtesy of Pat Hicton)

ful they would make it, due to the lethal fumes arising from the sludge in the sewer pipe. They searched for their rendezvous with Pat's agents to no avail and eventually hid under some bushes for the remainder of the night. They planned for the cleanest of them to search for help the following day. An alarm went off at the prison announcing their disappearance, and they listened and watched as the police cars and lanterns flashed throughout the countryside to the accompaniment of baying dogs. In the meantime, O'Leary's men waited under another clump of bushes, listening for the sound of prisoners still in the fort singing "Tipperary," the sign that the men had successfully escaped.[46]

Shortly after hearing their signal, the guides heard the voices of guards coming closer and so rushed away along winding paths, only to curve around and find themselves in the arms of the guards from whom they were running. They were released when their captors found papers from the Monaco police station among their belongings. The guides explained that they were on police business and feigned fury at the disruption in their affairs. Early the next morning, one of the escapees brushed the dried scum from his clothes, made himself as presentable as possible, and headed for Monte Carlo to find the rendezvous connection there. With great relief, O'Leary and his guides watched the bedraggled escaper approach the teashop in which they waited. Happy to see one of their lost lambs, the men retrieved the dirty, smelly prisoners who remained burrowed in the bushes. It was a perfect example of the snafus that could arise with any escape operation and the importance of flexibility and quick thinking in a helper.[47]

The Pat line successfully evacuated Higginson as well as the well-known pilot Whitney Straight, an American-born member of the RAF with an internationally known record as a race car driver. He had initially evaded on his own and almost succeeded before being arrested at a café within sight of the Spanish frontier.[48] Though Dr. Rodocanachi convinced the other members of the medical repatriation board that Straight was unfit for service, a disastrous raid by the RAF on a Renault factory at St. Cloud led to Vichy's withdrawal of his release permit. Instead, he was transferred to a hospital in Nice, where he drugged his guards with sedatives provided by a nurse associated with Francis Blanchain, a member of the Pat line. After escaping from the hospital, Straight entered the Pat line, which organized his return to England.[49]

Several people evacuated by the Pat line later returned to France to establish new escape lines. Sergeants Robert Vanier and Conrad Lafleur did so as radio operators—Vanier for the Fan-Fan line and Lafleur for the Possum line, both of which collapsed shortly after they were established. Helper Vladimir "Val" Bouryschkine tried to establish the Oaktree line in Brittany, but was arrested before the line could begin operating.[50] Two of the men evacuated by Pat were especially successful in establishing escape lines. Frenchman Georges Broussine escaped from prison in February 1942 and with the help of the Pat line went to England, where he became an active member of the Bureau Central des Renseignements et d'Action (BCRA).[51] Broussine wrote that the Pat line was very organized, and his passage through France and over the Pyrenees went smoothly. His group left early one morning, traveling by train from Perpignan to Banyuls, then continuing on foot over the mountains, arriving in Spain at the end of the day. A year later, Broussine returned to France and organized the Burgundy line, which evacuated about two hundred men.[52]

Lucien Dumais, another escaper, returned to France in October 1943 to establish an escape network, also with great success. He and Broussine had learned a number of lessons from the problems encountered by the earlier lines, which enabled them to resist enemy penetration more easily.

Though the workers on the Pat line were ever conscious of the need for secrecy and security to guard against penetration, to their horror the greatest treachery came from an enemy within their own organization. This situation was far different from that which arose when a helper, having been arrested, broke down under the strain of horrific physical and mental torture meted out by the Gestapo. In defense of helpers who suffered such trauma, Airey Neave wrote, "No one has any right to claim that they would not talk under torture or even under threat of it."[53] The human body and mind can only endure so much, and even the most honorable workers sometimes collapsed under such conditions, betraying those with whom they worked. Those who suffered such barbaric treatment and still maintained their silence were truly admirable, yet those who gave in could be forgiven. The man who betrayed the Pat line, however, was not one of these, and his actions were unforgivable. Neave wrote, "He was among the most selfish and callous traitors who ever served the enemy in time of war."[54]

Harold Cole, alias Paul Cole, was an enigma from the beginning of his association with the escape line. An Englishman, Cole had initially served with the British Expeditionary Force (BEF), but had run away even before the German invasion of France, taking with him the sergeant's mess funds. He hid in northern France, an area known for its close ties to the British, claiming to be a captain in British intelligence.[55] He was fond of women and earned a reputation as a ladies' man. But as the organizer of an escape network in the north, he was also admired for his bravery. Though he has been described as one with panache and a disregard for danger, his actions were perhaps more the result of a gambler's ever-present conviction that he cannot lose. Cole took extreme chances, on one occasion convincing two German soldiers passing on the street to carry a heavy stove into a house for him by showing them a document that stated he was deaf and dumb and using sign language to explain he could not move it himself. The Germans moved it willingly, not knowing that it was to be used by one of Cole's helpers to warm British soldiers she was hiding in her attic.[56]

Cole's workers were devoted to him, and he was apparently dedicated to the escape line. Mme Galant expressed the complete confidence everyone had in Cole, stating, "Some of my friends in the Resistance used to tell me, 'If Paul ever quits, we won't go on with all this dangerous work.'"[57] Several of the airmen who were repatriated as a result of Cole's efforts were also very grateful for his help. Among them was Taffy Higginson, who insisted that he owed his life to Cole even after he was informed of the extent to which Cole betrayed his fellow workers.[58] But these sentiments were not universal; in fact, they were far from it.

Cole recruited a young man named Roland Lepers to work as a guide. Like many others who became involved with escape work, Lepers wanted to go to England to join General Charles de Gaulle's Free French Forces and agreed to take a group of evaders to Marseilles in hopes of enlisting the aid of British intelligence in finding transport to England. Instead he met Garrow, who convinced him to stay in France and work with the line by escorting evaders from the north. After convoying several groups of airmen, Lepers told Garrow about Cole and agreed to bring him to Marseilles, where Garrow could meet him.[59] Langley, still in France at the time, agreed with Garrow that Cole's work in the north should be incorporated into the line. In spite of his support of this plan, Langley claimed he found Cole a "colorless character with a faintly subservient manner which I disliked . . . in no way my idea of a man capable of ruthless action, ingenuity and cunning. My judgement could not have been more wrong."[60]

Langley was not alone in his assessment. For each person who sang Cole's praises, there were others who instinctively disliked him. Georges Zarifi met him several times at the Rodocanachi's home and wrote, "He was not a pleasant personality. He seemed sly and my uncle and aunt, from the beginning, neither liked him, nor trusted him as they did Ian Garrow and Pat. But in these times, one had to accept the people who were willing to help, even if not particularly likable."[61]

Before meeting Cole, Donald Caskie also felt an instinctive distrust of him, based on what he had heard from others. After making his acquaintance it was even more pronounced. In writing of the relationships between the line's workers, he described Cole's lack of connection with the other agents:

In meetings with agents, one was always aware that there

was, of necessity, a missing dimension to their personalities, something withdrawn. We did not talk about our private lives. The less we knew of each other, the less could be extracted, under torture, by the experts of the Gestapo. But we were not on our guard against each other. The suppressed dimension had become an instinct. Cole lacked that instinct and, to me, he was insincere. The missing dimension worried him. He was always on the defensive, the difficulties of the journey he had made were as nothing, he proclaimed. That was untrue, as I well knew . . . Cole was, I felt, a half-man and when the unresolved half was defined, he might be a traitor."[62]

In contrast to Higginson's praise of Cole's work, RAF evader Flt. Lt. Denis Crowley-Milling found Cole's methods to be a terrible strain on his already taut nerves. Cole had no qualms about speaking his poor French around the Germans and insisted that the evaders mingle with the Germans in public, rather than engaging in the more passive and less risky approach of keeping to themselves. Crowley-Milling was amazed that the Germans seemed so oblivious to their identities.[63]

Pat O'Leary also had reservations about Cole from the first time he met him. Only Garrow seemed to trust him implicitly, never questioning his large requests for money and uncanny skill in extricating himself and the airmen from difficult situations. O'Leary questioned Garrow about Cole, explaining his concerns, and asked Garrow to use extreme caution in his dealings with him. Garrow was unconcerned, and responded that O'Leary simply had not had the opportunity to develop an appreciation for Cole's abilities.[64]

O'Leary was unconvinced of Cole's trustworthiness and looked for opportunities to check his reliability. After a particularly trying journey with a group of airmen that, according to Cole, included arrest by German guards and an exciting escape and getaway, Cole left the evaders at the assigned rendezvous.[65] He met with Garrow to explain the details of the trip and indicated that he planned to return to the north that night. While dining out that evening, O'Leary encountered one of Cole's mistresses and invited her to join him at his table. He eventually turned the topic of conversation to Cole, and the woman asked O'Leary if he was going to attend a party later that evening given in honor of Cole. Pat was surprised to hear that Cole had plans for such elaborate entertainment, considering he had told Garrow he was returning to the north immediately. The news troubled him and, as soon as he could, he passed the information on to Garrow.[66]

When Garrow learned what Pat had found out, he made plans for attending the party himself. He was appalled to find Cole entertaining in high fashion, particularly when he remembered the large sum of money he had turned over to him earlier in the day for funding the northern section of the escape line.[67] When confronted by Garrow at the party, Cole agreed to return to Lille the following morning, but his credibility was damaged and Garrow began to worry about the status of the line in the north.[68]

While relieved at his success in opening Garrow's eyes to Cole's dishonesty, O'Leary was dismayed at having his suspicions confirmed. At Garrow's request, he agreed to check immediately on the situation in the north, and within a short time he arrived in Lille. He went first to the home of François Duprez, only to be met at the door with suspicion and distrust by Duprez's wife.[69] O'Leary tried to put her at ease, but it was not until she detected his dislike of Cole that she agreed to let him in. O'Leary questioned Duprez about the finances of the line and was shocked to learn that none of the money sent by Garrow to support the line had arrived. Duprez was equally shocked and angry that Cole had lied to Garrow about depositing the money in his care.[70]

Pat's visits with the helpers of the north were eye-opening, and he realized that Cole's deceit went much further than any of them had imagined. Helpers were concerned about Cole's indiscretion around the Germans and the amount of money he spent on women and alcohol. In the meantime, they had to feed, shelter, and clothe evaders completely at their own expense. Duprez expressed a more chilling fear as well. He claimed some of the evaders were disappearing on the trip from Lille to Marseilles after having been given to Cole for transport.

In keeping with the regulations of the line, Cole had kept Garrow's headquarters a secret. At the same time, however, this security measure was detrimental to the members of the line, who had no way of getting in touch with the chief, Garrow, to make him aware of their fears.[71] O'Leary realized Cole had to be confronted with his treachery, and he convinced Duprez to arrange a temporary absence from his business and travel to Marseilles, where they could give Garrow an account of Cole's activity.

O'Leary arrived in Marseilles with a full report for Garrow, only to be greeted with devastating news. When he reached the Rodocanachi home, Fanny received him in tears and explained that Garrow had been arrested the day before. Though everyone had been aware that it could happen at any time, it was no less shocking when the arrest finally occurred. O'Leary now found himself in an even greater dilemma. No one knew the details about Garrow's arrest. O'Leary was left to speculate as to whether or not Cole had betrayed him, and if so, were more Gestapo or Vichy authorities on their way that very minute to arrest the remainder of the workers? Years later, O'Leary recalled his thoughts on hearing the news: "There I was, having only just arrived home with so much to report to Garrow, and he had been arrested twenty-four hours earlier. I simply couldn't take it in."[72]

With the arrest of Garrow in October 1941, O'Leary, as the senior ranking British officer, became chief of the line. Garrow's arrest was an isolated incident resulting from his connection with a French police officer who had pretended loyalty to the line long enough to trap Garrow. His arrest was a two-fold tragedy. Obviously the line had lost its chief and original organizer, but worse, Cole was left to continue his efforts to destroy the line from within. Before his arrest, Garrow had decided to eliminate him even without evidence of treachery. Without identifying Cole by name, Garrow told Dr. Rodocanachi that he needed to kill someone while making the death appear to be the result of natural causes. Rodocanachi told him that a large injection of insulin would accomplish this, after which a "gentle push" into the Mediterranean would solve the problem of what to do with the dead body.[73] Unfortunately, Garrow told no one of his plans, and after he was arrested, O'Leary had to deal with Cole without the benefit of Garrow's insight. One of Cole's northern agents, Alfred Lanselle, worried about the safety of the helpers in his section, also considered killing Cole, but another helper, Desiré Didry, convinced him otherwise.[74] Sadly, both were trapped in Cole's net when he betrayed many of those who worked for him.

Had O'Leary been aware of the cross currents blowing around him on the day he met with Cole at the Rodocanachi home, events might have turned out differently. Three days after Garrow's arrest, Duprez arrived in Marseilles. Cole appeared with a group of evaders shortly afterward, and O'Leary ordered him to report to Rodocanachi's house, where Australian agent Bruce Dowding, Mario Prassinos and Leoni Savinos, both trusted guides for the line, and Duprez waited.[75] Hoping to maintain the element of surprise and possibly shock Cole into honesty, Pat concealed Duprez in a connected bathroom where he could hear the exchange between Cole and the other men.[76]

As expected, Cole denied having taken the line's money for his own use, insisting that he had turned it all over to Duprez. Pat explained that Duprez claimed Cole had not done so, to which Cole snapped, "He's a liar."[77] But when O'Leary opened the door to Duprez's hiding place and let him enter, Cole's entire demeanor changed. His face turned white, and he moved toward O'Leary, apparently either to attack or attempt to escape. He did neither. O'Leary quickly reacted by hitting him in the mouth, after which Cole fell to his knees in tears pleading for forgiveness and crying, "I've done something terrible. I admit it . . . terrible. It was a moment of weakness. I'm sorry."[78] The rest of the men had jumped to their feet when O'Leary acted, but stood silently in the aftermath. It was at this moment that knowledge of Garrow's plan to kill Cole would have helped Pat. Locking Cole in the bathroom while they discussed the enormous problem of how to deal with him, Pat asked Bruce Dowding what he thought should be done. Dowding paused only a moment before saying, "I think we should kill him."[79] Prassinos immediately opposed this, feeling the punishment did not fit the crime. Moreover, without evidence of treachery, even O'Leary felt he could not kill Cole simply for embezzling funds. He suggested sending Cole back to England instead, taking him away from the line and its workers. Before further discussion took place, Dowding heard a noise in the bathroom and raced to the door in time to see Cole leap across the courtyard from the tiny fifth-floor bathroom window to a window leading into another area of the house. His effort was completely unexpected, as not only was the window unusually small, but fear of a fall to the brick courtyard below would have stopped all but the most desperate from attempting such a jump. Dowding rushed through the house trying to catch Cole before he could get out the front door, but he was too late. He hesitated at the door and then stopped. If he ran down the stairs and into the street after Cole, he would have drawn attention to himself and endangered the line. It appeared that the worst had happened, and yet the men realized the potential for an even greater disaster. Cole had been ejected from the line and could easily go to the Gestapo with the information he had.

O'Leary and Dowding immediately left for the north to warn the helpers in Cole's section of the events that had taken place. They tried desperately to convince the helpers to leave the area, take on new names, and become paid workers of the line, but for many such action was difficult. Alfred Lanselle knew that it would probably be only a matter of time before the Gestapo came searching for him, but he had a wife, five children, an elderly father, and a brother newly returned from a POW camp. Had he left, his family might have been punished instead, so he remained where he was and waited for the inevitable.[80]

One of the chief agents Cole had recruited in the north was a Roman Catholic priest, Abbé Peter Carpentier. As a peacetime hobby, Carpentier had dabbled in printing and become an expert craftsman. He had a small printer, and as part of the Pat line he created false identity cards complete with forged signatures of town officials. He was one of the first helpers visited by O'Leary and Dowding, but he refused to leave. Perhaps in his capacity as a priest Carpentier had difficulty rejecting Cole, particularly considering the positive aspects of their past relationship. Cole had no such qualms, and Carpentier was one of the first helpers he betrayed.[81]

Throughout November 1941, O'Leary and Dowding contacted Cole's workers throughout the northern region. O'Leary introduced Dowding as the new chief in the north and tried to restore the people's faith in the line. After Garrow's arrest, O'Leary had begun to depend more and more on Bruce Dowding, who had moved into the Rodocanachi house in Garrow's place. Having arrived in France to study before the outbreak of war, Dowding chose to stay and help fight rather than return home.[82]

Cole himself was hiding quietly during this period, but on December 6 Cornelius Verloop arrested Cole and the traitor's full wrath descended on the helpless workers who had trusted and worked for him. Verloop was a member of the French Foreign Legion who went to work for German military intelligence (Abwehr). He had been searching for Cole for some time, and when he caught him, all of O'Leary's fears were justified. Cole had no motivation for resisting German questioning and threats since he had been banished from the line. Verloop was astonished at the amount of information Cole provided. In his thirty-page deposition, Cole identified dozens of helpers, giving an almost complete outline of the northern branch of the line. Two days after Cole's capture by the Abwehr, the arrests began.[83]

Cole denounced about one hundred people at this time, almost all of whom were arrested. Those who were not executed were deported to concentration camps, from which few returned. François Duprez was the first of the victims. German authorities deported him to Germany in August 1942, and less than two years later, in April 1944, he died of exhaustion at Sonnenburg concentration camp.[84] Carpentier's arrest soon followed when Cole appeared at his house in the company of men who seemed to be evaders. At the time of their arrival, Dowding was visiting with the priest, and the two men decided to let Cole in but thought Dowding should hide in the back room in case of trouble. Carpentier spoke with some of the airmen, trying to determine their authenticity. Once convinced that they were genuine evaders, he began to make the false identity papers. Listening carefully, Bruce heard the sound of papers being shuffled about, then the command, "Put your hands up." He immediately bolted out the back window and escaped. Severely shaken by the affair, he was unable to act right away. He wandered about the streets of town for several hours before pulling himself together and spreading the alarm, going house to house warning the helpers of Cole's betrayal. It was exactly what the Germans had expected him to do, and when he reached the third house they arrested him.[85]

Carpentier was able to smuggle a letter out of prison with the help of a Catholic guard. In the letter, he identified Cole as the person who had betrayed him. Carpentier and Dowding remained in prison until June 30, 1943, when they were executed by beheading in Dortmund, Germany. Father Anton Steinhoff, the Catholic priest who witnessed Dowding's execution, later wrote a letter to the young man's parents in which he stated, "Your son met his death in such a proud and manly way, so triumphant a way that the Public Prosecutor present at the execution was annoyed. I shall never forget your son, nor his way of facing death."[86]

Yet another of Cole's agents fell into the Gestapo net in the first weeks after Cole's arrest. Captured and held in Fresnes prison, André Postel-Vinay wandered anxiously around his cell, waiting to be interrogated. Among his possessions that the guards had taken was a small notebook in which he had written the code names of several agents. The information alone was harmless, but Postel-Vinay feared that once the torture began he might not be able to hold back further information. His cell overlooked a thirty-foot-high balcony, and he chose to commit suicide rather than betray his friends. Jumping over the balcony, Postel-

Vinay fell three stories before hitting the stone floor, fracturing his spine, pelvis, and one leg. Ignoring his cries of agony, German guards handcuffed him and threw him back into his cell, where, unattended, he drifted in and out of consciousness for two days before being transferred to a hospital. Weeks passed in a blur of pain and unconsciousness, but eventually he began to recover under the care of a German doctor. When he regained the strength to get out of bed and hobble short distances, the doctor invited Postel-Vinay to come talk in his office a number of times, but always made an excuse to leave during the visit. Postel-Vinay noticed that he always left the door unlocked and concluded the doctor was trying to help him escape. Still weak and barely able to walk, he took advantage of the doctor's next absence and left the hospital. Postel-Vinay walked to the train station, hoping to ride the train to his sister's house with money collected from a group of boys playing on the street. Weakness forced him to ask for help from the stationmaster, who hid him in a closet until his sister could collect him later that night. After several weeks of recovery, Postel-Vinay escaped on the line he had almost given his life to protect.[87]

The principal people involved with the organization of the Pat line were extremely close. Though they understood the risks that went along with the work they were doing, they trusted one another implicitly, which was significantly advantageous in that they did not have to waste time with long explanations about matters pertaining to the line. It was to this kind of relationship among the agents that Cole caused the most harm. The damage was not permanent, and they remained united and strong. Nevertheless, Cole's betrayal of those who had complete faith in him was a tragic and painful lesson for all involved with the line.

5

In the Wake of Betrayal

The Pat O'Leary Line, 1942–1943

The aftermath of Cole's betrayal was devastating. O'Leary sent a new agent, Jean de la Olla, into the north to replace Bruce Dowding, reestablish connections among the helpers who remained free, and find new workers to replace those who were gone. In spite of these major changes, 1942 proved to be a successful year for the line, though expensive in terms of loss of agents. The Pat line extended its efforts into Switzerland, providing assistance to POWs from Germany, and established a route from Monte Carlo for POWs from Italian camps. With the help of Louis Nouveau, O'Leary also established networks in Brittany and Normandy that merged into the main line. His most ambitious plans for the line, however, involved mass evacuations by sea. O'Leary believed large groups of men could be evacuated with no greater risk than that involved in evacuating four or five at a time. But before establishing such an operation, he had to consult with Allied intelligence in Gibraltar. Leaving the line in the care of Louis Nouveau, Georges Rodocanachi, and Mario Prassinos, O'Leary crossed the Pyrenees into Spain in February 1942.[1]

While in Gibraltar, O'Leary met with Donald Darling and James Langley to discuss the future of the line as well as Cole's recent betrayals. Darling had been frustrated by the reaction of military intelligence to the problem with Cole. O'Leary had sent word to Darling about his plans for killing Cole, but Claude Dansey of MI6 would not allow it. Darling, who thought Dansey's decision was ill-advised, wrote, "It was all very well, I thought, to sit in London and issue instructions covering a situation only understood by the man on the spot, who was in danger."[2] Once they were together in Gibraltar, O'Leary, Langley, and Darling discussed the problem fully, and O'Leary showed them the letter Carpentier had smuggled out of prison denouncing Cole. Langley and Darling agreed that other escape lines should be warned about Cole, and Langley agreed to issue an order for his elimination.[3]

The men also discussed O'Leary's need for improved communications with England. Langley had brought a wireless radio operator so that O'Leary could have direct contact with London. The operator, M. Drouet, did not inspire a great deal of confidence in O'Leary, who upon loosening the man's tongue with several whiskies learned that Drouet had only volunteered as a means of getting back to France and his wife.[4] O'Leary told Langley the man would be useless, and he really had enough to worry about without having to deal with a lovesick radio operator. Unfortunately, O'Leary's options were Drouet or nothing, and Langley convinced him that anything was better than nothing. Against his better judgment, O'Leary consented to take Drouet back to Marseilles, but Drouet was so frightened of being arrested that he was unable to do his job. Furious at his dilemma, O'Leary found Mme Drouet and sent both her and her husband back to England.[5]

Other aspects of the meeting were successful, however, and O'Leary returned to Marseilles to prepare his series of mass sea evacuations off the Mediterranean coast of France. One of his agents, Gaston Negré, had found a suitable radio operator, Roger Gaston, and in June MI9 dispatched a second operator who worked well with the organization. The second operator, Jean Nitelet, was a RAF officer who had been evacuated by the Pat line. He had needed lengthy medical treatment, having lost an eye when his plane was shot down.[6] Unable to continue his war service in the air force, Nitelet volunteered to return to France as O'Leary's radio operator. He arrived by Lysander (a small aircraft used to deliver agents and supplies into occupied territory) with all the necessary radio equipment as well as detailed information about a mass evacuation at Pont Miou, on the coast between Marseille and Cassis.[7]

About the same time that Nitelet arrived, O'Leary began to lose some of his most experienced agents. Leoni Savinos and Pierre Lanvers were arrested in Paris while on their way to collect nine airmen in Brittany, and only Savinos's agreement to serve the Germans as a double agent within the line convinced them to let him go. Initially, German authorities wanted to hold Savinos's wife in his place as security, but agreed that this would raise suspicion among other workers on the line. Fearing for Lanvers, who had already been severely tortured, Savinos negotiated his release by pointing out that Lanvers's disappearance would also raise misgivings about his loyalty to the line. Both returned to Marseilles, where Savinos and his wife went into hiding until O'Leary could evacuate them to England.[8]

At the end of April, Donald Caskie, who had provided such great service housing airmen for the line, was arrested. Because he refused to return to England, Vichy authorities banished him from Marseilles, but before leaving he dispersed the nearly sixty airmen hiding in the mission to new safe houses. Always attentive to details, Caskie also made sure their clothing needs for crossing the Pyrenees were fully provided for before he left them.[9]

The Gestapo was tightening the noose around O'Leary's organization. Under such circumstances, the success of his mass sea evacuations was nothing short of miraculous. The effectiveness of the operations boosted morale immensely among the workers of the Pat line, even though the strain of carrying them out was oppressive at times. More importantly, the primitive operations evolved into a full-fledged evasion network less than two years after the first evacuation undertaken by O'Leary.

The sea evacuations were carried out by the *Tarana,* a British trawler commissioned into the Royal Navy to conduct secret operations along the Mediterranean coast. Manned by a dedicated Polish crew, the only disagreement to arise among the members had to do with who received the honor of transporting evaders and agents to or from the shore. A great deal of work went into preparations for carrying out these operations, since the trawler had to be disguised as a fishing boat each time it moved out into the Mediterranean to conduct its clandestine work. The *Tarana* carried numerous barrels of paint in its hold, and once out to sea the crew painted it to look like an ordinary fishing boat, completing the disguise by strewing fishing gear over the deck. After picking up the group of evaders, the trawler had to be transformed back into a naval vessel. Jack Misseldine, a RAF evader who evacuated from St. Pierre Plage in August, remembered being put to work with paint and a brush, covering the worn-out-looking trawler with a fresh coat of Royal Navy gray before it sailed into Gibraltar.[10] All of this was necessary to prevent enemy planes from attacking the *Tarana* or investigating the true purpose for its excursions along the French Mediterranean coast.

There were five such evacuations, and except for the last one, scheduled for the night of October 5 or 6 from Canet Plage, all went exactly according to plan.[11] A huge mass escape from Fort de la Turbie, a prison camp in Italy, resulted in forty-two new escapers finding their way into the line, bottlenecking the organization. MI9 confirmed O'Leary's request for an evacuation over the BBC, and in early October he and several agents moved the evaders to an empty vacation home provided by Mme LeBreton, manager of a hotel resort along the beach in Canet Plage. She also supplied meals for the evaders, which O'Leary and his agents delivered to them in the evenings. There was hardly room to squeeze thirty-two evaders into the house, and the tightly shut windows, combined with cigarette smoke and the presence of too many bodies in close quarters, resulted in ovenlike conditions. But it was important that the house maintain its vacant appearance, and the men were good-natured about the situation, realizing it was only temporary and convinced that they would be sailing for London within the next twenty-four hours. Lucien Dumais recalled the discomfort of the tight quarters, noting that men had to layer themselves in order to sleep. Some slept on the beds, others slept under them, some on the dining room table, others under it. Literally every flat surface served as a bed.[12]

O'Leary, Louis Nouveau, and the other agents spent most of their time at Mme LeBreton's Hotel du Tennis and then returned to the beach house at midnight. Leading the men through the back door, they began the long trek to the beach. O'Leary led the way and Nouveau brought up the rear, while agents Alex "Jacques" Wattebled and Mario Prassinos walked among the men.[13] On their way to the rendezvous point, the men had to wade across a 150-foot-wide area of the Tet River, which was known for its pockets of quicksand. Feeling their way carefully in the darkness, the men slowly waded across, with frightening moments for some whose feet sank too far in the soft sand. Once all had crossed to the other side, they regrouped and continued to follow O'Leary as he led them about one-half mile north of the river's mouth. The rendezvous was scheduled for 2:00 A.M., and the men huddled together in small groups along the beach, anxiously waiting. Every fifteen minutes O'Leary flashed his signal light while the men stared expectantly into the darkness waiting to see their ship appear out of the night.[14]

When an hour passed with no sign of the trawler, O'Leary became concerned, but having grown accustomed to the uncertainty of life in the Resistance, he did not panic. After all, the confirmation had been for the fifth or the sixth of the month. Possibly the evacuation was intended for the following night instead. The men's discomfort increased as the cool wind grew stronger, blowing up sheets of sand, which stung their bare skin and hurt their eyes, causing them to hunch down to protect their faces. Still looking out to sea, O'Leary glimpsed a red light flashing in the distance, northeast of their location. He jumped to his feet and raced toward it, fearing that the *Tarana* had missed the rendezvous point. It took several minutes of hard running to reach the signal light, but a rush of adrenaline helped him continue in spite of his exhaustion. Hoping to find the *Tarana* waiting offshore, O'Leary stopped short when he realized he had been chasing the blinking light of a buoy floating gently on the water. Frustrated and disappointed, he stood on the silent beach, the only sound being that of his own labored breathing. Disheartened, he turned and retraced his path back to the men still waiting on the beach. Concealing his disappointment, he continued signaling until 4:00 A.M., then gave up, leading the men back into the prisonlike walls of the beach house.[15]

Assuring the men that the boat would arrive for certain the following night, he left them to get some sleep, though this was easier said than done. The still, heavy air in the confines of the beach house was further aggravated by the heat of a bright sun blazing overhead and the crowded conditions within. The day was interminably long, but eventually the evening coolness began to seep in, and at midnight the men once again slipped out the back door and down the beach, fording the river and taking their places at the edge of the water, where they repeated the previous night's performance. Louis Nouveau saw a small boat skirting the shore and thought perhaps the meeting place had been confused. He slipped quietly out of the procession and moved toward the water's edge, where he softly called the password, "Where are the strawberries?"[16] Receiving no answer, he called again, expecting to hear the corresponding password "in the juice." But instead he heard the voice of a fisherman release a stream of French obscenities, very likely expressing his opinion of fools who searched for strawberries along the seashore. Without another word, Nouveau slipped back into the shadows and rejoined the men for another night of endless waiting.

As the men became more restless and impatient, O'Leary was concerned that discipline problems might arise. Again at 4:00 A.M. he called off the operation, and they returned to the beach house, where he explained to them that the operation had never failed before and that he was returning immediately to Marseilles to contact England about the situation. He wished he could relieve the doubt he saw in the eyes of the men, but he had nothing to offer them.[17]

While traveling to Marseilles, O'Leary and Nouveau discussed possible reasons why the operation might have failed. When they arrived at Nouveau's house, his wife Renée kept them supplied with fresh coffee while they engaged in the tedious and complicated task of encoding a message for London. The completed message read, "Waited nights 5 to 6 and 6 to 7 seven hundred yards from River Tet. No sign of boat."[18] Re-reading it, the two men decided it was far too mild to express the urgent situation in which they found themselves and added a postscript taken from a French army phrase that expressed anxiety: "No more sign of a boat than of butter on your backside." They later spent much time worrying that decoders would waste precious time trying to determine the meaning of the postscript, but James Langley checked the phrase with a French colleague and understood the problem immediately, though he laughed at their means of expressing their predicament.[19]

O'Leary turned the message over to the line's current radio operator, Philippe Vallat, who transmitted it immediately and then began the twenty-four-hour wait for a return message.[20] As a result of high levels of radio traffic, the Pat line was limited to one transmission per day. Waiting was difficult enough in the comfort of the Nouveau home, but O'Leary could only imagine the discomfort of the men shut away in the hot, crowded beach house.[21]

At times such as this, life in the Resistance underworld caught up with Pat O'Leary. For months he had been constantly on the run, shouldering the responsibility for airmen who, as evaders, were totally dependent on him. The physical and mental strain of quickly and efficiently coping with unexpected situations was taking its toll, and O'Leary may have realized that with large numbers of agents being arrested or forced to escape, the Gestapo might well be closing in. Still, he continued to fight, and two days later he received word that the *Tarana* was on her way back to Canet Plage.

The dispatch sent from England stated that the *Tarana* had made the rendezvous both nights and found no one waiting. Though halfway back to Gibraltar and low on fuel, the ship had turned around and would rendezvous again either October 11 or 12. Relieved, O'Leary and Nouveau returned to Canet Plage and found the situation at the beach house had deteriorated considerably. Two of the evaders were sick, and both toilets had backed up, causing a horrible stench that permeated the house. O'Leary patiently explained that the operation was to be repeated and they could expect the boat on either of two nights.[22] Trying to keep their spirits up, while reminding them that the boat might not arrive until the second night, O'Leary prepared the men for the possibility of yet a fourth hike to the rendezvous point. To O'Leary's great disappointment, that was exactly what happened. Arriving back at the beach house after spending a third night waiting for the *Tarana,* he could see that the men were depressed, listless, and haggard, having now spent ten days in miserable conditions. But even worse, he saw that they had lost faith in his ability to help them. Some of them no longer believed a boat was coming, and unsure himself, he could not convince them.[23]

The following night, the men sat on the beach for the fourth time while O'Leary flashed the prearranged signal. To maximize the operation's chances for successful completion, he had rearranged the men's positions on the beach. O'Leary had determined that if the problem was navigational, the boat might be returning to the same place again and again. To compensate for such a possibility, he spread the men at wide intervals along a mile-wide stretch of beach, with instructions for alerting the rest of the line if anyone saw the boat. At 3:00 A.M., the men on the outer southern portion of the beach saw a shadowy form materialize in the distance and realized with joy and relief that it was their ship. Passing the signal down the line, they organized themselves for transport to the *Tarana* by rowboat. The small craft was not meant to hold the large number of men that crowded in for the short trip out to sea, and one load in particular was so heavy that the men holding on to the sides felt water covering their fingers. Only the calmness of the sea kept them from sinking. All of the men were relieved to finally be leaving, and now that the ordeal was ended they could afford to joke, asking the rowers where the "bloody hell" they had been. But for some, the knowledge that freedom was so near inspired much deeper feelings, and tears flowed down the cheeks of one evader as emotions held at bay for so long broke loose.[24]

O'Leary, Nouveau, Prassinos, and Wattebled stood on the beach together, watching the boat silently drift into the night and disappear with its cargo. The evaders were safely aboard, and their jobs were over for now. But while the airmen returned to freedom, their courageous helpers remained in a world of shadows where fear of the future was a constant companion. Exhaustion from the strain of the last two weeks overwhelmed the men as they turned to make their way back across the beach.

Over the next few months, the Pat line continued evacuating large numbers of airmen over the Pyrenees, but O'Leary also felt responsible for those agents who had been arrested while engaged in evasion work or whose positions had become compromised. Shortly after the last sea operation, O'Leary evacuated Mario Prassinos to England and sent Renée Nouveau into hiding. Prassinos later returned to France for SOE, was arrested, and died of typhus in a concentration camp in 1945. Nouveau eventually evacuated to England, where she worked for de Gaulle's Free French organization.[25] However, Louis Nouveau refused to leave and moved to Paris instead, where he took over that region's operations. At about the same time, O'Leary moved his headquarters to Toulouse. He tried to convince Georges Rodocanachi to escape to England as well, but his wife, Fanny, was in poor health, and Rodocanachi refused to leave her alone. Rodocanachi was arrested in February 1943 on apparently "trumped up" charges. His interrogators never mentioned evaders in connection with him. Though there were no men hiding at his house on the day of his arrest, a guide arrived with six evaders the following morning. Dr. Rodocanachi died of illness in Büchenwald concentration camp in February 1944.[26] O'Leary also engineered the escapes of agents Gaston Negré, Pierre Lanvers, and Jean Nitelet, arrested together while taking part in a supply drop. But one of the most difficult escapes he organized was that of Ian Garrow in early December 1942.[27]

For his evasion activities, Vichy authorities had sentenced Garrow to ten years at Meauzac prison. It was by far the most formidable of the Vichy prison camps, and by German request usually reserved for only two groups of prisoners: those sentenced to life imprisonment and those sentenced to death. Conditions there were very harsh, and Garrow had suffered considerably since his incarceration a year earlier. When German forces moved into the unoccupied zone in France following the Allied invasion of North Africa, Garrow received word from one of the guards that he was to be deported to Germany, probably to Dachau. Garrow smuggled word of his imminent departure to O'Leary, who realized deportation meant almost certain death for his former compatriot. He viewed the arrangement of Garrow's escape as an opportunity to repay him for his efforts in establishing the line that had brought about the escape of so many others.

O'Leary's plan for organizing Garrow's escape was not unanimously supported by MI9. Langley and Claude Dansey, so often at loggerheads over support for the line's activities, opposed O'Leary's plan as presented by Neave and Norman Crockatt. Langley pointed out that if the plan failed, the whole line would probably collapse, sacrificing the safety of many for the rescue of one man. Crockatt agreed that Langley's fears were a distinct possibility, but stubbornly held to the opinion that it was a risk that must be taken, reminding them that it was Garrow who "with little money, scant encouragement and speaking no French began this line. I think we have a duty to take these risks."[28]

With permission from MI9 to move forward with his idea, O'Leary began developing a plan to effect Garrow's escape. He worked with Nancy Wake Fiocca, an Australian agent recruited by Garrow, whose French husband had been instrumental in providing financial support for the line. They met with a French jailer, "Pierre," from Meauzac to determine a means for rescuing Garrow. Pierre's skeptical response was not promising, and he told them not to waste their time, as they would never succeed. He added that he himself could not take part in such an effort because the likelihood of success was so slim. He feared that if the plan failed and he was arrested for helping them, his family would be left with no means of support. Thinking quickly, O'Leary asked Pierre the amount of his monthly salary. Knowing the financial difficulties for families throughout France, he thought money might inspire Pierre to assist them. O'Leary suggested he triple Pierre's salary for the next three years, offering to give his wife 100,000 francs immediately, and the remaining 116,000 francs on completion of the escape. It was a tremendous offer, and Pierre gladly accepted. O'Leary realized that acquiring an inside helper was a huge first step, but he also understood that Pierre could do nothing for them unless they devised a solid plan.[29]

Initial ideas were complex, as heavy security at the prison seemed to suggest the need for an ingenious plan. The camp was surrounded by three rings of heavy barbed wire, which narrowed the planners' options with regard to an exit point. After rejecting several ideas, they finally determined that the best possibility for success was to disguise Garrow as a prison guard and have him walk out with a group of off-duty workers at the end of a shift. They had little time in which to carry out the plan, and O'Leary agreed to deliver a guard's uniform to Pierre within forty-eight hours. He and Fiocca traveled immediately to Toulouse, where they contacted Paul Ulmann, a Jewish tailor connected with the line. With the help of his wife, Ulmann designed and sewed a uniform for Garrow within two days.[30]

O'Leary arrived at Pierre's home with the completed disguise in hand and with great consternation listened to Pierre explain that it was no longer of any use. German authorities had released the Vichy officials who had been acting guards for the prison, transporting French gendarmes from several regions to serve until German guards could be transferred in. Though it was difficult news to absorb, there was some advantage to the new situation. Since the guards were all new, they would be unrecognizable to those who protected the main gates, as well as to each other, increasing Garrow's chances of walking out unnoticed. However, an altogether different uniform was required and with little time to spare.

O'Leary returned to Ulmann and described the situation and need for a gendarme's uniform, complete with insignia, within forty-eight hours. Ulmann, so willing to assist in the first effort, claimed it would be impossible to provide a uniform of the type O'Leary requested within that short period. He had no fabric with which to begin his job and no clue as to where it could be found. O'Leary begged him to try, emphasizing the importance in having such a uniform. Surprisingly, Ulmann's employer provided him with the material, and Ulmann set to work. In the early morning, he struggled with tired eyes and slowed reflexes to create a uniform that met the necessary requirements, finally completing it within the period allotted.[31]

O'Leary set out once again, this time with agents Fabien de Cortes and Guy Berthet,[32] as well as his new radio operator, Thomas Groome,[33] who had arrived from England in late October. He intended to keep close contact with MI9 throughout the operation and needed Groome's expertise for this. Pierre had carefully observed the routine actions of the prison guards and felt the operation could be best carried out at the end of the day shift, which occurred at 7:00 P.M.[34]

From positions in the woods surrounding the prison, Berthet and de Cortes trained their pistols on the camp's two machine gun towers. O'Leary was also hidden in the woods, near the main entrance. The men were aware that their weapons were no match for the machine guns, but hoped they could create the illusion of a three-way attack in the case of an emergency. They also hoped to increase Garrow's chances for escape by drawing the gunfire to themselves and away from him.[35]

Pierre smuggled the uniform into Garrow's cell, and at 6:45 P.M., Garrow slipped into the bathroom to put it on. He was horrified when moments later someone tried to enter. The newcomer cursed and pounded on the locked door, then stood aside to wait his turn, muttering all the while. Garrow hardly dared move for fear of giving himself away. He had only a few minutes to change and join the exiting guards, and if his doorman did not leave soon, he would miss his chance. It was probably the longest five minutes of Garrow's life, but finally the man moved away. Shaken, Garrow completed his disguise and walked out. By this time the guards were preparing to leave, and he joined in the procession with Pierre falling into step behind him.[36]

Some people are readily recognizable even from a distance by the way they walk, and Garrow was one of these. O'Leary saw him immediately from his hiding place and knew it would be only a matter of time before Garrow's slow gait and gaunt face were recognized as those of a prisoner. He felt a moment of near panic when two gendarmes paused as though to visit a moment, but they moved on and Garrow continued. One of the guards manning the gate eyed him oddly but did not stop him, and within a few seconds he and Pierre were out of the prison and moving down the street.[37]

Pierre walked alongside Garrow, guiding him to a curve in the road, where they stepped into the woods and began running for the car that was hidden there to transport Garrow to the safe house. Once he saw that his friend was safely in the woods, O'Leary left his hiding place and ran for the car also, where he found Garrow changing into civilian clothing. Jean Brégi, the farmer to whose home they were going, turned the key in the ignition and the car started, then died. After repeated unsuccessful tries to restart the car, O'Leary began to worry that the whole effort had been for naught. Garrow's escape would be noticed very quickly because of his status as a high-profile prisoner, and the deafening sound of the starter could be heard from quite a distance. Brégi finally cranked the engine by hand, and the car roared to life. Hardly slowing down as he traversed the twenty miles to his home, Brégi squealed around corners and barreled through crossroads, finally arriving at the isolated farmhouse where his wife and Groome anxiously awaited their appearance. After a quick meal, Groome, O'Leary, and Garrow hid in the attic, where they radioed a message to England informing MI9 of the success of the first stage of the escape plan.[38]

Early the next morning, Brégi encountered German guards on the edge of his property, who told him of the escape of a British prisoner and asked if he had seen or heard anything. Brégi denied having any knowledge of the prisoner, after which the guards assured him that Garrow would be caught because of the vast number of searchers and roadblocks set up in the area. Brégi returned to his house, where he encouraged O'Leary, Groome, and Garrow to leave immediately. Outraged at Garrow's escape, the Germans retaliated by conducting extended searches with dogs throughout fields and farms and among homes in the territory surrounding Meauzac. Large numbers of innocent civilians, none of whom had any clue as to the escape or whereabouts of the British agent, were also dragged into Gestapo offices for questioning.[39]

Berthet and de Cortes had arranged their trips back to Marseilles on their own, while O'Leary and his two companions began a long day of travel, burrowing down in ditches and underbrush at the slightest sound of a voice or movement. Garrow was very weak from his yearlong imprisonment, which slowed their progress, and it was dark by the time they reached their second hiding place, further away from Meauzac. The next morning they caught a train for Toulouse and walked to the home of Françoise Dissart, their final destination. They were exhausted, particularly Garrow, but Françoise met them as though they were long-lost relatives, promptly feeding them and making them comfortable.[40]

O'Leary's rescue operation for Garrow was indicative of the closeness among the members of the line and the high regard they had for each other. Garrow remained with Françoise for three weeks, regaining his strength and preparing for the final stage of his escape—walking over the Pyrenees Mountains. When he had recovered enough to make the trip, O'Leary accompanied him to the Spanish frontier. They stood together on the silent, peaceful mountain saying with their eyes what they could not put into words. They had been through much together in their shared world of Resistance activity. With a final, meaningful handshake, Garrow turned and made his way down the Spanish side of the mountain with O'Leary's final words echoing in his ears, "Can this go on much longer?"[41] It was January 1943.

O'Leary continued his work while trying to provide the greatest possible security for his agents. Groome moved to Montauban, making his headquarters with the Cheramy family, dependable helpers who had hidden airmen on several occasions. He only occasionally sent his radio transmissions from their home, as German detector vans had become adept at locating transmitters. Groome's general routine was to change locations after every five transmissions. To reduce the amount of association between himself and O'Leary, and thus protect the security of the line, Groome received messages from London and decoded them, then gave them to his assistant, Edith Reddé, who took them to O'Leary at the Hotel du Paris in Toulouse.[42] O'Leary read the message and gave his response to Reddé, who returned to Groome.

While transmitting from the Cheramy home, Groome and Reddé, engrossed in their work, were shocked to feel guns pushed into their backs and to hear a voice telling them they were under arrest. Told to finish his transmission, Groome carried on with his work, but left out his security code, which informed MI9 immediately that he was in enemy hands. Along with the Cheramy family, they were taken to German headquarters for interrogation.[43] When the Gestapo tried to use Groome's radio to gain information, British military intelligence fed them misinformation instead. Unfortunately, because Groome was the line's only radio operator, MI9 could do nothing to transmit its knowledge of the arrests to O'Leary.

In early January, O'Leary became concerned at the long silence from Groome. He had gone to the room at the Hotel du Paris for several days in a row with no sign of Reddé. On his third trip, Reddé appeared, bedraggled and somewhat worse for wear, hysterically crying about arrests, escapes, and Gestapo. She could not say for certain whether she had been followed, and O'Leary made a hasty retreat, directing her to Françoise Dissart's house. Warning Mme Mongelard, the hotel manager, of the possibility of a Gestapo raid, he followed Reddé at a distance, determining that no one was tailing her. He could not tell whether she was telling the truth or working for the Gestapo. Reddé had never seemed like an aggressive sort of person, and it was difficult to believe that she could have escaped from the Gestapo when others far more creative had failed.[44]

At Mme Dissart's apartment, he found Françoise trying to comfort the distraught young woman. When Reddé could speak clearly, she told them her amazing experience. After taking them to Gestapo headquarters, the German authorities had placed them in separate rooms for questioning. Groome's second-floor windows overlooked the street outside, and in the middle of his interrogation he suddenly jumped to his feet and raced across the room, flying through the closed window. Though cut by the broken glass and hampered by a sprained ankle acquired when he landed on the concrete sidewalk below, he got up and kept running. While most of the Gestapo agents raced out of the building after him, Groome hid in a sheltered doorway, but was betrayed by a bystander who saw him run by.

In the meantime, the agents had completely forgotten about Reddé, sitting in her interrogation room awaiting questioning. When no one returned for her, she pushed the door open and peeked out into the hall. There was no one in sight except a group of girls walking by. Stepping into the hallway, Reddé walked out of the Gestapo offices onto the street completely unnoticed. Once in the streets she became frightened and hurried into the first hotel she could find, where she located an empty room and hid in a closet until she calmed down. When no one arrived to re-arrest her, Reddé ventured out of the hotel and into the quiet streets of town. Her first thought was to get word to O'Leary.[45]

O'Leary found her story fantastic and felt no more sure of her innocence than he had been before she told it. He finally decided that if the story were true, there would be news at certain cafés in Toulouse that were known for gossip about intelligence activity. Making the rounds of the cafés that night, O'Leary heard repeated accounts of the British agent who had jumped out the window during his interrogation. He was also relieved to hear reports of the girl arrested with him. The word in the cafés was that the agent had been rearrested but that the girl had escaped.[46]

After his recapture, Groome's interrogation was even more grueling than it might have been had he not tried to escape. O'Leary wrote, "His questioning as we would expect, was very hard, but I can affirm that he didn't tell the Gestapo anything very important, or we would have all been arrested that night."[47]

Though Groome's arrest caused yet another devastating loss to the line, the work of returning evaders to England continued. More and more airmen were being shot down as a result of increased bombing, particularly in the industrial northwest regions of France. For the most part, O'Leary's involvement in these areas was purely administrative. Though he had always taken an active role in conducting prison breakouts and evasions, he remained in the area south of Paris. Louis Nouveau had organized branches in Pas de Calais, Brittany, and Normandy under the individual leadership of agents Norbert Fillerin, Claude Bach, and Alex

Wattebled. All of these agents were extremely reliable, having been involved with the line since early in its formation. Their positions as regional agents were assigned to them largely because of their dependability,
initiative, and great dedication to the line.[48]

The high volume of evaders forced Nouveau to look for additional
recruits to serve as guides and liaisons between these regions and Paris.
In December 1942 he introduced Roger Le Neveu into the line. Le Neveu
had been a member of the French Foreign Legion for about three years
and had ties to other branches of the Resistance. He was highly recom-
mended, and Nouveau introduced him to his leading agents. Fillerin was
not overly enamored with Le Neveu, but he could not quite identify the
cause of his uneasiness. Jean de la Olla liked him well enough, and the
men agreed to give him a trial period.

During December and January, Le Neveu transported several groups
of airmen to Toulouse. His apparent eagerness to work hard, in combination with his success as a guide, caused the agents and Nouveau to feel
more confident in his abilities.[49] However, Le Neveu did not inspire those
feelings in Australian evader Colin Bayliss, who remembered him as
"rather cold and uncommunicative and somehow I did not feel the same
degree of confidence in him as I had in the previous people involved in
aiding me."[50]

Operations with Le Neveu seemed to be going well when in January he arrived in Toulouse without the evader he had been assigned to
transport. He claimed that the Germans had arrested him with the
evader,[51] but that he had managed to escape. Both Nouveau and de la
Olla were bothered by the occurrence, but Le Neveu successfully convoyed two subsequent groups with no difficulties. As is often the case
with hindsight, Nouveau later questioned his handling of the affair. At
the time, he chose not to interrogate Le Neveu about the incident, feeling
that if the guide had explained himself sufficiently to de la Olla, it was
not his place to interfere. He also hesitated for fear that further questioning would have placed a strain on the relationship among the agents. In
Nouveau's words, "What would it serve? The innocent would defend
themselves in the same way as the guilty...."[52]

In February 1943, a group of five airmen arrived in Paris for transport to Toulouse. De la Olla hid them overnight, and Nouveau arranged
to meet them the following morning at the train station. For almost an
hour Nouveau paced in front of the railroad station waiting for them to

appear. The agents were still adjusting to the new requirements implemented when the Germans took over the unoccupied zone of France,
and Nouveau realized the group of agents and airmen needed special
passes to enter the station, which would take extra time. De la Olla, Fillerin,
and Le Neveu were forty-five minutes late arriving with the men, which
complicated matters and might have caused the entire operation to be
cancelled had not Le Neveu taken the initiative to push his way through
the crowds and return minutes later with the passes. No one was concerned about Le Neveu's ability to get the tickets, partly because they
were in a hurry to get the airmen aboard and because all of the agents
present had done the same kind of thing at various times. It was part of
being an agent. Nouveau boarded the train with the five airmen and two
guides and, waving to the agents standing on the station platform, settled
in for the trip to Toulouse. He visited with one of the airmen and watched
the winter landscape outside the windows.[53]

The group changed trains at a small station along the way, entering
an empty carriage toward the back of the train. Nouveau heard the door
open behind him just before the train was to leave. Knowing there were
other vacant seats in the car, he did not turn around to acknowledge the
newcomers but remained where he was standing. It was a terrible shock
when he felt a gun push into his ribs and heard a man with a German
accent tell him to put his hands in the air. Nouveau recalled his horror
when he realized what had happened. He wrote, "I had the impression of
being in a terrible fall, a feeling of being in a falling elevator with a broken cable. . . . In a distress more violent than despair, I saw myself fallen
into an irreparable disaster, so irreparable that I tried, without success,
not to think so as not to realize that all was finished."[54] Nouveau, the two
guides, and all five airmen were taken to Gestapo headquarters, none of
them having any idea how they had been discovered. Back in Paris, the
other agents carried on with their evasion activities, completely ignorant
of the cancer that had worked its way into the inner core of their organization and would in a short time destroy them all.

O'Leary was stunned at the news of Nouveau's arrest. For this reason, he was willing to meet with Le Neveu when on March 2 agent Paul
Ulmann contacted him and told him Le Neveu had asked for an ap-
pointment with O'Leary and had information about Nouveau's arrest.
The two men had never met, since O'Leary delegated regions to his agents
and allowed them to conduct their affairs independently. Le Neveu was

considered a "minor" agent, and as such would not have had contact with the organizational or administrative portion of the line. Still, if he had information to share about Nouveau's betrayal, O'Leary wanted to talk to him. The three men agreed to meet in the early afternoon at a café in Toulouse known as the Super Bar. Ulmann was concerned about two suspicious-looking men wandering about outside, but O'Leary was armed and felt no need to worry. Entering the café, which was actually a very small place, they saw Le Neveu sitting at a back table and joined him there.[55]

Ulmann introduced the two, and they briefly discussed recent changes in the rules for crossing the demarcation line. German officials had implemented a new stamp for ID cards, and O'Leary examined Le Neveu's card to determine what difficulties might be involved in reproducing it. Finally he asked for details about Nouveau's arrest, and Le Neveu stated that he knew who had betrayed Nouveau and could identify him easily. At that moment, O'Leary felt a gun in his side and found that they were surrounded by Gestapo agents, including the two men that had been loitering outside the café when they arrived. He quickly realized that most of the people inside the café had been involved in their arrest. Only the pale, frightened proprietor and two other people appeared to be innocent bystanders. As the three men were led away to Gestapo headquarters, O'Leary searched his mind trying to figure out who the traitor was. He was now certain that there was a traitor, but could not imagine who it might be.[56]

The Gestapo interrogated O'Leary shortly after his arrest, but in a manner far less traumatic than he had imagined. At one point, the door to O'Leary's interrogation room opened, and he saw Le Neveu sitting outside visiting with a group of Gestapo officers. Realizing that Le Neveu was the traitor, O'Leary was gripped by a sickening fear that others in the line would soon be in the hands of the Gestapo, and there was absolutely nothing he could do about it. With no way of warning them, the entire organization was likely to collapse as a result of Le Neveu's betrayal.

Three days later, Alex Wattebled sat in a café in Paris waiting for Norbert Fillerin, Jean de la Olla, and a third agent, Costa Dimpoglou. He knew about the arrest of Nouveau, but was more disturbed by a rumor that had just reached him concerning O'Leary's arrest. He simply could not believe that it had happened. But having thought carefully about recent events, he felt certain that he knew who the traitor was. For several reasons Wattebled thought it was probably Le Neveu, and he was surprised to see him entering the café. Trying to determine whether or not he was innocent, Wattebled asked him some leading questions that resulted in unsatisfying answers. When he saw Fillerin and de la Olla approaching, he suggested that Le Neveu use a phone located on the lower level of the café to contact another agent. As soon as he was out of sight, Wattebled rushed out the door to quickly tell of his suspicions and send them to warn others. When Le Neveu returned, Wattebled was sitting quietly in his chair waiting for him. Soon after, Dimpoglou arrived, and on the pretense of calling for de la Olla, he and Wattebled walked to the phone and exchanged thoughts about Le Neveu. When they reentered the café from the lower floor, they saw Le Neveu speaking with a member of the Gestapo. The agent turned and pointed his gun at them, but having decided he would rather die than be captured, Dimpoglou raced out the door and down the street. The Gestapo official tried to hold on to the thrashing Wattebled, who wrestled with him, shoving his arm aside and directing the revolver away from Dimpoglou, allowing him to safely escape. Two French gendarmes, misunderstanding the situation, came to Wattebled's aid, but five more German Gestapo officials quickly entered, stifling their efforts. In the confusion, Wattebled broke free and ran down the street with the Gestapo in pursuit. He slipped into an apartment house, telling a woman outside that he was a patriot and

Alex Wattebled, chief agent for the O'Leary escape line, initially worked as a translator for the Germans. He was an invaluable and trusted member of the line until his arrest in March 1942. (Courtesy of Alex Wattebled)

asking her not to give him away. As he ran up the stairs toward the roof, he heard the woman call out his location.[57]

Pausing on the roof, Wattebled burned his papers while frantically deliberating the course of action left open to him. He could wait for the Gestapo to appear and endure all that was certain to follow, or he could jump off the roof and kill himself. He felt the end result would be the same and decided he would rather die quickly. Throwing himself off the roof, Wattebled hit a veranda halfway down and felt his back twist painfully while broken glass shattered all around him. Seconds later, the veranda collapsed, sending him crashing through the ceiling of a restaurant. Severely injured and yet very much alive, he was collected by the Gestapo and without sympathy delivered to headquarters for immediate interrogation. His injuries were severe. Blood ran from an open cut in his head, and two fingers were completely numb from the damage to his spinal cord. None of this stopped Wattebled's captors from inflicting still more damage, viciously beating and electrocuting him over a period of days while he continued to withhold what he knew.[58]

In the meantime, de la Olla and Fillerin warned everyone they could find who had not already been betrayed. The next morning, March 4, 1943, the two of them were arrested almost immediately after arriving at a small café.[59] Taken to Gestapo headquarters, both were savagely interrogated. De la Olla's torture began with a whipping. The blows were so hard his entire body was spun around, and when the beating ended there was hardly a part of his body that had not been hit. He was alternately sprayed with ice-cold water in a basement cell and then removed to a heated room while Gestapo agents directed questions at him, nonstop. When he still refused to speak, they wrapped chains around his neck and pulled from both ends, choking him with each question he did not answer.[60]

Finally the Gestapo allowed the three men to see each other, perhaps hoping that the shock of seeing the pathetic condition of their friends might induce them to talk. Though physically broken, the men's spirits remained strong. Again they were tortured—seven, nine, fourteen hours. Still they remained silent.

O'Leary was also horribly tortured as he worked to maintain his silence. He reminded himself that he was the leader of the organization. All of his people believed in him, and he could not betray them. Groome, Nouveau, and others had kept their silence in order to protect him, and he could do no less for those who remained free. But for the first time he truly understood what their silence had probably cost. He reflected that before the torture started, fear of it created a desire to tell everything there was to tell, but once the torment began, a fierce resistance developed inside that was initially stronger than the pain being inflicted. By the time the excruciating pain began to dim the urge to resist, unconsciousness was fast approaching and with it a release from the need to be strong.[61]

O'Leary had false papers that identified him as Joseph Cartier, but after learning that Le Neveu was the traitor, he chose to admit to being the leader of the organization in the hope of protecting some of his other workers. His interrogators had released the names of several of his agents during their questioning, and he realized that the line had been seriously penetrated. Gestapo agents later associated him with several other agents arrested near Marseilles and transferred him to a prison there. After several weeks, he and some other captured members of the line were sent by train to Fresnes prison in Paris, a way station before deportation to Germany. On the way, O'Leary and Paulette Gouber, one of his former helpers, helped Fabien de Cortes jump off the train. O'Leary had briefed him on the events that had taken place and asked him to go to Spain or Switzerland in order to get word about Le Neveu's betrayal to MI9 in England. De Cortes went to Switzerland, where he told Victor Farel, the British Vice Consul, about the arrests and then returned to Toulouse. Attempting to reach Spain and safety, he traveled almost to the Spanish border before he was rearrested. MI9 passed the information to other escape lines operating through France, but for the Pat line it was too late.[62]

Airey Neave has said that Françoise Dissart and her cat were almost the sole survivors of the O'Leary organization, and in large part that is true. Françoise was devoted to O'Leary and picked up where he left off, evacuating a large number of airmen before the war ended. However, O'Leary left a legacy that was bravely fulfilled by the men and women he had spent almost two years of his life protecting. Lucien Dumais, Georges Broussine, and Val Bouryschkine each returned to head newly created escape lines. Georges Jouanjean, an invaluable leader in the Brittany section of the Pat line, resumed his work in Brittany and formed a core group who worked with Bouryschkine and later Dumais in developing their lines. Conrad Lafleur and Robert Vanier both returned to work as radio operators for escape lines, while former helpers Nancy Wake Fiocca, Andrée Borel, and Mario Prassinos trained with SOE and returned to conduct operations in France, the latter two losing their lives in the service.

The Pat line evacuated over three hundred Allied servicemen, and the escape lines that formed under the leadership of Dumais and Broussine evacuated approximately five hundred airmen. These men carried forward the determined spirit and commitment to aiding escapers and evaders when O'Leary could no longer do it himself. O'Leary was highly regarded by military intelligence, as is evident by U.S. Army Lt. Col. R.H. Betts's tribute: "His bold conceptions, his unstinting courage and his extraordinary capacity for organization and leadership marked him as one of the most outstanding leaders in the invaluable work of escape and evasion."[63]

6

Riding the Tail of a Comet

The Comet Line, 1941–1944

A young couple crawled stealthily through the heavy grasses growing on the banks of the Somme River, searching for a rowboat. Already the searchlights of German sentinels on patrol along the river had nearly exposed them, and they soon concluded that the boat was not there. After a hasty conference, they returned to the group of Belgians hidden nearby and explained that the boat was missing and all would have to swim across the river, where a young woman was waiting to hide them for the night. Because most of the group did not know how to swim, one of the guides, Arnold Depée, left to find some equipment to help the men cross the river. The other guide, Andrée "Dédée" de Jongh, remained with them to manage any emergencies that might arise.[1] The thirteen men in the group were young Belgians who wanted to escape to England and join the war effort. Dédée and Depée were attempting to organize an escape line to evacuate Belgian patriots and the many British servicemen who had been hiding in and around Brussels since the fall of Belgium and France the previous summer. This effort was a trial run, for though Depée had made one trip through France and over the Pyrenees, Dédée had not, and for the line to work effectively, both needed to be familiar with the route.[2]

Returning with a rope and the inner tube from an old tire, Depée tied one end of the rope around a sturdy tree and swam across the river, where he anchored the other end. Dédée helped a man onto the tube and, holding onto the rope, began propelling him through the water. The feeling of excitement helped to counter any fear she felt and created a rush of energy that enabled her to swim across the river twenty-five times that night, pushing the men across while offering encouragement to calm their fears. It helped that the German sentinels who usually patrolled every hour did not appear during the nearly two hours it took to complete the operation. Dédée later called their actions "pure madness," claiming, "We made, in spite of all our efforts, a dreadful noise."[3]

After spending the night in the farmhouse provided by Depée's friend Nenette, the two guides led the men to Bayonne, from which Depée took them across the Pyrenees and left them at the Spanish border. He gave them directions for reaching the British consul and returned to Bayonne to pick up Dédée for the trip back to Brussels. Uplifted by the apparent success of their operation, the two guides returned to Belgium, making plans for a second trip.

Dédée de Jongh was a twenty-five-year-old commercial artist who had volunteered her services as a Red Cross nurse soon after the Germans invaded Belgium. Armed with an intense hatred for all things German, she had organized a group of friends, including Depée, to hide servicemen in their homes around Brussels. Though she did not discuss her work with her parents, she soon realized they knew what she was doing. Dédée recalled an exchange with her mother that revealed her parents' awareness and concern: "I was phoning somebody and there was no answer. I tried again. No answer. My mother was sewing and quite naturally she said to me, 'Perhaps they are arrested.' I made as if this was a joke and said, 'You're saying funny things.' She said, 'But my daughter, you have to know it always finishes like this.'"[4]

Dédée de Jongh, chief of the Comet escape line, exhibited a tenacity and courage not often found in one so young. The route she organized for evaders enabled about nine hundred men to return to England and continue the fight against Germany. (Courtesy of Andrée de Jongh)

While Dédée and Depée worked together to establish an escape line between Brussels and Spain, it was Depée who made one of the most valuable of the line's helper connections. In June 1941 he traveled to Bayonne in the southwestern corner of France, where he contacted M. Appert, secretary of the General Society Bank, who was known to be in contact with a resistance group. Depée's visit coincided with an earlier visit to Appert by Elvire de Greef, who had also offered her services to assist Belgium. Remembering her visit, Appert gave Depée a password, "GoGo is dead," prearranged by himself and Elvire, and sent him to the de Greef home.[5]

The de Greef family had fled Belgium in May 1940 with the help of Albert Edward Johnson (code-named "B"), an Englishman working in Brussels for Count de Baillet Latour, president of the International Olympic Committee. At the Count's request, Johnson had taken several people, including the de Greefs, to the Spanish frontier hoping to evacuate them to England. When they found the borders closed, the de Greef family settled into an abandoned house in Anglet, near Bayonne, where Fernand de Greef found work as an interpreter for the German commander in that region. Elvire, known to all as "Tante Go" as a result of the unusual password, became active in the black market trade, which proved useful for feeding airmen en route to Spain and, on occasion, as a means of blackmailing German soldiers. Johnson moved into the house with them, serving as a general handyman. However, he also took part in the line's work, often convoying men over the mountains.[6]

The work of the de Greef family proved vital to the escape line. From his office, Fernand stole blank identification cards, permits for crossing into the Atlantic zone, and stamps for making false papers. Tante Go housed airmen and organized several safe houses in the Bayonne region where men stayed during the final stop of their journey before crossing the Pyrenees. In addition, she maintained the finances of the line and kept a record of all the men evacuated by it. The de Greef children, Fred and Janine, both in their mid-teens when the war broke out, served as couriers and guides for the line.[7]

In August 1941, Dédée and Depée prepared to convoy a second group of men to Spain. Because they disagreed on the safety of the main route, Dédée took three men down a longer rural route, Mons to Valencienne, while Depée took six more along the main thoroughfare, from Brussels to Lille, intending to link with Dédée in Corbie, just south of the Belgian border. When Depée did not appear, Dédée took her men to Bayonne, where they rested briefly at Tante Go's house. She felt frustrated at the lack of news about Depée, and the feeling increased when Tante Go gave her disappointing news about the Belgians they had aided on their last trip to Spain. All of them had been placed in a concentration camp just after they crossed the Spanish border. Dédée realized that if the escape line was to work properly, she had to make contact with the British consulate in Spain so British authorities could collect the evaders as soon as they entered Spanish territory.[8]

Tante Go introduced Dédée to Tomas Anabitarte, a smuggler from St. Jean de Luz, who was experienced at crossing the mountains and had agreed to guide the men into Spain. However, Tomas was not thrilled at the idea of taking a woman along with him. Dédée convinced him that she could keep up, and he allowed her to accompany him on the long trip—twelve hours the first night, then eight more the following night—at the end of which Dédée presented herself to the British consulate at Bilbao.[9]

The British vice consul, Vyvyan Pedrick, listened in amazement as the young woman told him where she was from and why she had come to his office. He first thought she was a German plant, for surely this small, blue-eyed blonde wearing ankle socks and saddle oxfords could not possibly have led three men all the way across occupied France and over the Pyrenees. But Dédée's youthful, almost fragile appearance belied her extraordinary strength of character.[10]

Dédée explained that she had established an escape line from Brussels, but that she needed help with financing the line and a contact to whom she could release the men after they arrived in Spain. She did not want to see the men she rescued land in prison camps after they crossed the border. Unlike O'Leary, who was glad to receive any form of assistance MI9 could provide, Dédée wanted only financial help to pay for food and transportation costs for the men traveling across France and over the mountains.[11]

Of the three servicemen Dédée accompanied over the Pyrenees, only one was a British serviceman. The consul agreed to pay a specific amount for his return, but could not reimburse her for the two Belgians escaping from German occupation.[12] He asked her to return in a month with more men, preferably airmen, and agreed to forward her request to MI9 in London. Having spent a good deal of time listening to her story, he was convinced of her authenticity, but knew it would not be easy to convince his superiors in London.

When he heard of the exchange, Claude Dansey of MI6, who was associated with MI9, caustically retorted that the consul had been a "damned fool" to pay Dédée for the one serviceman she had returned. However, Norman Crockatt's examination of interrogation reports established that a girl named Andrée de Jongh had sent letters to the parents of three wounded servicemen one year earlier. The letters had been friendly and comforting to the anxious families, who prior to that time had received no word on the health of their sons. Convinced that a German agent would most likely not go to such lengths to gain the confidence of the British, Dansey gave the consul at Bilbao permission to financially support her endeavors.[13]

Dédée was adamant about maintaining the independence of the escape line. The Belgian government-in-exile made repeated attempts to get control of it, but her stubborn determination was more than they had bargained for. Belgian officials saw her resistance as arrogance, but Dédée claimed she could not comply with their directions because they "were given by people who were not aware of the situation, and did not understand the spirit that drove the team, nor the . . . situation under which the work was being done."[14] Her insistence that the line remain independent also frustrated Langley of MI9, who wrote: "We never had the faintest intention of issuing orders since we knew only too well that it would be a waste of time and energy as we had no means of ensuring they were carried out. . . . My admiration for their bravery and unconquerable spirit in the face of disaster never wavered, but at times, their intransigence and failure to make use of some of the help we offered them . . . nearly drove me frantic."[15]

Returning to Bayonne after meeting with the British consul, Dédée learned Depée had been betrayed and arrested, and that her family in Brussels had been questioned by the Gestapo concerning her whereabouts. Realizing that it was no longer safe to go home, she contacted her father, Fréderic de Jongh, who agreed to take over the Belgian portion of the line. His job was to organize the rescue of airmen, while Dédée established a new headquarters in Valenciennes, near the Belgian border, from which evaders would be transported to Bayonne and over the mountains.

In establishing her new center of operations, Dédée enlisted the aid

Fréderic de Jongh took over leadership of the Comet line after his daughter Dédée was arrested. He served as chief for about six months until he was arrested due to a traitor in the line. De Jongh was executed for his activities several months later. (Courtesy of Andrée de Jongh)

of a brother-and-sister team, Charles ("Charlie") and Elvire Morelle. Charles had been a military prisoner in Germany, and when he escaped in the spring of 1941 Dédée provided him with a safe house in Brussels before assisting his escape into France, where he was reunited with his wife and two children.[16] Charles became her right-hand man, housing evaders and traveling from one end of the line to the other with messages and men, while Elvire served as a guide in the Somme region.

During this time, Dédée made repeated trips over the Pyrenees escorting men into Spain, where she delivered them into the hands of Michael Creswell. Creswell was a British diplomat attached to the British Embassy in Madrid. Code-named "Monday" for MI9's purposes, he had a warm and caring personality, which endeared him to all who came in contact with him. He played a valuable role in the evasion efforts, serving as liaison for the Comet line and initiating the release of airmen and helpers imprisoned in Spanish concentration camps.[17]

Though Dédée's original guide, Tomas, had been capable and efficient, his price for transporting the men over the mountains was higher than Dédée felt was appropriate. With the aid of a Basque customs agent, she acquired the services of Basque smuggler Florentino Goicoechea, without whom the Comet line probably would not have been so successful.[18] Florentino's knowledge of the mountains was extensive, and though he spoke only Basque, he earned great respect from the evaders, who recalled that he always seemed to know where he was going. No matter what the weather conditions, Florentino continued onward, stopping occasionally to reclaim a bottle of cognac that he had hidden behind a rock or under a tree stump. Passionate opposition to fascism, more than a desire for money, motivated Florentino to offer his services as a guide and may well explain his remarkable success. He had earlier taken part in the Spanish Civil War as a member of the Republican army and saw his work with the evaders as a continuation of that fight.[19]

The trip across the Pyrenees was a grueling, arduous task for men and women in the best of health. The evaders were often weak from injuries or inadequate nutrition, which further increased their discomfort as they traveled. Many repatriated airmen expressed amazement at the apparent ease with which Dédée made the trip, often helping stragglers and boosting men larger than herself over rough spots. Canadian Angus MacLean recalled that his feet hurt terribly, and he felt he could go no farther, but each time he thought about stopping, a glance at the petite figure of Dédée working her way up the mountain gave him the strength to keep moving.[20]

The difficulty of the hike over the mountains and the shortage of guides who could accompany the evaders on the arduous journey meant that the line, called Comet, evacuated only about three groups of men over the mountains each month. On the night of the planned crossing, Dédée and the evaders would meet Florentino at the farmhouse of Francia Usandizaga, a Basque woman with three young children who had lost her husband earlier in the war. She would provide them with a good meal and strong coffee, and the men relaxed by playing with the children until it was time to leave. They spent several hours walking in the mountains, which was difficult enough, but toward the end of the journey, just before entering Spain, the men had to cross the swiftly running Bidassoa River. Though not more than waist deep, its rocky bottom was very uneven and its fast current unusually treacherous even in good weather. In bad weather the river turned into torrential rapids and sometimes could not be crossed at all. The nearest bridge was five hours away and heavily guarded by the Germans.[21]

When Florentino reached the bank of the river, he would hold up his hand for silence, then carefully search the distance for German patrols that guarded the nearby Spanish road. When he determined that all was clear, he and Dédée would lead the men one by one across the river.

Florentino Goicoechea served as Comet's Pyrenees mountain guide. His dedication to the line was partly due to his hatred of fascism. Florentino is well remembered by former evaders for his strength and uncanny ability to travel across the
mountains at night without losing his way. (Courtesy of Andrée de Jongh)

On one occasion, when a Welsh evader could not cross due to injuries, Florentino amazed his fellow travelers by picking the young man up and carrying him across the swiftly running river on his shoulders.[22]

Once across the river, the group had yet another dangerous task ahead of them. So near to Spain that they could see the twinkling lights of a frontier town, they still had to scramble up a rocky hillside, cross a railway and the frontier road, and then climb another steep embankment before reaching the border. The difficulty was increased by loose gravel spread along the hillside and German soldiers patrolling within hearing distance. On reaching the top of the hill, the travelers could relax, and after a few more miles of walking they stopped to rest a couple of hours at Sarobe Farm before continuing on to San Sebastian, where a Spanish farmer, Bernardo Aracama, fed them and provided shelter. While the men rested throughout the day, Dédée walked further down the mountain and contacted the British consul in Bilbao, who reported to Creswell in Madrid. Later in the day a Spanish taxi driver working for the line would deliver Dédée and the men to a quiet section of road where they met Creswell. After a brief conference, Creswell would leave with the evaders while Dédée and Florentino returned to the mountains and to France.[23]

Dédée crossed the mountains thirty-two times for the line. Tante Go recalled that she never seemed to tire and in December 1941 convoyed a group of evaders over the mountain on Christmas Eve.[24] Albert Johnson relieved her occasionally by guiding the men with Florentino, and Elvire Morelle also offered to serve as a "passer" in the Pyrenees. Rotating crossings between three people would allow the line to continue evacuating airmen regularly without exhausting any one guide. Unfortunately, Elvire fell and fractured her leg during her first trip, leaving Dédée without a third passer.[25]

Despite the inconvenience of losing Elvire, the Comet's first year passed relatively smoothly. There had been a number of changes in the network—some helpers had been arrested, and new workers had been incorporated into Comet's workforce—but the organization had not suffered a massive betrayal, as had the Pat line by this time. Minor complications developed early in 1942 when the Abwehr and the Gestapo increased their efforts to close down the line. As a result, Dédée's father, Fréderic, went into hiding at the home of one of his main helpers, Henri Michelli, then fled to Paris on April 30, leaving the Brussels headquarters in the hands of Michelli and Charles Morelle. Six days later both new leaders were arrested along with several of their helpers at a reunion dinner at Michelli's home.[26] The arrests caused a serious break in the line because only Michelli knew Fréderic's address in Paris. By a stroke of luck, one of Fréderic's earlier helpers recalled the appearance and location of Charles's brother-in-law's house in Paris, and with this information the connection with the de Jonghs was restored.[27]

Dédée joined her father in Paris in May, where they re-established the line's French headquarters. She found it a pleasure to have him with her, as she had not seen any of her family for four months. An effort to secretly visit them earlier in the year had almost ended in disaster when the Gestapo appeared at the house. Dédée had escaped quickly out of the back garden as her sister stalled the officers in the house.[28]

While Dédée continued transporting men over the Pyrenees, Fréderic began expanding the organization's work in France. Rather than allow France to remain simply a transit area, he hoped to establish collection points from which men could be introduced into the line. Elvire, fully recovered from her leg fracture, joined them in Paris and established a safe house in a nearby suburb. A large number of French people began to be incorporated into the line, and a core group of helpers grew in Paris under the de Jonghs' leadership. Raymonde Coache served as guide, safe house keeper, and organizer of supplies. Robert Aylé and his wife Germaine were also members of this inner circle, providing supplies and contacts with people who housed airmen and members of active resistance organizations.[29]

While Fréderic organized the line in Paris, Baron Jean Greindl, affectionately known to his workers as "Nemo," reorganized the Brussels section. Recently returned from the Congo, where he had managed a coffee plantation for many years, the thirty-five-year-old Greindl was the oldest of the helpers involved with the main organization in Brussels. Employed as the manager of the Swedish Canteen, a Red Cross organization dedicated to feeding and caring for poor and sick children living in Brussels, he used his office as a headquarters for the line. His introduction into Comet was the result of his friendship with Peggy van Lier, a young girl acquainted with Dédée's married sister, Suzanne de Wittek.[30] Initially Greindl provided food for safe house keepers from the canteen's supplies, but after the Brussels group was arrested he suggested to van Lier and de Wittek that they should try to reorganize the Brussels section of the line. De Wittek had contact with several of the line's former workers, particularly Nadine Dumon, Fréderic's principal assistant during the period when he was chief of the Belgian sector. In an effort to protect the newly created portion, Greindl kept his identity secret from the helpers associated with the original line. De Wittek served as the liaison between Greindl and the original group of helpers, referring to him as Mlle Jacques when conducting business with them.[31]

Greindl was a very able chief and greatly admired by his young helpers. While he appreciated their spirit of adventure and willingness to serve, his own actions were tempered with a more mature understanding of the dangerous activities in which they were involved. According to a post-war report by his brother Albert, Greindl "inspired a wonderful fraternity and patriotic ideal. His orders were always given with kind friendship. He had magnanimous sympathy and every one of his men would have done everything to protect him." Greindl was well organized and created a system of rescuing airmen throughout Belgium by dividing the country into regional collection centers at Namur, Liege, and Massert. A center was already in place at Gand, organized by Jean Ingles, one of Fréderic's original helpers. Greindl developed a very successful and secure system of collection from these areas by arranging contacts with the local teacher, doctor, and priest. Any of the townspeople who found themselves with evaders on their hands would get in touch with one of these town leaders to find out what they should do, and this would result in the evaders being filtered into the main line in Brussels.[32]

During the summer of 1942 there were further arrests in Brussels. The line lost Nadine Dumon, her parents, and de Wittek when the Abwehr, under pressure from the Luftwaffe, increased its efforts to crush the escape lines. The Brussels sector had tried to arrange the transfer of airmen from helper to helper in such a way as to protect against infiltration, particularly after Harold Cole had created such havoc in the Pat line. MI9 had issued directions to all the escape lines urging caution and stressing the need to interrogate the airmen carefully to ensure that they were indeed airmen and not German plants. It is important to remember, however, that the escape lines were operated largely by amateurs. None of the people in the Comet line's leadership positions had been trained in military intelligence. They and those who worked with them were simply caring, honorable people who wanted to serve the Allies in whatever way they could. In spite of the fact that they were fighting against a formidable enemy, they adapted well to the clandestine life they were forced to lead. It is a tribute to them that many intelligence operations established by trained agents suffered penetrations just as disastrous as those of the escape lines, though such knowledge is no comfort to those who suffered or live with the memory of loved ones who died for the cause. Nadine Dumon recalled the terrible sadness of remembering those who died in the years following the war: "Whenever I felt the slightest bit gay, suddenly I would think to myself . . . my Papa did not come back either. He thought that after the war he would do this or that, and he never did. That he would go to this or that place that he never got to. Each time you were happy, pouf! Suddenly you're no longer happy. . . . And that went on for years."[33]

The Maréchal family was an ordinary family that rose to the occasion when Belgium was invaded by German forces. Eighteen-year-old Elsie Maréchal and her parents had been involved with the Comet organization since its early days. Their work as safe house keepers was valuable, but Mme Elsie Belle Maréchal, an Englishwoman, and her daughter Elsie were particularly useful because their ability to speak English enabled them to interrogate airmen to determine their authenticity. Elsie worked in other capacities as well, carrying supplies to hidden evaders and convoying men to safe houses.[34]

In 1942, the Maréchals fell victim to a trap set by German police intent on destroying the line. Quite often the family had evaders hiding at their home waiting to be transferred further down the line. However, when they were arrested during late November there were no airmen lodging with them and Elsie had received no notice of new airmen arriving anytime soon. Midway through the afternoon of their arrests, she was greatly surprised to find a green envelope in the mailbox announcing the arrival of two airmen on the upcoming Thursday. Her shock was more the result of finding the letter in her box than the knowledge that evaders were on the way. Increased bombing raids meant that airmen were being shot down regularly and might arrive at any time, but letters relating to escape work were never delivered to the Maréchal house. Nelly Boceuninck was the official letter liaison for the Brussels sector. All information about incoming evaders was delivered to her house, and she took the communications to Elsie.[35]

Elsie showed the letter to her mother, who expressed concern. Neither could understand why they had received it. Mme Maréchal told her daughter to take the note to Greindl at the Swedish Canteen, but before Elsie could leave the doorbell rang. When she opened the front door, Elsie stared in surprise at her liaison, Albert Marchal, who was standing on the front porch with two American airmen behind him. Something seemed to be very wrong. Not only had the letter arrived at the wrong place, but the airmen had been delivered earlier than expected, and directly to her home rather than at a neutral meeting place.[36]

Albert was confused as well. He had taken the men to the Frére Orban Park, near a church where Elsie usually met him, and waited for her to come interrogate them, but she never arrived. Unsure of what to do, he took them to Nelly, who was not home, and then to Elsie. He felt uneasy about the situation and, before leaving, expressed additional concerns to Mme Maréchal about the men, who seemed unlike others he had helped. Worried, Mme Maréchal sent Elsie to Greindl with the letter.

Greindl was extremely troubled about the situation. The entire operation had been conducted out of order, and he was bothered by the fact that the letter's script had a German look about it. He instructed Elsie to return home and interrogate the airmen very carefully, warning her that she and her mother should leave immediately if the men's answers seemed at all suspicious.[37]

Frightened, Elsie returned home, unaware of the events that had taken place since her departure. In spite of her concerns, Mme Maréchal had cared for the men in her usual fashion, cooking them breakfast and making them feel welcome. They were the first Americans she had sheltered, and she wanted them to feel at home. She had heard Americans described as friendly and talkative, but these men were quiet, almost sullen. Her worst fears were confirmed when, after finishing their meal, the men, Luftwaffe agents Brenner and Mohr (Paul), suddenly stood up and announced that she was under arrest. Shortly afterward, a large group of policemen entered the house and made themselves at home while waiting for the rest of the family. Thirty minutes later an unsuspecting Elsie walked through the front door and was arrested. Unable to warn anyone, she and her mother sat helplessly while M. Georges Maréchal and Elsie's fifteen-year-old brother, Bobby, also walked into the trap. The whole family was taken to German police headquarters, while a number of policemen remained at the house in the hopes that other members of the organization would appear.[38]

In spite of fierce interrogations by German agents Ziegelmeyer (Wastel) and Kallabis, the Maréchals denied having any information about the escape line. However, a seemingly insignificant detail from Bobby led the German agents back to Elsie. Bobby had told them that his sister served meals each day at the Swedish Canteen. Already suspicious of Griendl, they harshly questioned Elsie about him. Though they beat her unmercifully, she insisted that she knew nothing. Finally, telling her that denials were useless and claiming they would arrest Greindl the following day, they returned her to her cell. Bruised and battered, Elsie cried for the rest of the night, knowing she was powerless to save Greindl or any of the other helpers with whom she had worked.[39]

After Elsie had left the Swedish Canteen, Griendl had sat in his office with Peggy van Lier and Victor Michiels, a new guide recently recruited to work in the Brussels section. All of them were worried and waited anxiously for some word from Elsie to ease their minds. As the afternoon passed slowly by, they heard the cheerful voices of children on the lower floor of the canteen, a stark contrast to the seriousness of their own conversation in Greindl's office. Finally, late in the afternoon, Greindl sent Michiels to the Maréchal home to investigate the situation. Elsie's silence made him very uneasy, and while he did not want to put Michiels into danger, he needed to know what was happening. He instructed Michiels to study the house and any activities taking place around it, but that if he saw anything suspicious he should leave at once. Under no circumstances was he to approach the house unless absolutely certain it was safe.[40]

Eager to be of some assistance, Michiels went to the Maréchal home, agreeing to report back soon. He walked along the street in front of the house, searching for signs of activity. It was a quiet night and everything seemed to be in order, so he crossed the street and raised his hand to ring the doorbell; but before he could do so, three German police appeared in the doorway with their revolvers raised. Not wanting to be captured, Michiels began to back away from the door. Night had fallen and he thought he had a good chance of escaping into the shadows if he ran. Turning away, he dashed across the yard and down the street, but the police shot at him, hitting him three times before he fell dead at the edge of the road.[41]

In the meantime, Greindl waited in his office at the canteen. He had already sent van Lier home, but hoping that Michiels would report back, he stayed late. Eventually, he too went wearily home. Van Lier, tossing in her bed all night, remembered with sickening fear that Elvire Morelle was scheduled to arrive at the Maréchal home early the next morning. Because of the curfew, there was no way to get to the train station early enough to intercept her, and Elvire was arrested as soon as she appeared at the Maréchal house. Though she might have been able to bluff her way out of the situation, the packages she carried, holding escape aids for her brother Charles, incriminated her. She was taken to police headquarters, interrogated, and imprisoned.[42]

On the morning of Elvire's arrest, van Lier met Greindl at the canteen and convinced him, against his better judgment, to allow her to go to Michiels' parents' house to find out if he was there. When she arrived, German police met her at the door and interrogated her as to her reason for visiting the family. Van Lier had prepared her alibi in advance and told them she wanted to speak to Michiels' sister, Josée, about a university course. As added protection, she carried in her purse some photographs of herself with German officers taken before the war and tried to answer the officers' questions in German, though she did not speak the language very well.[43]

After lunch, German police took van Lier to their headquarters in Brussels, where they interrogated her about her relationship with Michiels' family. Shaken by the sight of Elvire in the waiting room and even more so by the news that Michiels had been killed, van Lier was shocked when the police, satisfied with her answers, released her that night. Leaving the police station, she walked down the street shaking with relief and found a church where she stopped to pray before reporting to Greindl.[44]

The following day, fearing for their safety, Greindl sent van Lier and his two other main guides, Georges and Edouard d'Oultremont, down the line to England. He then closed his headquarters at the Swedish Canteen, heeding Dédée's warning not to go there again, and reestablished his organization from an apartment in town. The line had been severely penetrated, and he spent the next three months trying to put it back together, finding new guides and safe house keepers. He suspected that his own days of working with the line were numbered, and his wife, who had recently given birth to their second child, pleaded with him to leave. Greindl recalled Dédée's recent words to him, "You realize that there are nine chances out of ten that you will never come out of this alive?"[45] Still he remained, dedicated to the work of the escape line and refusing to leave Belgium until he had found a successor to replace him as chief of the Brussels sector.

The false airmen responsible for the Maréchal affair had been introduced into the line in Luxembourg and traveled from there to the Namur region and then to Brussels. Though Dédée and Fréderic continued to refuse the assistance of a radio operator, Airey Neave felt that their use of one might have prevented the Maréchal tragedy by allowing the line to check the evaders' identities with the London office. Due to the speed with which the Maréchal situation deteriorated, that is probably not the case, although radio checks were indeed more efficient than the interview method. O'Leary was able to radio London to check men's identities, but Comet used questionnaires that were initially too general to do much good. Later questionnaires were more detailed and included cultural questions in addition to those dealing with locations and kinds of aircraft. A radio also would have allowed them to transmit information on traitors and make more timely reports to MI9 about problems, as well as allow MI9 to offer more timely solutions. The courier system used by Comet was time-consuming and inefficient, but it was difficult to convince Dédée that MI9 had only the line's best interests at heart rather than a desire to take it over.[46] Over one hundred people were arrested for helping the false airmen—a high price for the sixty flyers the line had evacuated over the previous half year. Unfortunately, the arrests in Brussels were only the first of a series of catastrophies to befall Comet over the next few months.[47]

In January 1943 Dédée finally convinced her father that he should leave France. Fréderic worried about Dédée and was dedicated to helping her, but she feared for his safety. He did not want to go, and Dédée later remembered, "He left Paris with a heavy heart. He hated the thought of leaving me."[48] Though she appreciated his help, Dédée felt the line could continue to function without him, and that she could work more effectively if she knew he was safe. In September Greindl had sent Jean François Nothomb ("Franco") to Paris in response to Dédée's request for an assistant. Nothomb was a twenty-three-year-old Belgian whose dark complexion gave him a Spanish appearance. From the beginning, he proved a great help to Dédée and Fréderic, sharing his home with them after Elvire Morelle's arrest and serving as a passer over the Pyrenees.[49]

Leaving the Paris section in the able hands of Nothomb and Robert

Aylé, the de Jonghs traveled to Bayonne with three evaders, intending to cross the Pyrenees that night. However, torrential rainstorms beat down on the southern region, and considering Fréderic's age and health, Dédée and Tante Go persuaded him to wait at the de Greef's house until the next trip. Tante Go drove Dédée and her evaders to Francia Usandizaga's farmhouse in the foothills of the Pyrenees, then went to the nearby resort town of St. Jean de Luz for the night rather than return to Bayonne in the storm. Even Florentino was not anxious to try crossing the mountains in such weather, and he and Dédée decided it would be safer to delay until the next night. Florentino left, and Dédée and the men made themselves comfortable at Francia's house, where her children were delighted to have the airmen to entertain them.[50]

The weather improved the following day, January 15, though it was still dreary, and the airmen and Dédée passed the morning visiting and drinking coffee. During the midday meal they heard the sound of a car, and one of the evaders said jokingly, "It is the Gestapo," while playfully holding up a knife. It came as a terrible shock when the door opened and German gendarmes stepped in, pointing machine guns at everyone in the room. In stunned silence, everyone around the table got up and, with their hands in the air, marched down the road toward St. Jean de Luz. A smuggler who had been dismissed from the line for dishonesty had betrayed the group to the Gestapo at St. Jean de Luz. Luckily, Florentino had escaped arrest by returning to his own house the night before, but Dédée's work with the line was over. She had rescued 118 evaders since her first trip to Spain in August 1941. Francia suffered the most as a result of the betrayal. Illness and poor treatment led to her death at Ravensbrük concentration camp. As a widow, it is likely that she spent much of her time in the camp worrying about the safety and care of her three young children. Though deprived of their mother, the children received a good home with a neighbor and were later educated with the financial assistance of former Comet helpers.[51]

Tante Go learned of Dédée's arrest the following day and broke the news to Fréderic, who decided to return to Paris to take over leadership of the line. Florentino immediately crossed the Pyrenees and contacted Creswell of the British Embassy, who sent a telegram to MI9 in London. Dédée had been a driving force behind the line, and her arrest was distressing news to Neave and Langley, who were still worrying about the recovery of the Brussels sector after the penetrations only six weeks earlier.[52]

Though with the help of a Red Cross worker they were able to communicate with Dédée, all efforts to help her escape were unsuccessful, much to the frustration of Tante Go, Nothomb, and Jean Dassié, a helper in Bayonne. Further arrests followed when German interrogators forced information from one of the evaders captured with Dédée. As a result, Dassié, his wife, and his sixteen-year-old daughter were arrested at their home. All were brutally tortured and beaten before being deported to concentration camps in Germany.[53] Not long afterward, Albert Johnson was arrested with Tante Go in St. Jean de Luz. Drawing on her experience with the black market, Tante Go won their freedom by threatening to betray their captors' black market purchases to their superiors. But Johnson's position as passer and guide was compromised, and in May 1943 he crossed the Pyrenees for the last time. He had traversed the mountains twenty-eight times, convoying 122 evaders to Spain.[54]

It seemed that nothing else could go wrong, but on February 6, 1943, just three weeks after Dédée's arrest, Greindl was arrested at the Swedish Canteen. Since November, he had found a new group of workers and agreed to have a radio operator from MI9, who parachuted into Belgium in late January. Neave looked forward to improved communication with the Brussels sector of the line, but he received only one transmission from the operator, which said, "Nemo [Greindl] arrested sixth of February."[55]

It is unclear why Greindl returned to the canteen, but while sitting in his old office talking with one of his helpers, the Luftwaffe police burst in and arrested them both. They also arrested Greindl's wife, though she had not participated in his work, forcing her to spend a week in the infirmary of St. Gilles prison with her month-old baby. Within a few days the entire Brussels sector collapsed as several more helpers were apprehended by the secret police, victims of a betrayal from within. Greindl had used a priest, Father William Cracco, as a liaison with the line's workers imprisoned at St. Gilles. In fact, Cracco worked for the Germans and betrayed Greindl as well as his two young nephews, José and François Cracco. José had served as courier between the elder Cracco and Greindl, but was unaware that his uncle was turning all of the correspondence over to the Germans. This, in addition to information obtained earlier during interrogations of young Bobby Maréchal, enabled German intelligence agents Ziegelmeyer and Kallabis to trace Greindl and arrest him. After the arrest, Greindl's brother Albert collected most of Greindl's papers and money from his apartment before police arrived. He then left Brussels and escaped safely to England, where he reported the recent events to MI9.

Neave claimed that he heard nothing else from the radio operator, and in April 1943 the man's dead body was found. He had been arrested shortly after Greindl and agreed to turn double agent for the Germans. Though he gave up his security code, only a few messages were sent, then silence. José and François were deported to Germany, where they died.[56]

Greindl's behavior during his arrest and imprisonment evoked feelings of respect even among the Germans who witnessed his interrogations. Dr. Pfaw, a German, stated that following his arrest four or five German agents beat Greindl with their hands and a steel spring. They showed him a letter they claimed he had written but that he had not yet signed. They said they would beat him again if he didn't sign it.[57] In spite of such threats, Greindl refused to cooperate with his interrogators. Werner Theiss, the Luftwaffe's translator present at Greindl's interrogations, claimed Greindl told agents nothing they did not already know, and added, "I can confirm that the Baron Greindl always maintained a very dignified manner."[58]

Greindl died September 7, 1943, when an Allied bomb fell on the army barracks at Etterbeek, where he was imprisoned after being condemned to death by a council of the German Luftwaffe. In the presence of a Belgian inspector, his family identified his body, which was then released to them for burial by order of the Luftwaffe. Only six weeks later, on October 20, nine other Comet workers, including Georges Maréchal, were executed by firing squad in Brussels.

The events in Belgium and France had a devastating effect on the morale of those who worked on the line, and many became fearful of helping evaders. In less than two months, not only had Dédée and Greindl been arrested, but also Pat O'Leary and Louis Nouveau of the Pat line. The latter had collapsed and Comet, the only other well-established escape line, was in desperate need of help. But there was little MI9 could do to assist. The arrests had resulted in a loss of confidence in the escape networks and prompted a violent backlash from the War Office criticizing the escape organizations as a threat to intelligence gathering and sabotage. Neave's suggestion that returned aircrew were more relevant to the war than much of the intelligence that was gathered was not appreciated by his superiors.[59]

The Germans' massive campaign against the escape lines produced a heavy backlog of evaders in France, since the destruction of an escape line had no effect on the number of air operations conducted by Allied forces. The Comet line had delivered three to five groups of men to Spain per month before November 1942, but in the five-month period between November 1, 1942, and April 1, 1943, it averaged only one group per month.[60]

Fréderic desperately needed a means to evacuate the stranded airmen and turned to the Burgundy and Brandy escape lines for assistance. The Burgundy line, established by Georges Broussine, took sixteen of Comet's evaders, granting some relief to the organization, while Brandy, led by Mme Camille Spiquel, took about twenty more. About this time, Spiquel agreed to lodge a guide, Jacques Desoubrie, known as "Jean Masson," who claimed to have a reliable route to the north and a steady supply of blank identity papers for that region. Knowing Fréderic's connection to Brussels had been broken, Spiquel contacted him about Desoubrie, suggesting the new agent might be of help in reestablishing the connection. Eager to restore communications between the Paris and Brussels sectors, Fréderic met with Desoubrie and, with the approval of Aylé, incorporated his services into the line.[61]

After successfully convoying two groups of evaders from Brussels to Paris, Desoubrie contacted Fréderic in early June 1943, reporting that he would deliver a large group of airmen on June 6. He asked that there be several helpers on hand to whom he could deliver them, and Fréderic made the required arrangements, sending Raymonde Coache and Madeleine Bouteloupt to Lille to help Desoubrie guide the men to Paris. Desoubrie suggested that Coache remain in Lille until a second group arrived later in the afternoon, and he and Bouteloupt boarded the train for Paris. Coache walked to a small café to wait for the next convoy to arrive, but shortly after she sat down a group of German police entered and arrested her. They interrogated her for ten hours that night, tightening the handcuffs painfully around her wrists when she refused to talk. Coache did not know who had betrayed her until several days later when Desoubrie visited her in the presence of SS agent Hermann Gentsell. He told her to give them names and addresses, but Coache refused. She was condemned to death and deported to Germany.[62]

Sadly, Coache was only the first in a vicious series of betrayals conducted by Desoubrie. Madeleine Bouteloupt, along with the airman she convoyed, was arrested before the train left the Lille station. Desoubrie's treachery was all the more tragic because of the great trust his fellow helpers had for him. The line's Paris headquarters had received communication about a traitor working for an escape line somewhere between Brussels and Paris, but they never suspected Desoubrie.[63]

While Coache and Bouteloupt were being arrested, Fréderic sat in his apartment filling out information on false papers to be used by the airmen. Realizing it was nearly time to meet Desoubrie, but knowing he would return shortly, he left the papers on the table and a small pot of leftover vegetables from lunch sitting on the stove. When he arrived at the station, Aylé and his wife, Germaine, were waiting for him on the boarding platform. When the train arrived, Desoubrie stepped off with six evaders and joined the group, shaking hands with them and receiving their congratulations for his work. Minutes later, several German police surrounded them in the station and handcuffed the evaders and helpers, including Desoubrie, then took them to Gestapo headquarters. Fréderic, Aylé, and Germaine sat in a holding room in disbelief, waiting to be interrogated. Like Coache, they could not imagine who had betrayed them, but their confusion ended when the traitor entered the room, freed from the handcuffs and smiling contemptuously at them. Desoubrie boastfully admitted his deceit and Aylé, unable to contain his anger, stood up and hit him. It proved to be Robert Aylé's only opportunity to strike out at the man who betrayed him. On March 28, 1944, both he and Fréderic de Jongh were executed for their dedication to the Comet escape line.[64]

While the three helpers suffered brutal interrogation by the Gestapo, the repercussions of Desoubrie's treachery continued, moving beyond Paris and causing the complete collapse of the newly established Brussels sector within twenty-four hours of the Paris arrests. Over one hundred people associated with Comet were arrested as a result of Desoubrie's betrayal. Antoine d'Ursel ("Jacques Cartier"), chief of the Brussels sector, received advanced warning that enabled him to go into hiding, but his wife and daughter were arrested in his place.[65]

Georges Broussine of Burgundy had a meeting scheduled with Fréderic and Aylé on the afternoon of June 6. As was the prearranged method for confirmation, he telephoned Aylé's apartment thirty minutes in advance of the planned rendezvous. Instead of Aylé, a German voice answered the phone and asked his name, inviting Broussine to come to Aylé's apartment. Broussine knew immediately what had happened, hung up the phone, then contacted his Comet liaison through a third party to end all connections with her. Broussine's correspondence with the Comet line was well organized with careful security measures. Fréderic and Aylé did not know Broussine's code name. They made contact with him through a woman named Dr. Bertrand-Fontaine. If Broussine needed to get in touch with Aylé or Fréderic, he phoned Aylé's apartment and indicated his need without using his name. The three men confirmed the meeting place for their next rendezvous each time they met, and when Broussine called to confirm his meetings, he again did so without giving his name. The fact that the German voice asked him to go to Aylé's house indicated to Broussine that something was wrong, as all of the men were aware that Broussine did not know where Aylé lived. Broussine claimed it was only the courage of Fréderic and Aylé that kept the Burgundy line from being attacked as well. Had either of the men released the name of Bertrand-Fontaine, Burgundy would have been in great danger of collapse.[66]

Desoubrie extended his efforts into the Brandy line, turning over to the Gestapo all the information he had collected about the line before he transferred to Comet. Consequently, the entire northern portion of Brandy collapsed as well, with many more helpers arrested and deported for aiding evaders. For MI9, the nightmare that had begun in early 1943 with the arrests of Dédée and Griendl had grown beyond comprehension.[67]

Georges Broussine, chief of the Burgundy escape line. (Courtesy of Georges Broussine)

About one week after the collapse of the Paris and Brussels sectors, Nothomb returned to Paris after leading a convoy to Spain and spending time with Tante Go in Bayonne. Entering the apartment he shared with Fréderic, he found the false papers still spread out on the table where Fréderic had left them when he departed for what he had thought would be a quick meeting with Desoubrie. Nothomb was not concerned, expecting that his associate would return shortly, and walked into the kitchen. There he found the leftover vegetables standing in the pot, covered in mold, and understood all too well that something had gone terribly wrong in his absence. Collecting all the money, stamps, and papers that he could carry, Nothomb fled the apartment and went to the home of Max Roger, one of the helpers who had not been compromised by Desoubrie. Together they went to Aylé's apartment, but found Gestapo seals had been placed on the door. They tried to return to the apartment shared by Nothomb and Fréderic but, finding Germans at the apartment house, left again. Later that night, Nothomb was able to enter the apartment and search all of the hidden compartments for money and papers. As he left, he removed the newly placed Gestapo seals from the door.[68]

Exhibiting the resilient spirit that had come to be associated with the Comet line, Nothomb spent the next few months trying to reorganize the line once again. For the first time, the line agreed to let MI9 assist it by sending an agent trained by military intelligence to work on the line. Nothomb did not wholeheartedly embrace the suggestion, but he was exhausted and in poor health. Confronted by Neave during a brief trip to Gibraltar, Nothomb agreed to at least try to work with the new agent, Jacques Legrelle ("Jerome"). Luckily, the personalities of the two men meshed well, and they divided the Paris–Bayonne route between them. Nothomb took control of the line from Bordeaux to Bayonne, while Legrelle took over the organization in Paris. A new leader emerged in Brussels, Yvon Michiels ("Jean Serment"), and the three sections of the line were reconnected.[69]

Michiels had become involved in Comet during the period of Antoine d'Ursel's leadership. He had been associated with the Belgian Resistance since 1941, running an intelligence gathering service, and when he joined Comet many of his compatriots became escape line workers also. When d'Ursel went into hiding, Michiels took control of the Brussels section of the organization. He had experienced help from Lily Dumon ("Michou"), sister of Nadine. After her parents and sister were

arrested, Lily kept their escape section together under the code name
Marc and rejoined Comet when d'Ursel took control of the line. She
escaped arrest when the Brussels sector collapsed in June and became an
active guide for Michiels.[70]

Albert Mattens ("Jean Jacques") also became very active in the line.
Mattens was a member of Michiels' intelligence network, but after joining Comet he held an active role as guide and liaison. He established
several new routes for convoying men from Brussels to Paris and had
several guides placed under his control. After delivering men to Paris, he
met with Legrelle, who gave him directions and documents to deliver to
Michiels in Brussels.[71]

Under the control of these men and their helpers, Comet was able
to continue its work of evacuating valuable airmen. While Tante Go and
Nothomb continued to work in the southern region, which had been
largely untouched by the disasters in Brussels and Paris, Legrelle recruited
new guides and safe house keepers in the Paris area. M. Crampon ("Henri
Grapin") was one of three housing chiefs in Paris. He met the evaders
when they arrived in Paris and escorted them to safe houses, either at his
own home or another in his section. Crampon was also responsible for
providing supplies to the various safe houses and escorting the men to
their point of departure when they left Paris.[72] To the relief of Neave and
Langley, Comet recovered once again and continued its vital contribution to the war effort by evacuating large numbers of airmen.

On Christmas Eve 1943, Nothomb made arrangements for Antoine
d'Ursel to escape to England with a group of airmen.[73] Florentino, Comet's
dependable guide, was ill, and two other guides took his place. Though
Nothomb was familiar and comfortable with them, they were not as skilled
as Florentino, and the Bidassoa River was running swiftly due to recent
heavy rains. After helping the two Europeans and four American airmen
across, Nothomb watched as one of the guides returned to help d'Ursel,
while the other led the evaders over the road. Halfway across the river,
they heard four gunshots and d'Ursel lost his grip on the guide. The
guide continued across, and Nothomb sent him to investigate the gunfire while he himself searched for d'Ursel. Nothomb was relieved when
d'Ursel responded to his whistle. He recrossed the river and attempted to
convince d'Ursel to return to France and rest a few days before trying
again. Though suffering ill effects from an earlier bout with malaria,
D'Ursel was adamant that he should get to Spain and insisted on con-

tinuing forward. The men were shaken when more gunshots rang out as they entered the water. In his weakened and fearful state, d'Ursel was once again swept away by the raging current. Nothomb searched frantically for his friend, but to no avail. Finally he traveled back across the mountains to get help from Florentino, who, ill and running a fever, crossed the mountains to search. Unknown to both at that time, one of the American evaders, Jim Burch, had also somehow fallen into the river and drowned. German border patrols found both men's bodies later that night.[74]

The loss of d'Ursel was a terrible blow to the line. Throughout the line's history no one had died while crossing the river. That one of the victims had been one of their own helpers was even more difficult to accept. As had so often been the case with Comet, the loss of d'Ursel was the first of a new set of tragedies for the line. Nothomb, Legrelle, and Michiels were aware of Desoubrie's previous association with the line and kept their eyes open for renewed attacks. When Legrelle noticed a young blond woman following him on several occasions, he feared the line had been infiltrated. An effort to assassinate Desoubrie with the help of a French Resistance group failed when Desoubrie captured the assassin. In early January, Legrelle received word that Mattens had been arrested when he was stopped on a train for having false papers. Mattens was carrying several other important documents, which he secretly gave to a woman standing next to him, but unwilling to be caught with the papers, she threw them down at his feet and those of the Gestapo.[75]

Legrelle realized that he needed to leave France but, like Greindl, did not want to do so without finding a successor and reestablishing contact with Brussels. He chose M. Crampon, his chief of housing, to replace him as chief in Paris and explained all of the Paris activities to him. Legrelle then traveled to Brussels and chose a new liaison and chief convoy agent, after which he returned to report to Crampon in Paris. Before meeting Crampon at an apartment kept for such activities, Legrelle telephoned his home to ensure that everything was as it should be. Mme Crampon assured him that all was well and her husband was waiting at the apartment to see him. When he arrived at the apartment, Legrelle was arrested by two Gestapo agents and taken to their headquarters for questioning.[76]

Questioned and tortured by six men, Legrelle was astounded at the amount of information the Gestapo had. They knew everything about the Paris organization and were familiar with MI9's Neave, Nothomb, and d'Ursel. Legrelle underwent brutal torture as the Gestapo tried to make him elaborate on the information they had. He recalled that much of the torture took place in a bathroom. After whipping him, they tied his ankles to his thighs so that he could not straighten his knees and handcuffed his hands behind his back. Seventeen times they forced his head into a bathtub full of water, and each time he lost consciousness they threw him to the ground and kicked him until the water was forced out of his lungs. Legrelle regained consciousness amid much pain, only to have the act repeated. The first interrogation lasted ten hours and left him with several broken ribs, but the only information he gave was his own true identity. He convinced them that d'Ursel was dead, which was in fact true, and that he was the only person who had knowledge of Nothomb's address. Unfortunately, at 8:00 A.M. the following morning, just as Legrelle's first painful interrogation was ending, Nothomb arrived for a meeting with Legrelle and was arrested in the same apartment from which Legrelle had been taken.[77]

The Gestapo had been searching for Nothomb for some time, knowing that if they could arrest him the line would falter or perhaps collapse. Nothomb wrote, "The Gestapo was well aware of my position in the line and the two men who arrested me said to me 'Oh Franco, finally we take you,' and they knew very well that arresting me they had an end for awhile to the activity of the Comet Line."[78]

Though Desoubrie took part in the interrogations of Legrelle and Nothomb, he was not directly responsible for their arrests. Crampon had been arrested while Legrelle was in Belgium, and in the course of his interrogation the Gestapo had threatened his pregnant wife with harm. Unlike the cold betrayal of traitors such as Desoubrie, Crampon had collapsed under the psychological strain of fearing for those he loved. Lily Dumon learned that Crampon had been betrayed by Desoubrie and wrote, "It seemed to me that 'Henri' had burned everyone."[79] Years later, Nothomb expressed no anger for the disaster Crampon had brought to the line, only sorrow for the situation he was in, stating Crampon was "a good man. I was sorry for him. He was afraid. They tortured him and he gave them names." Crampon was tried for treason after the war, and Nothomb testified in his behalf to convince the military tribunal that Crampon was not a cold-blooded murderer like Desoubrie. Crampon was condemned to two years' service for betraying the line.[80]

Over the next few months, as they had so many times before, new Comet helpers rose to the forefront and reconnected the broken portions of the line. Though they continued transporting men through France and over the Pyrenees, new efforts were directed at establishing a forest camp in which to conceal men during the anticipated Allied invasion of the continent. Lily Dumon was instrumental in helping to reorganize the line by recruiting helpers such as Philippe and Virginia d'Albert Lake, who were highly influential in the forest camp's success.

On June 4, 1944, two days before Allied forces stormed the beaches of Normandy, the last five Comet evaders to travel the full length of the line crossed the Pyrenees Mountains.[81] During the years of Comet's existence, hundreds of people had contributed to its success, keeping the flame of resistance burning in spite of countless arrests and huge loss of life. Their efforts led to the rescue of 756 people, all but 68 of whom were Allied evaders.[82] The courage and steadfastness of the young men and women who operated the line made Comet the most successful of the escape lines in terms of the numbers of men repatriated. That they consistently and successfully reorganized the line in the face of constant adversity is a testimony to their resilient spirits and dedication to the Allied cause.

7

Out of the Ashes

The Shelburne Line, 1944

Fifteen-year-old Pierre Moreau watched with silent interest as the evasion network chief, "Val Williams," and two other intelligence agents secured the shutters to the kitchen windows of his home and unrolled secret plans and maps on his mother's dining room table. The documents detailed a new evacuation operation to be conducted, in cooperation with the Royal Navy, off the Brittany coast near the small village of Plouha. Though young in age, Moreau had lived all of his teenage life under the shadow of German occupation and understood very well the seriousness of the events taking place in his home. He had earlier promised his mother that he would never tell anyone what went on in their home concerning the Resistance, and he intended to keep that promise.[1]

In an effort to relieve the overburdened Pat and Comet escape lines, Langley and Neave of MI9 had devised a new line to be established in Brittany, where many Allied planes were being shot down on a daily basis. The success of Pat O'Leary's mass sea evacuations suggested that such operations could be done on a larger scale, and Langley and Neave felt the Brittany coast was the ideal area from which to carry them out. They chose Vladimir Bouryschkine ("Val Williams") to oversee the operation. Bouryschkine had been a member of the Pat line until his position became too well known by the Gestapo, forcing him to leave for France on board the *Tarana* in fall 1942. He volunteered to return to France as chief of the new line, code-named "Oaktree," and Canadian Raymond Labrosse, whose levelheaded ways contrasted with the less restrained nature of Bouryschkine, agreed to go with him to serve as radio operator.[2]

Prior to their departure, both men received special training, particularly regarding naval operations. Langley recalled that Bouryschkine's volatile nature made him difficult to train and that "he was forever making enemies by pointing out the deficiencies in our methods, usually justifiably, but nonetheless irritatingly, to those responsible."[3]

In spite of MI9's efforts to provide the men with training to meet any difficulty, bad luck and poor security doomed the mission from the beginning. A failed attempt to transport the men to France by Lysander led to their parachuting into the country instead. Nine times they left England, only to return a few hours later when poor visibility interfered with the pilot's ability to find the drop zone. Langley began to despair of the two men ever making it into France. However, on March 20, 1943, they were able to parachute with their equipment.[4] Unfortunately, one of the two folding bicycles sent in with them for traveling purposes was irreparably damaged when it hit the ground, as was Labrosse's radio set. Bouryschkine rode the remaining bicycle to Paris to organize means of lodging and transporting evaders, while Labrosse tried with no success to contact London using the damaged radio.[5]

Within a week Bouryschkine made contact with Paul Campinchi ("François"), a lawyer, who agreed to take control of operations in Paris, organizing safe houses and arranging for feeding the men and transporting them to Brittany. Bouryschkine then returned to Brittany to establish the network in that area, and there he made a fatal mistake. MI9's plans for Oaktree were already in place when the Pat line collapsed in early March 1943. Langley told Bouryschkine that instead of making contact with the Pat line and using it as a base of operations from which to establish his network, as was originally intended, he would have to establish a completely new organization. The extent of Roger Le Neveu's treachery had been such that no one in the Pat line could be contacted for participation in the new line. Unfortunately, instead of following the order to avoid the remnants of the O'Leary line, Bouryschkine depended on these workers to form the core of his network in Brittany, with devastating results.[6]

With the help of the BCRA information network, "Mithridate," Labrosse finally got word to MI9 that he and Bouryschkine had arrived safely, but were without radio contact. The crossing of intelligence lines was not well received in London, and MI9 searched for a way to smuggle a new radio into France for Oaktree.[7] As large numbers of airmen filtered into the new line, Bouryschkine requested an evacuation operation off the Brittany coast through radio messages sent to London by "Mithridate." On the night of the planned evacuation, Oaktree's agents listened for the BBC message that would give confirmation of the operation. Instead they heard the phrase "Denise is dead," which told them that the operation had been aborted. In the absence of solid radio communication with Oaktree, British intelligence had been unwilling to risk such a large operation.[8]

This created a new problem for Bouryschkine and Oaktree. There were ninety men backlogged in the line, with no immediate prospect of evacuation. Countess Betty de Mauduit, an American woman married to a Frenchman serving with de Gaulle's FFI, had thirty-nine evaders staying in her sixteenth-century chateau.[9] She had not planned to keep that many in her home at one time, but circumstances changed her plans. Georges Jouanjean, a Pat line agent who joined the Oaktree network, recalled trying to deliver four airmen to de Mauduit's house in early May 1943. He had hidden the evaders under the porch before entering her house, where he found that she already had thirty aviators hidden in the chateau. Though usually very gracious, she seemed irritable and tired, and on learning he had four more evaders waiting outside in need of shelter, she told him to leave and not come back. Desperate to find a place for them to stay, Jouanjean convinced her to take them in by slipping into her bedroom late that evening. She laughingly rejected his offer of company for the night, but claimed that if he was willing to go that far to find shelter for his boys, she thought she could make room for them.[10]

Bouryschkine decided that to handle the backlog of evaders, a line should be established to take the men over the Pyrenees. He arranged to convoy the men to Pau in southern France, where he transferred them into the care of the Françoise network,[11] which organized their escape over the mountains. While convoying a group of evaders to Pau by train, Bouryschkine was arrested by the Gestapo on June 4, 1943. They interrogated and imprisoned him, first at Fresnes and then at Rennes prison. At the same time, Le Neveu renewed his efforts to betray what remained of the Pat line, resulting in a number of arrests and the collapse of Oaktree.[12]

When Labrosse learned of Bouryschkine's arrest, he saw no other course of action but to escape to Spain himself. He established contact with Georges Broussine of the Burgundy network and informed him of the situation in Oaktree. Broussine agreed to evacuate the stranded evaders, but gave Labrosse the job of moving them to Paris. After Labrosse arranged for the men's transfer into the Burgundy line, Broussine successfully evacuated both the evaders and Labrosse over the Pyrenees. Labrosse was aware of the security risk involved with contacting Broussine, but stated, as have others, that what was taught in intelligence training could not always be done.[13]

After returning to England, Labrosse briefed MI9 on the status of the Oaktree line. Though Le Neveu had destroyed much of the Brittany sector, the nucleus of which had been formed from the remnants of the Pat line, the Paris sector, under Campinchi, was largely untouched. Labrosse convinced Langley and Neave that another attempt should be made to create an evacuation organization in Brittany and volunteered to return to France as radio operator for a new chief.

Believing that Brittany evacuations could be successfully established, Neave and Langley selected Canadian Sgt. Maj. Lucien Dumais, a member of the Fusilier Mont Royal, to organize the new operation. Dumais had been captured during the Dieppe raid in 1942, but escaped from a train en route to a POW camp. He had a vigorous, aggressive nature and used it to help him evade on his own for several weeks before finding his way into the Pat O'Leary line, which evacuated him to England on board the *Tarana*. Dumais was a member of the evacuation party from Canet Plage that had suffered through so many nights on the beach and was well acquainted with some of the hazards of mass evacuations. Even at the time of his evacuation, Dumais had ideas for making improvements in the operation and did not hesitate to share them forcefully with MI9 upon his return to England in 1942.[14]

Dumais's insistence on efficiency made him the logical choice to head the new effort to establish a Brittany evacuation route. His strong personality complemented Labrosse's easygoing nature, and on November 19, 1943, after two aborted efforts, the men were delivered to France by Lysander near Chauny.[15] Almost immediately, they too ran into difficulty when their French contacts were arrested shortly after they arrived. In addition, radio transmission problems meant Labrosse could not make contact with London to inform MI9 of their situation and get advice concerning their next move. They had been given strict instructions to avoid Paul Campinchi, as Neave feared he might have been compromised in the earlier Oaktree arrests. But in the absence of a better plan, Labrosse suggested that they contact him. Dumais was unsure of the wisdom in opening communications with Campinchi, but options were minimal.

Labrosse was convinced that Campinchi was trustworthy, and having no better plan, Dumais agreed.[16]

It had not occurred to Dumais and Labrosse that Campinchi would be hesitant about trusting *them*. After the collapse of Oaktree, Campinchi and his family had been forced into hiding. Though he had taken part in resistance activity since 1941, he was unsure as to whether he wanted to get involved in another attempt at rescuing evaders. The meeting between the three men was successful in that Dumais sensed Campinchi's sincerity and welcomed him into the network, assuring him that every effort would be made to insure security for the line's workers. After considering the offer for several days, Campinchi agreed to take charge of the Paris sector, just as he had for Oaktree.[17] Relieved at having established a solid connection to handle the Paris sector, Dumais and Labrosse moved to Brittany to organize services there. After repeated efforts Labrosse was finally able to contact London by radio, which cheered both men immensely, and they went on to organize the operation along the coastal area from which the evacuations were to take place.

The mechanics of the new Brittany operation, code-named Shelburne,[18] involved hiding evaders in Paris until the moonless period of the month, then collecting them at the village of Plouha, where they could be picked up by a British motor gunboat off the coast of Anse Cochat, code-named Bonaparte Beach. Unfortunately, the Germans were not so cooperative as to shoot planes down only when they were flying over Paris, so measures were taken to collect the airmen wherever they landed and convoy them to Paris, where they were sheltered until time for the evacuation. Occasionally men were transferred into the Shelburne line from the Burgundy organization when they reached Paris.[19]

Campinchi's job of setting up the Paris sector was eased by the fact that much of the Paris portion of the Oaktree organization had survived intact. One of his most efficient agents was a young woman named Marie-Rose Zerling ("Claudette"). She obtained false papers, food, and clothing for the evaders and arranged for their shelter and transportation to their next stop. Zerling had attended Wellesley College in the United States, but had returned to France by the time the war broke out. In the early days of the occupation, she helped with the distribution of a clandestine newspaper and later assisted evading airmen. Campinchi recruited her to work for Oaktree and reengaged her when the Shelburne network was organized. Because she spoke fluent English, part of Zerling's job also included interrogating the airmen to prove that they were genuine. An American airman, Joseph Birdwell, helped her for several weeks and claimed that she always "worked steadily, reliably and cautiously. She knew the situation in which she was working, and she believed in adequate precautions."[20] In spite of this, Zerling was the victim of a "fake" airman, Olaf Hanson ("Fred"), planted by the Germans. American evader Edward J. Donaldson met Hanson while staying with a French helper, Mme Schmidt. Hanson claimed to be a Norwegian who flew with the USAAF, but Donaldson stated that "Fred's stories to us are all self-contradictory, so we were all suspicious and careful."[21] Through radio contact with London, Dumais determined that Hanson was indeed a German traitor, but Hanson disappeared before he could be eliminated. His denunciation of Claudette and Mme Schmidt led to their arrests in February 1944, followed by the arrest of Claudette's parents shortly thereafter. She was tortured by the Germans and sentenced to be executed, but was instead deported to Auschwitz along with her parents. Though her father died at Auschwitz, Zerling and her mother were repatriated when the Allies liberated the camp in August 1945. Bertranne Auvert claimed in her memoirs that Zerling was extremely disturbed by the belief that she was responsible for her father's death and after the war refused to have anything to do with the group with which she had worked.[22]

Because of her status as a section leader, Zerling's arrest led to a great deal of confusion in the line. Campinchi replaced her immediately with Frenchman Marcel Cola ("Yvon"), but in many cases Zerling had been the only contact her helpers had with the line, and Cola had no idea where to find some of the airmen she had hidden throughout Paris.[23] Security in the Shelburne line was so tight as to make it difficult to reconnect the line in the aftermath of Zerling's arrest.

Bertranne Auvert was one of the helpers Zerling had recruited for lodging airmen in Paris, and she had two of Shelburne's evaders staying with her at the time of Zerling's arrest, which she learned about from a mutual friend. But the friend was unable to help with Auvert's dilemma over what to do with the airmen. Zerling had been her only connection with Shelburne, and without her assistance Auvert did not have enough money to feed them. Evader Neelan Parker (USAAF) was one of those stranded at Auvert's home. He remained there for six weeks, along with a fellow crew member, while Auvert carefully questioned those she trusted in an attempt to contact another Resistance network.[24] Her continued efforts to establish connections with an escape line eventually led her to Cola, who gave her instructions on where to transfer the airmen.[25]

One month after Dumais and Labrosse arrived in France, they concluded that Shelburne was functioning well enough to proceed with the planned evacuations. The first operation, scheduled for December, was cancelled due to gale force winds, and the organization had to wait a full month before a second attempt could be made. But during the January new moon conditions were favorable, and the first evacuation was carried out successfully to the delight and relief of all involved.

When an operation was scheduled, guides moved the evaders from Paris to St. Brieuc by train, a distance of about 250 miles. As on other lines, the men carried false identification papers and pretended to be deaf-mutes or asleep in order to discourage questioning from friendly passengers on the trains. American evader Dick Smith remembered that he was told to "rough up" his false papers in order to age them, and that when the German police checked papers on the train he should just hand them the papers without looking at them. He recalled that it was a long trip and felt his fellow travelers must have thought him very rude, because they offered him food and wine and he ignored them.[26]

Once the men arrived in St. Brieuc, they boarded a small local train for Plouha as they had been instructed in Paris. At least this was the initial plan of action. After the second evacuation the Germans closed down the local train route between St. Brieuc and Plouha, so new plans had to be made. Rather than disembark at St. Brieuc, the men stayed on the train until they reached Guingamp or Châtelaudren, the two stops following St. Brieuc on the main train line. Though inconvenient to have the men traveling to two different stations, it was a necessary precaution since it would have looked odd to see so many healthy young men arriving in one station at the same time. From the two stations, the airmen were collected at central locations in the towns and later transported by truck to Plouha.[27]

François Kerambrun, a self-employed mechanic, used his truck to transport supplies for the Germans during the day and, because of his service to them, was able to use the truck at other times as well. He took advantage of his permit by transporting the airmen on the Guingamp-Plouha leg of their journey, about twelve kilometers. Though this trip was usually taken at night, with the airmen buried under potatoes and straw in the back of the truck, Kerambrun sometimes transported the men during the day due to the curfew. During daytime trips the men were disguised as workmen. Although he had a permit from the Germans to drive his charcoal-powered truck, Kerambrun was still subject to searches by the local police. On one such occasion two police stopped him to ask for information about his passengers. Kerambrun told them the truth about his cargo and later claimed, "If they were not patriots, we would have killed them with our bare hands."[28] As it turned out, the police in this case were patriots and Kerambrun passed through safely with the evaders.[29]

Once the airmen arrived in Plouha, they began yet another period of waiting. George Buckner recalled that Kerambrun had dropped him and his three traveling companions off on a deserted road, where they met a young girl, Marie Thérèse Le Calvez,[30] who instructed them to follow her. Although Marie Thérèse was only seventeen years old, she held a crucial position in the organization. Her mother also participated in the line's work, as a safe house keeper, and it was to her house that the young girl led them. After hiding them in an upstairs room, Marie Thérèse presented them with a meal. Soon after, the men heard banging on the door downstairs, and their young hostess raced up the steps to warn that Germans had come. The evaders were sure that they had been caught, but the "Germans" turned out to be one soldier who only wanted to use an air pump for the tire of his bicycle.[31]

While the airmen were hiding quietly in attics and backrooms throughout the village of Plouha, members of the Shelburne Resistance were preparing for a busy night. At 7:00 P.M. and 9:00 P.M., the radio show *The French Speak to the French* aired on the BBC, after which London relayed its litany of unrelated sentences, each of which had meaning to intelligence organizations throughout France. The Shelburne organization had three possible communications they listened for on the BBC. "Good evening to everyone at the house of Alphonse" meant that the operation would take place that night, while "Yvonne always thinks of the happy occasion" meant the operation would be postponed twenty-four hours. The phrase "Rigoulet has a good head" meant the operation had been cancelled altogether.[32]

On the night of the planned evacuation, Dumais and Labrosse waited anxiously at the café of François Le Cornec, listening to the BBC. Le Cornec was the organizer of the group known as the "beach party," which handled the embarkation process of the evacuation. Initially,

Labrosse and Dumais were the only people who knew the coded phrases, but they later shared the information with others in the group so that they could work more quickly and efficiently. At the prearranged time, the confirmation was heard, "Good evening to everyone at the house of Alphonse." The men were elated, but they still had to wait for the message to be repeated during the 9:00 P.M. program, confirming that the motor gunboat designated to meet them that night had not turned back to England for any reason.[33]

The section of the Royal Navy appointed to carry out the Shelburne operations was the 15th Motor Gunboat flotilla, created in 1942 specifically for conducting clandestine operations between France and England. It performed operations associated with carrying supplies and agents in and out of France and provided support for SOE operations and, later, operations of evasion networks like Shelburne. Its success was largely due to the fact that British intelligence had discovered a means of breaking the German ENIGMA codes, providing the flotilla with German naval recognition codes before the motor gunboats left to conduct their secret activities.[34]

After receiving confirmation on the BBC that the motor gunboat was indeed on its way to the Brittany coast, guides collected the men from various safe houses around Plouha and took them to a small stone house on the edge of the beach. It belonged to a young married couple, Jean and Marie Gicquel, whose friendship with Le Cornec led him to ask permission to use their house as a rendezvous point. Jean also served as part of the beach party, while Marie, who was several months pregnant, cared for the occasional airman who lodged with them for more than just an evening. At 11:30 P.M., all of the men were collected at the Gicquels' home, which became known in the evaders' world as the "house of Alphonse." At midnight the evaders were led to the beach. It was no simple task to get there, as the men were required to walk about two miles in darkness along a rough path and then descend a steep cliff to Bonaparte Beach. Dumais instructed each of them to walk single file, with one hand on the coattail or shoulder of the person ahead of him. He emphasized the importance of hanging on to the person ahead, as the moonless night made it easy to get separated. He assured the evaders that if they should lose contact with the person in front of them they were to stop and wait until the guides returned for them. Most important of all, they were to keep silent.[35]

(*Above*) Bonaparte Beach was the site of a series of escapes conducted by British motor gunboats off the west coast of France during the first eight months of 1944. (*Below*) Evaders descended this steep cliff at the edge of Bonaparte Beach on their way to meet the motor gunboats waiting offshore in the English Channel.

When they reached the cliff, the guides told the airmen to slide down on their backsides, using their hands and heels for leverage. The trip was difficult for men in good health, but for those recovering from injuries it was especially difficult. Val Bouryschkine had broken his leg while escaping from prison in December 1943. He had managed to make contact with the new line through Campinchi, but the rough path to the beach was nearly impossible to negotiate on his crutches. Le Cornec and Le Calvez fashioned a stretcher on which they carried him along the path, then maneuvered him down the steep cliff to the beach.[36]

The cliff was a daunting barrier for the men, and had they seen it in daylight they might have been more skeptical of their ability to descend it. Keith Sutor, an American evader, returned to France in 1979 and, standing at the top of the cliff, wondered if he would have attempted it had he known what it looked like ahead of time. "But I would have," he wrote, "because I wanted to go home and that was the only way I was going to get there."[37]

A number of guides went with the men to the beach. Pierre Huet and Le Calvez led the procession of airmen, while Le Cornec brought up the rear so he could move ahead and reconnect any breaks that might occur in the line. Joseph Mainguy, a former merchant marine captain, remained at the top of the cliff to signal the incoming boats, using a flashlight with a cardboard tube taped around it to ensure that the light would only be seen from the sea. Dumais accompanied them as well to oversee the delivery of supplies and money sent by the Allies and the evacuation of the airmen.[38]

Upon reaching the beach, airmen and Resistance workers scattered among the boulders and awaited the arrival of small rowboats. When the boats arrived, Dumais met them at the edge of the water with the prearranged password, "Dinan." The response, "St. Brieuc," was a welcome one, and after the Resistance workers unloaded the supplies that had been sent on the boats, the airmen piled in and helped row to the British motor gunboat waiting about one and a half miles out.[39] The hulking shadow of the 120-foot-long boat was a welcome sight for the tired, anxious men who had been waiting to make the trip home. Like the agents for the Pat line just over a year earlier, the Shelburne helpers watched their charges disappear into the night.[40] Many years later, Labrosse expressed the mixed feelings that he experienced as he watched the men leave, saying, "There were a few times when I wished it were me going home . . . this farewell was always emotional for us, because we had the urge to get in the boat, too, and say, 'I'd like to rest awhile.'"[41]

There were nine operations conducted off Bonaparte Beach between January 28, 1944, and August 9, 1944, most of them completed without difficulty of any kind. However, on the third operation, the motor gunboat was fired upon by German batteries along the coast. Bonaparte Beach was located within a small cove along the Brittany coastline and sandwiched between two German gun posts overlooking the English Channel. On the night of March 16–17, the evaders had already reached the beach and hidden along the shoreline when Dumais received the password from the gunboat by walkie-talkie informing him of its imminent arrival. A few minutes later the men on the beach heard an explosion that broke the quietness of the night. The gunboat radioed that it was being fired upon and would try to return later. Ralph Patton remembered that the blast of the German defense batteries "lit up the beach like daylight."[42] He and the other men waited anxiously, fearful that one of the blasts had hit their boat. About one hour after the firing stopped, the gunboat again radioed to Dumais asking about conditions on shore and announcing the immediate arrival of the rowboats. Within a few minutes the rowboats appeared on the beach, and the group of worried evaders climbed aboard.

Shelburne conducted five evacuation operations of airmen from January to March 1944,[43] after which MI9 issued orders that operations be put on hold. Military intelligence did not want to risk the discovery of any clandestine operations along the coast that might endanger the European invasion scheduled to take place in late spring. During that time, Dumais organized passage for the evaders across the Pyrenees and also directed men into the forest camp organized by the remnants of the Comet line.[44]

Anticipating an Allied assault on Europe across the channel, the Germans initiated defensive measures, which further complicated the work of the Shelburne line. In February 1944, Gen. Erwin Rommel insisted that the only means of repulsing an Allied invasion was to create barriers that would enable German counterinvasion tactics to interfere with landing abilities. The following April, at his orders, mines were placed along the Brittany coast, including the area near Plouha. Pierre Huet and Joseph Mainguy studied the newly established minefield and, with the help of a mine detector parachuted in from MI9, located seventeen mines, which they mapped so that they could mark them the next time an evacuation was carried out.[45]

Within two weeks after the European invasion, Shelburne had again activated its coastal operations, evacuating three groups of agents and airmen in June and July.[46] The little stone house at the edge of the beach continued to serve as the rendezvous point. Marie Gicquel had given birth to a daughter in June, adding the responsibility of caring for a newborn to that of providing for the airmen delivered to her home.

On July 23, Dumais and Le Cornec left three British officers at the Gicquels' home to be hidden until the evening operation. Only a few minutes after they left, White Russian soldiers appeared at the house with their German commander. Jean answered their knock at the door, but slammed it in their faces when he realized who they were. The British officers rushed up to the attic, and the soldiers burst into the room, firing their guns in the direction of the roof. In the melee, one of their own soldiers was wounded, and they carried him into the house and forced Marie to care for him. One soldier remained at the house to guard Marie, while Jean, with a gun at his back, led the others to a neighbor who had a wagon with which they could transport their wounded comrade. The guard threatened Marie and her daughter, and Marie wrote, "I thought I had seen my last hour with my five-week-old daughter at my side."[47]

When the men returned with the wagon, the soldiers loaded the injured man onto the bed and left, but Marie was certain they would come back. Jean led the British officers into a wheat field and took Marie and their baby to his parents' house. Within hours the soldiers returned and set the house on fire, destroying it, but by this time Marie and the baby were safely hidden and Jean was far away in England, where Dumais had sent him after learning of the evening's events.[48]

The operation that ended with the destruction of the "house of Alphonse" was the last of the clandestine naval operations of the Shelburne organization. On August 9, 1944, a final evacuation took place from Bonaparte Beach, but it was conducted during the daytime and after invading Allied forces had pushed their way inland, dismantling the German defense batteries that had threatened each of the earlier operations. During the nine months of its existence, the Shelburne line rescued a total of 307 men,[49] 118 of these by Operation Bonaparte and the rest on foot over the Pyrenees or through concentration in forest camps. Despite localized arrests, the line never suffered from major enemy penetration, which earned it accolades as one of the most successful evasion lines of World War II.[50] Labrosse addressed this many years later, stating that Shelburne was not a superior line, but it had the benefit of learning from other evasion lines that had paved the way. By studying the work of pioneer lines such as Pat O'Leary and Comet, Shelburne was able to avoid the tragedies the earlier lines had encountered.

In 1964 a group of former evaders aided by Shelburne were reunited for the first time since their evacuation in 1944. Though the reunion was attended mostly by Americans, the tribute to the people of Shelburne written by former Shelburne evader William Spinning and printed in the souvenir booklet displayed a universal appreciation for the people who helped evaders without regard for their own safety. It read: "Shelburne is not well remembered by the statisticians. It was not the turning point for military tacticians. It was, instead, a blazing beacon of the absolute limits of man's courage—of man's willingness to gamble his own life and the lives of those dearest to him in order to save strangers who believed in the same ideals of liberty and personal dignity. . . . Theirs were calculated feats of audacious, rash fearlessness—carried out under the very eyes of the German occupational forces. . . . The odds against success were staggering. The penalties for failure were almost incalculable. . . . We of America can never repay these noble people. Nothing can ever balance the score, and nothing will ever dull the glory. In greatest humility we say, 'We'll never forget.'"[51]

8

We Will Never Forget

The Aftermath

When Georges Jouanjean took over the care of English evader Gordon Carter, he had no idea of the role Carter would later play in his life. Likewise, Carter, fearful about his immediate future, was blissfully ignorant of what awaited him at his quickly arranged temporary safe house with Jouanjean's married sister, Lucette. Jouanjean's beautiful second sister, Janine, caught his eye, and the two enjoyed each other's company from the beginning. When Jouanjean arranged for Carter to move to new quarters, he asked Janine to ride along with them to counter any suspicion that might arise from two young men riding together. Carter slowed his bicycle-riding pace to meet Janine's rather than riding ahead with Jouanjean, and over the next three weeks, until his departure, they spent much of their time together.[1]

After returning to England, Carter rejoined an air combat unit and was shot down a second time. Unfortunately, he was captured this time and spent the remainder of the war as a POW. In May 1945, after returning to England, Carter applied for a special dispensation to return to France and find Janine. Though it had been two years, their feelings had remained strong, and they decided to marry immediately. Carter wrote, "The circumstances of our marriage were rather preposterous."[2] Arranging the marriage was quite complicated, as he had to get an extension of his leave—termed "compassionate" leave—obtain special certificates, and arrange wedding plans in a very limited amount of time. Finally, on June 11, 1945, Janine put on her wedding dress and married her evader in a ceremony performed by the local attorney general, who was newly returned from a concentration camp. Fifty-four years later, Gordon and Janine are still happily married and living in France.[3]

Gordon Carter (*top row, second from left*), with his original crew. Carter was flying with another crew when he was shot down over France. (Courtesy of Gordon and Janine Carter)

During a visit with the author in July 1999, former evader Gordon Carter displayed a remnant of his downed plane's wing and his parachute. Though a bit snug, his World War II RAF jacket could still be worn.

Janine Jouanjean Carter fell in
love with evader Gordon Carter
when he hid at her sister's home
after his original safe house had
been discovered by Germans.
They married at the end of the
war and live in the Brittany region
of France. (Courtesy of Gordon
and Janine Carter)

Janine Jouanjean Carter in front of her home in Brittany, France,
in July 1999.

Not all of the war's escape and evasion stories had such happy endings. Many of the helpers who returned from the concentration camps were ill and dying. Some had sustained injuries due to brutal treatment by their German guards, injuries from which they never recovered. Jean de la Olla of the Pat line was left without the use of one arm and contracted a virulent form of tuberculosis, which rendered him "unfit for employment," while Jean Dassié of Comet died shortly after returning to France.[4] Dr. Gabriel Nahas, a medical student who worked for the Dutch–Paris and Françoise lines, recalled going to Dachau concentration camp immediately after it was liberated to assist with medical needs of the inmates. He said the people were in such terrible condition, there was little that could be done other than try to make them as comfortable as possible.[5]

Women who were deported returned to find that their children had been dispersed by the Germans. In desperation, they turned to the French Red Cross to help find them. Eleanor Cheramy, of the Pat line, had suffered a terrible injury resulting from a blow to the head by a German guard. Following the liberation of Ravensbrük, she was flown to England for emergency surgery, after which she waited anxiously to be reunited with her son Michel, now four years old. She recalled seeing him again for the first time after the war and the relief she felt at learning his grandmother had been caring for him since her deportation. Still, it was difficult, she said. "He was very shy of me and my heart flipped a little when he said to his grandmother, 'I don't understand a word that mother says.' But I did have a wonderful moment of being recognized as a mother."[6]

For Donald Darling, who set up an agency in Paris to provide assistance for helpers in need, there were wonderful surprises as people who had not been heard from in months and years returned from Germany. Pat O'Leary arrived from Dachau, thin and tired, but alive. He took back his own name, Albert Marie Guerisse, and rejoined the Belgian army as a medical officer. He was awarded numerous citations for his work in World War II and again in the Korean War for rescuing an injured man under fire. He was promoted to major general before retiring from the military.[7] O'Leary married Sylvia Cooper, secretary to Airey Neave during the war, and in 1949 they had a son, whom they named Patrick. O'Leary died in March 1989, aged seventy-seven years. At his request, his body was cremated, and humble in death as he had been in life, no one was

Alex Wattebled at his home in Pontorson, France, during a visit with the author in July 1999.

informed of the funeral service. Nevertheless, about five hundred people appeared at the church to pay their respects to this kind and courageous man.

Alex Wattebled spent eleven months in solitary confinement at Fresnes prison before being transferred to a series of concentration camps in Germany, including Büchenwald and Flossenberg. While a prisoner, he was befriended by a German soldier who tried to protect him by getting him the lightest jobs and having him moved from the front lines of the work force when a group was to be selected for death. The German officers took the first ten rows of workers when they made this kind of selection, and Wattebled was saved three times as a result of the German's intervention. They agreed that they would do their best to help each other during the war and after the liberation. Unfortunately, Wattebled was unable to keep his word, and the young soldier was killed before his eyes in the chaos that occurred when Russian soldiers liberated the camp. He returned to France, where he married and had two children. Wattebled still lives in France with his wife, Esther. Each morning he walks to the nearby café, greeting local merchants as he passes by, and enjoys coffee with his friends in town.

Louis Nouveau returned as well, in spite of his damaged lungs, and lived several more years in Marseilles with his wife, Renée. In 1946 former British evader Peter Scott Janes was pleasantly surprised when he received a package with Nouveau's return address. Janes had kept a diary of his evasion and left it with Nouveau for safekeeping. After Nouveau returned home from the concentration camp, he found the diary and mailed it to Janes. Though Janes died several years ago, his son Keith recently found the diary and is preparing it for publication.

Georges Broussine survived the war without bring arrested, and his escape line, Burgundy, succeeded in evacuating about three hundred men. After the war he worked as a political journalist, and he now lives in Paris with his lovely wife, Genéviève, in the very area where both Burgundy and Comet were active during the war. Both are very active, and Georges still enjoys climbing mountains and has recently published a memoir in which he recounts his work on the Burgundy line. It is easy to imagine this lively and energetic man organizing and running a clandestine organization.

Sadly, Georges Rodocanachi, who so generously volunteered his

Georges Broussine and his wife Geneviéve at their Paris home during a visit with the author in July 1999.

Dédée de Jongh on the balcony of her Brussels apartment. (Courtesy of Andrée de Jongh)

house as a headquarters for the Pat line, died at Büchenwald in February 1944. He was one of many who sacrificed their lives to aid the Allied forces in liberating the country that meant so much to them. His wife, Fanny, moved to England after the war, where she remained until her death in April 1959.

Dédée de Jongh returned from Ravensbrük, appearing at Darling's Paris Awards Bureau in the summer of 1945. She arrived in the middle of the night still wearing the striped pink and white dress from the concentration camp. She was thin and had medical ailments from which she still suffers today, but she had survived. Though it was well known that one of the evaders arrested with her had betrayed several of his helpers, Dédée refused to allow an investigation into his identity, saying, "All is forgiven."[8] After recovering from her treatment at Ravensbrük, Dédée became a nurse and worked in a leper colony in the Belgian Congo for many years, after which she continued to serve the sick in underprivileged countries. Dedée is a delightful woman, and her mind is still very

Sarobe Farm was the first rest stop for Jean François "Franco" Nothomb and his evaders after they crossed the Bidassoa River. Nothomb revisited Sarobe in September 2000, where he reminisced about his wartime activities with the author.

sharp although physically she has difficulty getting around. She still refers to the former evaders as her children and holds a tender place in her heart for each of them. When she speaks of her work on the Comet line, it is as if it happened yesterday. Listening to her talk, it is obvious that she has fond memories of her war work and that she still holds to the words she once wrote about the Comet escape network: "Our team was, during its activity, a perfect homogeneity. The memory of our brotherhood is one of the most beautiful ones that we keep of this era of public work."⁹

Like so many other evasion network leaders, Jean François Nothomb, chief of the Comet line after the arrest of Fréderic de Jongh, has also devoted his life to the service of others. He entered the priesthood, becoming a member of a small order called the Little Brothers of Jesus. About 1980, he left the priesthood to get married and is now the father of two daughters. He still visits occasionally with former evaders whose passage he arranged. Nothomb currently lives in retirement in

Rome, Italy, and keeps in close contact with his former comrades from the Comet line.[10]

Nadine Dumon returned to Brussels after spending over two years in concentration camps. She is a tiny woman but every part of her being shines with life. Her eyes dance and she is never without a smile or kind word for those around her. Nadine is the driving force behind annual reunions of the Comet line and also played a significant role in organizing a retracing of the Comet line in September 2000. Though almost sixty years have passed since the war, Nadine still mourns her father's death at the Germans' hands.

The traitors of the evasion lines died as violently as they had lived. According to Nancy Wake Fiocca of the Pat line, Roger Le Neveu was tortured and executed by the Maquis group she formed after she parachuted into France as a member of SOE. The Maquis were not known for being kind to traitors, and one can only imagine the violent end to which he came.[11]

Nadine Dumon helped organize the first retracing of the Comet escape route, which took place in September 2000. Here she sits on the rocky bank of the Bidassoa River awaiting the arrival of hikers who participated by climbing the Pyrenees.

Unlike Le Neveu, Jacques Desoubrie and Harold Cole were not caught until after the war ended. Desoubrie, a young man in his early twenties during the war, was the illegitimate son of a doctor and had been abandoned at a young age by his mother. During the war, he lived part of the time with his girlfriend, Marie Thérèse Laurent, the French wife of a POW, by whom he had two children, Jacques and Adolphe, both under five years of age at war's end. Nothomb attended the trial in Lille, France, where Desoubrie was condemned to death and executed in 1945 for his betrayal of the evasion networks.[12]

Harold Cole was the most fascinating of the escape line traitors and has been described as the worst traitor of World War II. While working for the Pat line, a young coworker, Suzanne Waringham, fell in love with him. He used her affection to help him carry out his betrayals without her knowledge, even marrying her with a falsified marriage certificate. On the day his young wife told him she was pregnant with their child, he set her up to be arrested by Vichy police. After Cole deserted her, Suzanne gave birth to their child, a son, and struggled to support the infant with the help of members of the Pat line. Sadly, the baby died when only a few months old from illness and exposure in a cold apartment.[13]

Cole turned on one ally and then another with no sense of remorse. By the time the war ended, he was wanted by military authorities in four countries. The British wanted him for desertion and treachery; the French, for betraying the evasion organizations and other Resistance groups; the Germans, for murder of an officer; and the Americans, for stealing cars and conducting black market operations in which he involved American servicemen.[14]

Cole slipped out of the authorities' hands at least three times, once from a high security prison operated by combined British and American military services. In January 1946, French detectives received word that a suspicious man was living in a Paris apartment. Unaware that the occupant was Cole, two officers went to the apartment to investigate. Cole realized he was trapped and opened fire on the men, hitting one of them in the arm; the second detective fired back, killing Cole instantly. Ironically, the man who traveled to Paris to identify the body was Pat O'Leary.[15]

In the aftermath of the war, France and other occupied countries had to come to terms with the damage done by the occupying forces— not only as individuals recovering from the loss of loved ones, but also from a collective societal perspective. Many people had supported the Allies during the war, while their neighbors and friends had served the Germans. People who had shared their lives together before the war found themselves on opposite sides during the conflict, and it has been difficult for them to heal the wounds of betrayal. A number of people were ostracized after the war for associating with German soldiers, while others stood trial for supporting the enemy. For some, the anger associated with such betrayal still exists more than fifty years later.[16]

Though the war left a rift within French society, it created a bond between the people of western Europe and the Allied countries that survives to this day. Immediately following the war, the Royal Air Force formed the Royal Air Force Escaping Society (RAFES.) Its purpose was to maintain the relationships that had developed between the evaders and helpers during the war and to aid helpers who needed financial or medical assistance due to consequences suffered as a result of helping the airmen.

Supported by former evaders, air force personnel, and private citizens, the organization served a large number of helpers in its more than fifty years of existence. On one occasion it provided an enjoyable vacation for seventy-five children of helpers, and time and again the organization provided financial aid for helpers in need. In addition, helpers have visited their evaders in England, and evaders have returned to Europe to visit the people who once risked all they had to provide for the young strangers who had landed among them. Eventually Canadian and Australian branches of the RAFES were formed. They are still active today, providing for helpers' needs and maintaining contact between former evaders and helpers.[17]

The American counterpart to RAFES was created in 1964. USAAF evader Ralph Patton returned to France in 1961 and met some of the Resistance people who assisted in his evacuation through the Shelburne line. One of them had kept a list of addresses of the evaders they assisted, and when Patton returned home he contacted two of the men on the list. The three men worked together to organize a reunion of those evacuated from Bonaparte Beach. Patton advertised his search for evaders in *VFW Magazine,* and coincidentally, an ad placed by Frenchman Leslie Atkinson appeared on the same page. Atkinson had assisted evaders during the war and was trying to contact some of them. Their correspondence resulted in a relationship that continues more than a half-century later.[18]

In May 1964, the Air Force Escape and Evasion Society held its first reunion in Buffalo, New York. Since then, the organization has grown to almost a thousand members. Each year it hosts a reunion where evaders, helpers, family members, and other supporters all join together for several days of remembrance and tribute.

At the May 1998 reunion in Washington, D.C., Fred Gleason met his helper, René Charpentier, for the first time since 1944, when he was in France as a young airman evading capture. During each reunion, old relationships are renewed and new ones forged as the children of evaders and helpers come to know each other and carry on their parents' legacies of appreciation and honor.

In recent years, museums in some of the Allied countries have established special displays devoted to the area of escape and evasion. Eden Camp, a World War II museum located in North Yorkshire, England, hosted a reunion of helpers and evaders of all networks in conjunction with the opening of a permanent escape and evasion exhibit. Its success made the reunion a yearly event. Also, the opportunity to retrace evaders' routes across the Pyrenees is now possible through the efforts of those who want to see the history of evasion during World War II preserved. Each July since 1994, a group has crossed the Pyrenees in remembrance of evaders and helpers. In 1999, for the first time, an American contingent was represented in the crossing. It included the elderly wife and eleven-year-old granddaughter of former evader Ralph Patton, as well as his children and those of several other former evaders.[19]

The relationship between the airmen and helpers is unlike any other. Many men returned home and named their daughters, born after the war, for the motherly women who cared for them when they needed help.[20] A large number of the helpers grew to love the evaders as if they were members of the family. Mme Leona Quillien, who sheltered American evader Gus Bubenzer, often said about the men, "They are all my sons."[21] The feeling of family ties extended beyond the airmen to the wives they later married and the children born to them. Hélène Arnould recalled that British evader Leonard Williams returned to see them every two years, bringing with him his wife, children, and parents. He died on the same day as Hélène's father, and when her mother died, William's son and daughter-in-law attended the funeral. Williams once told Hélène, "The war is something horrible, but if there had been no war, we would have never known each other and now we are part of one family."[22]

The airmen share feelings of gratitude and admiration for the sacrifices the helpers made for them. American Keith Sutor tried to thank his helpers for what they had done for him, but wrote, "Our efforts to thank these people for their help during World War II were met with resistance.... You simply cannot out-thank the people over there."[23] But they try, and through their efforts, the bond between the evaders and helpers remains strong. Evader Paul Kenney captured the feeling well when he wrote, "I will always admire the courage, heroism and sacrifices of the brave people in the underground who fought for the freedom of their country. I will always remember them with gratitude for all that they did for me."[24]

The men who worked for MI9 also ended the war with fond feelings for the helpers they had assisted from afar throughout the years of the war. Donald Darling commented that some people had remarked negatively about the small percentage of people who aided escapers and evaders. But, he wrote, "That low percentage is something to be thankful for, since the task of showing our gratitude to those thousands after their liberation proved colossal and left me with a deep personal feeling of inadequacy."[25]

Others shared Darling's feelings. Jim Langley claimed the work of MI9 was too little, too late. No one realized that evasion would become a matter of routine rather than a lucky break. He felt the delay in this understanding resulted in the arrests of many helpers that might have been avoided had there been replacements to move in and take over the lines when agents' positions became compromised. As things stood, there were no replacements.[26] When Langley left MI9 to form Intelligence School 9 (IS9), an escape and evasion attachment to Supreme Headquarters Allied Expeditionary Forces (SHAEF), MI6's Claude Dansey accused him of loving his agents—in his opinion, an act of weakness. But Langley believed otherwise, and those acquainted with this part of the history of World War II can easily understand his words on the matter. He wrote, "If ever people deserved to be loved, it is those brave men and women whose courage and self-sacrifice enabled so many to live and fight another day."[27]

9

Conclusion

The home where Georges and Fanny Rodocanachi once sheltered evaders and from which the drama of Paul Cole's betrayal of the Pat line unfolded is now part of an office building. A ward of the local hospital where Rodocanachi worked has been named for him, and every day people walk or drive along the Boulevard Rodocanachi in Marseilles. It is unlikely that many who see his name have taken time beyond a passing thought to learn who Dr. Rodocanachi really was. In Brussels, Belgium, the school where Comet chief Fréderic de Jongh once served as headmaster now carries his name. Yet the children who run in the playground probably give little thought to the man whose name is displayed on the outside wall of their school building or to the part he played in freeing their country from oppression. Memorials such as these exist throughout western Europe, paying tribute to those who aided in the evasion of Allied airmen, each with its own unique story.

Every human emotion that makes for great drama, and therefore great history, can be found in the story of the helpers and their efforts to provide sanctuary and, ultimately, deliverance for the Allied personnel with whom they came in contact. The quiet courage of the helpers, the cold calculations of the traitors, the inspired determination of the evaders, and the dogged persistence of the Germans provide all the ingredients one needs to depict the grim realities of war fought on a very personal level.

For the helpers who manned the escape lines, the war was fought in anonymity, day by day, evader by evader. The work was taxing, both mentally and physically. Their successes did not appear in the headlines of any newspapers, nor were they broadcast over any of the major news services. There were no avenues of retreat if their plans failed. Nor was the prospect ever far removed from their conscious thoughts that they could, unknown by those they had helped or by the comrades with whom they had worked, face alone the horror of a slow and agonizing death at the hands of the enemy. Little wonder that Raymond Labrosse could candidly admit that he watched with envy as a boatload of evaders made its way from the beach to a British gunboat waiting to take them to safety. Many helpers may have entertained similar thoughts, since their work frequently brought them to the very threshold of escape. However, they, like Labrosse, reflected on such thoughts only briefly and then returned to the task of dealing with the inevitable flow of evaders making their way through the lines. Ordinary people responding with determined resolve to extraordinary challenges, not least among them denying one's own personal safety in the interest of others; little else explains the success of the escape networks so well.

It would be difficult to say whether any one evasion line was more successful than another. The various networks were responsible for the rescue and evacuation of hundreds of Allied airmen, but each was unique in its methods. The Pat O'Leary line was the most diverse in its efforts to evacuate airmen, conducting mountain crossings, sea evacuations, and prison breakouts. The line conducted these varied operations with great success, and though it ultimately collapsed, the willingness to try new and different measures to make the line more efficient was one of the Pat line's greatest legacies.

The Comet line's strength lay in its perseverance. Though it was infiltrated and lost its leadership to enemy penetration on several occasions, the line had the benefit of strong personalities working within it. Each time the organization seemed to be irreparably damaged, new, strong leaders emerged to carry on the work of those who had led before them. When the war ended, the Comet line was still functioning and had evacuated more evaders and agents than any other line.

The Shelburne line is remembered as the only line never to be penetrated by the enemy. Though a few people were arrested, the line was never completely broken and its leadership never changed throughout its existence. While this was certainly an extraordinary feat, it is important to remember that circumstances contributed greatly to Shelburne's success. The line existed for less than a year, while the Pat line survived for two and a half years and Comet endured for four. Had Shelburne been created earlier, it might have encountered difficulties similar to those of the earlier lines.

Military intelligence agents in London provided a valuable service to those evasion networks with which they had radio contact by authenticating evaders' identities quickly, thus reducing the problems associated with "fake" airmen infiltrating the line. Unfortunately, there was little the intelligence agency could do to protect the lines against internal traitors, particularly if the traitor had worked his way into the upper level of the network's administration. By the time MI9 learned the identity of the traitor responsible for the collapse of the Pat line, there was no line left to save. Had the various regional departments of the line had radio contact with London, their chief agents could have been warned of the traitor's presence. They did not, and the traitor continued his betrayal.

Protecting the lines was even more difficult when there was no radio communication with London. Comet's refusal to accept a wireless operator from MI9, on the grounds that the intelligence agency would try to take control of the line, remained an issue throughout the war. The lines were highly compartmentalized as a means of security; however, such security measures made it difficult to warn other sections of the line of impending disaster in case of betrayal, often resulting in whole sections of a line being cut off. That a line could not be reconstructed after a major penetration did not necessarily suggest that the evasion network was incompetent. Instead, it could have indicated a high level of security. Either way, the work of the evasion organization was seriously impeded.

It is important not to dismiss the contributions of military intelligence in taking information provided by evaders and agents and applying it to avoid similar mistakes and problems in the lines it created. Evaders made suggestions that led to changes in escape kit provisions, and their experiences enabled intelligence personnel to instruct new airmen who might find themselves downed in occupied Europe in the future. The Pat O'Leary and Comet lines had no such collection of information to consult as they moved forward day by day conducting evacuations and dealing with unexpected situations. That they not only survived for a lengthy period, but thrived, is a testament to the dedication of those who devoted themselves to running the lines.

Should the helpers be regarded as part of the Resistance movement in France? Certainly they were not part of the armed resistance movements that one usually thinks of when the French Resistance is mentioned. However, there is no denying that the activities of the helpers constituted a form of resistance or that the Germans responded to it as such. Perhaps the work of the helpers did not win the war, but the return of some five thousand Allied personnel to the war effort, the intelligence provided by the returnees, and the positive effect on morale contributed significantly to the Allied cause.

The Second World War produced many horrifying examples of man's inhumanity to man. Still, we are reminded by the courage and compassion of the helpers that fear, violence, and hatred, however great the measure, cannot quench the fire in the human spirit.

Epilogue

Fifty-Five Years Later

The summer of 1999 offered me a wonderful opportunity to travel to France and visit some of the people and places about which I had read and written during the previous two years. The trip was as rewarding as the research that led me to take it. The French people I contacted made me feel wonderfully welcome, meeting me at train stations, organizing accommodations, and treating me like a queen. From the small village of St. Girons in the Pyrenees foothills to Paris, Brittany, and Normandy, I was received by former French helpers who, much to my surprise, held receptions and ceremonies in my honor, some of them driving several hours to attend. Time and again they responded to my claims that I had not done anything special by saying they wanted to "thank [me] for letting the American people know what [they had done] during the war."

In the faces of their own past sacrifices, it was a rather humbling experience. They took me to the places where they had conducted their escape operations, and though I could have visited these places alone, it was far more meaningful to do so with them at my side. Napoleon's tomb became more than just a historical shrine when Georges Broussine began telling me where the caretaker's cottages had stood and how the caretaker's daughter had fallen in love with one of the evaders and threatened to betray the line if he were taken away. Bonaparte Beach became far more than just a historical monument when I walked along the rocky beach to the foot of the cliff, scaled by the evaders over fifty-five years ago, alongside Jean Tréhiou. And history replayed itself in my mind as I stood on the site where the "house of Alphonse" once stood, listening to Marie Gicquel tell about the last night she spent in her home. It is still difficult to explain the feelings I had when I looked above the cliff at the

American, French, British, and Canadian flags flying over the memorial. In response to my question as to why the flags were there, former evader Gordon Carter said, "They are for you . . . they were raised this morning in honor of your visit."

In Normandy I had the pleasure of visiting with Alex Wattebled, now eighty-eight years old, a former Pat O'Leary agent who was arrested and tortured for his activities. I may not see Alex again, but I will never forget the light in his eyes as he told me about his Resistance work, nor his tears over the execution of a young man in a neighboring prison cell whom he had never seen.

The three days I spent in Paris with Georges and Genevieve Broussine were more like a family reunion than a first-time meeting. I refer to him as my adopted grandfather and am delighted to hear him call me his American granddaughter.

I learned that there is something in each of the people I met that loves humanity. They loved it then and it remains in them now. I began to understand what kind of people became helpers by being with them. These people shared so much of themselves with me over the last three years, and in many cases I have the only recorded version of their stories. It is truly an honor to be the guardian of these personal and historical treasures. Their experiences have become a part of me, and I will forever be a different and, I hope, better person for knowing them.

The completion of this book by no means ends my study of these fascinating events and the people who lived through them. It is a topic that is still very much alive for me, with many different aspects yet to be examined. It was the chance to study one of these different aspects of escape and evasion that led to an experience I will never forget for the lessons it taught me, even while I never want to repeat it.

On July 8, 1999, with a group of about forty-five American, Belgian, Dutch, English, and French hikers, I left the town of St. Girons in southern France and began retracing the evacuation route over the Pyrenees Mountains used by escapers and evaders of the Pat O'Leary line during World War II. Each of the hikers had his or her own reason for making the hike. Many had fathers or other family members who were evaders. Others undertook the trek as a challenge, and a few, like myself, engaged in this physical torture because they wanted to gain a historian's perspective of an act about which they had studied and written.

To everyone who asked why I would to do such a thing, I explained that I wanted to know what it was really like to be an evader. I thought that to successfully cross that mountain would give me the answer. I knew my experience would not be quite the same. After all, I had taken the time to buy a good pair of hiking boots, which I spent several weeks breaking in. I had been working out in a gym for some months in preparation, so unlike the airmen, who had been hiding in small places with no exercise, I would be in good condition for such a workout. I had no injuries from which I was recovering, and I would have plenty of food, carried in a backpack that I had been hauling around full of weights in preparation for the hike. Lastly, I would not be saddled with the fear that there might be a German patrol around every bend. This hike would be a far cry from that taken by the wartime evaders!

Little did I know when I left the little bridge in St. Girons just how well I would learn the lesson I had so often claimed as my purpose for participating in the hike. Fortunately, during the two days before the start of the climb, the hikers from the various countries had had the opportunity to mingle and become friendly with one another. As the first hours of the climb were more scenic than difficult, we continued to visit with one another as we walked. But after only a couple of hours walking, I could already feel the warning signs of a blister on one heel. When I mentioned this at our first break, one of my new Dutch friends offered me some tape to provide additional protection, which I gladly used. The walk continued, and though most of it was not difficult, the last hour before our lunch stop became quite arduous with a winding climb up a rocky incline, followed by a steep hike through what must have been several years' layers of fallen leaves. Throughout the morning my heel had become more and more tender, and I had begun to worry about what I would find when I reached the stopping point. In addition, the climb was tiring and difficult, and two hikers decided they would go no further once they reached the lunch stop. I admit that I, too, questioned the wisdom of continuing on if the rest of the day promised more of what the last hour had delivered.

As is usually the case, a good rest and lunch refreshed most of us. My heels were blistered, one of them completely raw and very tender. Another new friend, this time an Englishman, patched up both of my feet, and I pulled my boots back on, ready to keep going, though still not sure if I was making a smart decision. I just hated to quit. I felt a little better when I learned one of the Belgian team also had sore feet. I suppose the old adage about misery loving company is true no matter the setting.

Dutchman Gert Overeem and Englishman Roger Stanton became my guardians for the afternoon. Roger was determined that I should make it over that mountain and placed me in the front of the line so I would be able to take advantage of the periodic breaks taken to allow stragglers to catch up. I suspect I slowed the group somewhat, but I appreciated the encouragement from both men as I walked on through the afternoon. Each made a point of asking how I was or just telling me I was doing well. I began to see the stories I had read of stronger evaders helping weaker ones come to life. My energy began to wane later in the afternoon, and I again worried that I might be better off dropping out, though already I was growing close to some of the people in the group and did not like the idea of letting them continue without me. "Besides," I told myself, "the evaders had trouble with blisters and they managed to make it. Be tough." My raw heel had continued hurting in spite of the patch, but not wanting to be labeled a complainer, I kept quiet.

By the time we reached our checkpoint for the night, my heel had blisters within blisters. The patch had slipped off and I had spent the afternoon hours walking with the tender raw skin rubbing against the back of my boot. Once again Roger patched up the raw spot. The other heel was still covered and had not worsened. We had a large meal with plenty to eat and a cabin of sorts with cots on which to sleep, but I did not rest well. My feet were tired, hot, and sore and I lay awake most of the night.

The next morning I unloaded all but the bare necessities from my pack: sleeping bag, food, water, and a jacket. The first day we had not had to carry a pack, as several cars had driven to this checkpoint and delivered them to us. Remembering the difficulty of the day before, I did not want to carry any more than I had to. Roger assured me that if I ran into a problem they would divide my pack so that I would not have to carry such a heavy load and that they would manage to get me over the mountain.

Initially the hike went well, but during our first break I was forced to ask for help with my heel again. The second patch had fallen off, and I knew I could not walk with that much pain in my foot. This time my wounds became an international affair. While everyone else stood by watching, Roger and the Belgians patched and taped my heel so that no bandage could possibly fall off, and Lynn David, the son of a former American evader, provided a second pair of socks. As we set off again, I began to think that things might be looking up, as I could barely feel the soreness anymore.

Though the morning's hike was not as grueling as some of the previous day's walk had been, I noticed that I was growing more and more tired as we climbed up numerous hills. As we rounded each ridge, I would look ahead to see if the path was going to level out soon. After a few disappointing glances at more uphill slopes, I stopped checking. My pack did not feel too heavy, but when I leaned over on my walking stick for a quick break, I was not strong enough to stop the pack from tipping me over onto the ground. Set back on my feet by Roger and Gert, I kept going. "Just plod on," Roger told me, and I plodded. All of my concentration became focused on putting one foot in front of the other. As I watched Roger's feet in front of me, I was reminded of one of the evaders who had written that only by watching his guide's legs in front of him was he able to continue.

After a particularly long and trying hill—at least for me—I had to ask Roger for a break. I had not wanted to ask for special assistance of that kind, but knew I would not be able to stay on my feet much longer. Oddly enough, tired as I was, another evader, Roland Barlow, came to mind. When Roland had fallen to the ground in exhaustion and his guide threatened to shoot him if he did not get up, Roland had simply laughed at him. It was not a question of wanting to get up. He could not.

Fortunately for me, Roger called a break instead of waving a gun at me, and Johan Samyn, my footsore Belgian friend, stepped forward to ask what I had eaten for breakfast. Correctly convinced that I had not eaten enough, he gave me some of the high-energy snacks that had been provided him and his companions by the Belgian Air Force. I did not feel particularly hungry, but his instructions to "eat this and this and drink this down to here" did not sound like commands with which I should argue. Besides, I had no energy for being difficult, and I did recognize, even at that point, that I was in trouble. I was gaining valuable insight into being an evader without realizing it.

I hoped Johan's snacks would help, but shortly after we began walking again I lost my balance a second time. This time when I was assisted, I noticed with some surprise that I had no strength in my legs with which to help the men set me on my feet. Paschal Herman, another Belgian, told me to take off my pack. I felt bad about burdening someone else with my pack and I think I protested once, but he insisted and I let it go. Other members of the Belgian group stepped in to help as well. Bob Croes carried my pack on his chest and his own pack on his back. Alain Anckaer gave me a package of cookies and told me to eat them constantly, while Johan found a ring with which to attach my water bottle to my belt and carried the sleeping mat that had been removed from my pack. Gert and Roger continued to walk one ahead of me, one behind, and each time I got tired they stopped with me until I was able to continue. I thought it poignant that fifty-five years ago it was Belgian and Dutch helpers who had helped Americans to evade capture and cross the Pyrenees into neutral Spain. Now another American struggled to make the same trip, once again with the aid of Dutch, Belgian, and English helpers.

I finally reached the place called the Col de la Core, where the group stopped for lunch. Roger was willing to help me along through the afternoon until we reached the evening's campsite. There I could spend the night and decide in the morning whether I wanted to continue. But as I sat on the grass staring at my lunch, I knew that my hike was over. The last thing I wanted was food, but I was already weak, and without eating I certainly could not climb any further. I spent the lunch break teary-eyed, sitting with my many "helpers" and thanking them for their assistance.

When they left, I stood miserably on the side of the hill and watched everyone go. I had become fond of so many of them and they had been genuinely sorry to leave me behind. The last thing I saw as the group rounded the bend was one of the Dutchmen blowing me a kiss and giving a wave. Then, just as had happened to so many evaders during the war, I was left behind while my companions continued on their way into Spain.

In my frustration at having to quit hiking, I did not see that I had done what I had come to do. In fact, it took a comment from one of the hikers who did make it over the mountain to make me aware of what I had accomplished. He told me that of everyone, I had probably come closest to experiencing what it was really like to be an evader. That may or may not be true. I know that it was a long and difficult climb for those who continued. But if I really attempted the climb because I wanted to learn what it was like to be an evader, then I was very successful. I suffered from the terrible blisters and exhaustion as they had. I had the good fortune to experience the close relationships that developed between the evaders, as those who could helped those who could not, and I developed the same bonds with my fellow hikers that led evaders to maintain contact with each other long after the war ended. Even dropping out of the hike had its own lesson, for how else could I understand the anguish felt by the evaders forced to stay behind because of injuries or weakness had I not been forced to experience a degree of such misery myself. The only element of difficulty I had not shared with the evaders of World War II was the fear of capture by Germans, though perhaps it was this lack of motivation that allowed me to quit.

It took the better part of the next couple of months for me to get over the fatigue that resulted from my attempt to cross the mountains, but I will never regret having tried. I was not able to feel the exhilaration of crossing the French–Spanish border at the top of the mountain, nor did I get the satisfaction of being able to sign the little blue book that records the names of those who followed the Freedom Trail to its end. But I know that I gave it all I had, and I can honestly say that I have experienced what it felt like to be an evader crossing the Pyrenees.

In October 2000 I got the chance to give the mountains a second try when English, Belgian, French, and Spanish organizers established a route retracing the Comet line. I began my journey in Brussels, where I watched members of the Belgian Air Force parachute out of a plane in memory of the World War II evaders.

The friendships I made during the previous climb stood me well as Belgian Air Force officers Maj. Eddy Lievrouw and Comm. Johan Samyn arranged for me to be attached to their crew as an American historian. They undertook to provide me with the perfect evasion experience. We traveled by train to Dax, France, from which, like the true evaders, we bicycled to Anglet. Truthfully, I rode only a small fraction of the distance, but was thankful for the opportunity and the good-natured attitude of the other eleven crew members who accepted me as one of them.

In Anglet I was reunited with the French and British groups with whom I had climbed in 1999. I also met Jean François Nothomb, or Franco as I call him, in person for the first time. Once again it was like greeting an old friend.

The grave of Florentino Goicoechea marked the starting point for the 2000 Comet Freedom Trail. A memorial service was held at the gravesite, after which about seventy people crossed the Pyrenees Mountains in a tribute to the Comet helpers who risked their lives to help evaders during World War II.

Our group began hiking at the cemetery where Florentino was buried, stopping for lunch at the farmhouse at which Dédée and Francia Usandizaga were arrested. Francia's daughter Mayie Goya joined us on the walk, as did two of Florentino's grandchildren. The day ended when the hikers crossed the Bidassoa River late that afternoon. I am well acquainted with that tragic night when Antoine D'Ursel slipped from Franco's shoulders and drowned. But the story came to life as I sat on a rock along the bank of the Bidassoa and listened to Franco recount the story for me in the very place where it happened.

After spending the night alongside the river, the hike resumed. We later enjoyed lunch on the grounds of the Sarobe Farm, where Franco and his evaders rested in the barn after their long night of travel. Though the farmhouse has been modernized, the barn is intact and Franco reminded me not to forget Sarobe.

A few more hours walking and we arrived in Renteria, Spain, where a reception awaited us at the mayor's office. It was a very special moment when at long last I was able to sign the book saying I had taken the Freedom Trail to Spain, a moment made all the more special because I was the only American to walk. Few historians are fortunate enough to be able to touch the history that they study. I have been lucky to not only touch it, but also to share in the emotional, mental, and physical journey taken by the evaders and helpers. For this I will always be grateful.

Appendix A

List of Abbreviations

AFEES	Air Forces Escape and Evasion Society
BCRA	Bureau Central des Renseignements et d'Actions
E and E	Escape and Evasion
FFI	French Forces of the Interior
IS9	Intelligence School 9
JIC	Joint Intelligence Committee
MI6	Military Intelligence Section 6
MI9	Military Intelligence Section 9
MIS-X	Military Intelligence Section–Escape and Evasion
OSS	Office of Strategic Services
POW	Prisoner of War
RAAF	Royal Australian Air Force
RAF	Royal Air Force
RAFES	Royal Air Forces Escaping Society
RCAF	Royal Canadian Air Force
SD	Sicherheitsdienst (Intelligence section for the S.S.)
SHAEF	Supreme Headquarters Allied Expeditionary Forces
SIS	Secret Intelligence Services
SOE	Special Operations Executive
SS	Schutzstaffel (Elite German protection organization)
USAAF	United States Army Air Force

Appendix B

Evaders Evacuated through the Burgundy/Shelburne Connection

John T. Amery
Leonard F. Bergeron
Shirley D. Berry
Joseph A. Birdwell
William T. Campbell
Philip A. Capo
Kenneth P. Christian
Robert L. Costello
Charles W. Cregger
Paul F. Dicken
Edward J. Donaldson
_____ Evans
Robert K. Fruth
Francess P. Hennessy
Glenn B. Johnson
Norman R. King
William C. Lessig
Robert O. Lorenzi
John A. McGlynn
Jack McGough
Carl W. Mielke
Frank J. Moast

Paul R. Packer
Russell L. Paquin
Neelan B. Parker
Ralph Patton
Clyde C. Richardson
Elmer D. Risch
Manuel M. Rogoff
William J. Scanlon
Richard F. Schafer
William H. Spinning
Everett E. Stump
Edward J. Sweeney
Dean W. Tate
Carlyle A. Van Selus
Isadore C. Viola
Harold R. Wines
Charles B. Winkelman
Earl J. Wolf Jr.

Source: "Burgundy,"
    National Archives.

Notes

Introduction

1. John Brown, correspondence with author, June 30, 1998. In author's files.

1. Science Fiction or Military Strategy: The Activities of MI9 and MIS-X

1. Donald Darling, *Secret Sunday* (London: William Kimber, 1975), 83. Postel-Vinay's account will be told in greater detail further in the story.

2. M.R.D. Foot and J.M. Langley, *MI9–Escape and Evasion* (Boston: Little, Brown, 1980), 4–5.

3. Airey Neave, *Saturday at MI9* (London: Hodder and Stoughton, 1969), 19; and Foot and Langley, *MI9–Escape and Evasion,* 56.

4. J.M. Langley, *Fight Another Day* (London: William Collins Sons, 1974), 132.

5. Foot and Langley, *MI9– Escape and Evasion,* 24.

6. Ibid., 24.

7. Ibid., 24–25.

8. Langley, *Fight Another Day,* 154.

9. Ibid., 136.

10. Foot and Langley, *MI9–Escape and Evasion,* 58.

11. Neave, *Saturday at MI9,* 75.

12. Darling, *Secret Sunday,* 9, 11, 19.

13. Langley, *Fight Another Day,* 29.

14. Neave, *Saturday at MI9,* 70.

15. Langley, *Fight Another Day,* 55.

16. Ibid., 138.

17. Ibid., 34, 35, 37. Since the reunification of Germany, Colditz has been opened as a historical site and can now be toured by the public.

18. Neave, *Saturday at MI9,* 71.

19. Ibid., 64.

20. Lloyd Shoemaker, *The Escape Factory: The Story of MIS-X* (New York: St. Martin's, 1990), 7–9.

21. Ibid., 11.

22. Ibid.

23. Gerald Astor, *The Mighty Eighth* (New York: Donald I. Fine, 1997), 3; Margaret Rossiter, *Women in the Resistance* (New York: Praeger, 1986), 54.

24. Foot and Langley, *MI9–Escape and Evasion,* 46; Shoemaker, *The Escape Factory: The Story of MIS-X,* 14.

25. Shoemaker, *The Escape Factory,* 5, 17. Very little information remains on the MIS-X organization. Shoemaker worked for the agency at Fort Hunt and when researching *The Escape Factory* ran into numerous "brick walls" while searching for documentation on the agency. Most of the information was destroyed at the end of the war by the staff at Fort Hunt on an order from Major General Strong, issued just five days after Japan's surrender. Other material on the organization seems to have disappeared—perhaps, it was suggested, in the 1974 fire at the St. Louis military records center.

Though some of the work of MIS-X remains in the National Archives in the form of E and E reports and traitor reports, the papers on the organization itself were so effectively obliterated that three years after the end of World War II there was not enough information available to reactivate the agency for possible use in the Korean War. To my knowledge, only two books carry information on the formation of the agency, one of which is Shoemaker's. In many respects it is based on the recollections of people who participated in the agency's work, but Shoemaker also did much research of documents in the military archives to recreate the agency. Foot and Langley's *MI9–Escape and Evasion* also includes information on the creation of MIS-X and the personalities involved with it.

26. Langley, *Fight Another Day,* 191.

27. This followed a line of division already established by higher powers in the war alliance.

28. Foot and Langley, *MI9–Escape and Evasion,* 177; Langley, *Fight Another Day,* 206–7.

29. Foot and Langley, *MI9–Escape and Evasion,* 26, 54.

30. Shoemaker, *The Escape Factory,* 12.

31. Foot and Langley, *MI9–Escape and Evasion,* 29.

32. Ibid., 29–30.

33. Ibid., 32–33.

34. Brendan Murphy, *Turncoat* (San Diego: Harcourt Brace Jovanovich, 1987), 35; Foot and Langley, *MI9–Escape and Evasion,* 32, 35.

35. [Black Book], H.Q., Air Force Service Command, no date, IRIS No. 00239706, in USAF Collection, Air Force Historical Research Agency (AFHRA), Maxwell Air Force Base, Montgomery, Alabama.

36. "Escape and Evasion Report 485 Wesley Coss," Folder Wesley Coss #485, Box 15, Entry ETO MIS-X, Record Group 338, National Archives, Washington, D.C.

37. Roland Barlow, unpublished manuscript, 3. In author's files. Barlow died in April 2000.

38. David Turner, audiocassette of evasion experience. In author's files.

39. [Black Book], AFHRA.

40. R.M. Johnson, "Phrase card." Sent by Randy Johnson, son of R.M. Johnson. In author's files.

41. [Black Book], AFHRA.

42. Barlow, unpublished manuscript, 44.

43. "Escape and Evasion Report 502 John McGlynn," Folder John McGlynn #502, Box 15, Entry ETO MIS-X, Record Group 332, National Archives, Washington, D.C.

44. Kenneth Skidmore, *Follow the Man With the Pitcher* (Merseyside, Eng.: Countyvise, 1960), 12.

45. Brown correspondence.

46. Barney Rawlings, *Off We Went Into the Wild Blue Yonder* (Washington, N.C.: Morgan 1994), 203.

47. "Interrogation Forms," Folder: Military Attaché–WDLO, Letters to, from (28 May 44 to 19 June 45), Box 3, Entry ETO MIS-X, Record Group 332, National Archives, Washington, D.C.

48. Ibid.

49. Ibid.

50. Darling, *Secret Sunday,* 52–54.

51. "Letters From American Airmen," Folders A-Z, Box 1, Entry ETO MIS-X, Record Group 338, National Archives, Washington, D.C.

52. "History of French Evasion Networks," Folder Liberation Vengeance, Box 2, Entry ETO MIS-X, Record Group 332, National Archives, Washington, D.C. The event is referred to as the Peyrehorade Affair.

53. David Turner, E-mail to author, August 9, 1997. In author's files.

54. "Interrogation Forms," National Archives.

55. "Escape and Evasion Report 505 George Jasman," H.Q., Air Force Service Command, April 6, 1944 to August 26, 1944, IRIS No. 00116857, in USAF Collection, AFHRA; "Escape and Evasion Report 654 Hobart C. Trigg," H.Q., Air Force Service Command, April 6, 1944 to August 26, 1944, IRIS No. 00116857, in USAF Collection, AFHRA.

56. Foot and Langley, *MI9–Escape and Evasion,* 13.

57. "Means of Escape of Anglo-American Flying Personnel," Box 3, Entry ETO MIS-X, Record Group 332, National Archives, Washington, D.C., 4. This booklet is tucked in between the folders of MIS-X files in the National Archives rather than contained within a folder, as are the other files in the box.

58. Ibid., 24.

59. Ibid., 24.

60. "Pre-Capture Training Lecture," folder unlabeled, Box 3, Entry ETO MIS-X, Record Group 332, National Archives, Washington, D.C., 1.

61. Rossiter, *Women in the Resistance,* 23.

2. It Was Raining Aviators: The Evaders

1. "Rapport de Andrée de Jongh," Folder Comet, Box 1, Entry ETO MIS-X, Record Group 338, National Archives, Washington, D.C.

2. Helen Long, *Safe Houses Are Dangerous* (London: William Kimber, 1985), 66.

3. "Means of Escape of Anglo-American Flying Personnel," National Archives, 4; Rossiter, *Women in the Resistance,* 23; Russell Miller, *The Resistance,* World War II–Time-Life Books Series (Alexandria, Va.: Time-Life, 1979), 105.

4. Jack Stead, unpublished manuscript. Sent by Jack Stead. In author's files. USAAF required men to fly twenty-five missions, after which they were sent home. This seldom happened, as many were shot down before reaching this number. Many airmen were frustrated at being shot down on their last or near last mission, which delayed their return home by however long it took them to evade, a period which extended to months for some. Many of the English and Commonwealth airmen died in subsequent missions.

5. Brian Todd Carey, "Operation Pointblank: Evolution of Allied Air Doctrine," *World War II,* November 1998, 50; Art Horning, *In the Footsteps of a Winged Boot* (New York: Hearthstone, 1994), xxii.

6. Gail Tabor and Kathleen Ingley, "Leslie Says It Rained Aviators," *The Air Forces Escape and Evasion Society Communications* (vol. 11, no. 3), September 8, 1997, 5. Atkinson is currently the French liaison for the American Air Force Escape and Evasion Society.

Each year at their annual reunion, he arranges for a number of European helpers to travel to the U.S. and visit with the airmen they rescued.

7. George Buckner, "Down and Out in Forty-Four Days," unpublished manuscript. Sent by George Buckner. In author's files.

8. Neave, *Saturday at MI9*, 85; Darling, *Secret Sunday*, 58.

9. "Means of Escape of Anglo-American Flying Personnel," National Archives, 25.

10. Neave, *Saturday at MI9*, 144.

11. David Goldberg, correspondence with author, March 26, 1998. In author's files.

12. Foot and Langley, *MI9 Escape and Evasion*, 12–13.

13. "Escape and Evasion 239 Report Peter Seniawsky," H.Q., Air Force Service Command, April 6, 1944 to August 26, 1944, IRIS No. 00116857, in USAF Collection, AFHRA; Airey Neave, *They Have Their Exits* (Boston: Little, Brown, 1953). Neave relates his escape from Colditz POW camp and subsequent evasion to Switzerland and then through France and across the Pyrenees Mountains; "Pre-Capture Training Lecture" (National Archives) uses stories of men who escaped and evaded from Germany.

14. [Black Book], AFHRA; Foot and Langley, *MI9 Escape and Evasion*, 10.

15. Neave, *Saturday at MI9*, 18; Darling, *Secret Sunday*, 31; Foot and Langley, *MI9 Escape and Evasion*, 51.

16. Rossiter, *Women in the Resistance*, 12; Long, *Safe Houses Are Dangerous*, 19. The Milice was a French paramilitary group that embraced fascist ideology and worked to rid France of those who resisted the new regime. The French people greatly feared the Milice, which served as a local Gestapo. It was a voluntary organization established in January 1943 by the Vichy government. The Milice was more threatening than the Germans, because they usually worked within their own communities and were therefore more familiar with the area and its people. They took part in betraying their own countrymen, which earned them a hatred beyond that which the French felt for the German occupiers.

17. Long, *Safe Houses Are Dangerous*, 207; Albert Leslie Wright, correspondence with author, May 19, 1998. In author's files. Wright died in October 1998.

18. "Escape and Evasion Report 323 William Howell," Rossiter papers, Harlan Hatcher Library, University of Michigan at Ann Arbor.

19. "Escape and Evasion Report 671 Bernard Rawlings," Folder Bernard Rawlings #671, Box 22, Entry ETO MIS-X, Record Group 338, National Archives, Washington, D.C.; Rawlings, *Off We Went*, 122; "Escape and Evasion Report 449 Charles Adcock," Folder Charles Adcock #449, Box 13, Entry ETO MIS-X, Record Group 338, National Archives, Washington, D.C.

20. Colin Bayliss, *No Flying Without Wings* (Perth: Colin Bayliss, 1994), 124; Virgil Marco, "A Little Bit of History," unpublished manuscript. Sent by Virgil Marco. In author's files; "E and E 494 Norman King," Folder Norman King # 494, Box 15, Entry ETO MIS-X, Record Group 338, National Archives, Washington, D.C.

21. Barlow, unpublished manuscript, 14.

22. Paul Kenney, unpublished manuscript. Sent by Paul Kenney. In author's files.

23. Ibid.

24. "Escape and Evasion Report 203 James McElroy," Rossiter papers; Martin W. Bowman, *Home by Christmas* (Wellingborough, Eng.: Patrick Stevens, 1987), 119.

25. The Maquis movement began with the young men who fled to the mountains to escape German labor conscription. Maquis groups later included men and women of all ages who were hunted by the Germans. They took part in sabotage missions and were known for guerrilla-type warfare. As the European invasion approached, the Allies in-

creased parachute drops of ammunition and food supplies as well as intelligence agents to help the Maquis groups organize themselves to fight against the Germans. They often worked under the leadership of OSS or SOE agents, which resulted in the crossing of intelligence lines. The term "Maquis" meant "men of the scrub brush."

26. Wayne Eveland, "Memories and Reflections," unpublished manuscript. Sent by Wayne Eveland. In author's files. 79. Eveland died in July 1999.

27. Ibid., 69, 79.

28. Carpetbaggers were Allied airmen who dropped supplies and agents to Resistance groups such as the Maquis on night operations.

29. Frank Hines, unpublished manuscript. Sent by Frank Hines. In author's files; John Meade, unpublished manuscript. Sent by John Meade. In author's files. Meade was awarded the Silver Star for his action with SOE after he was shot down.

30. Hélène De Champlain, *The Secret War of Hélène De Champlain* (London: W.H. Allen, 1980), 128–31, 138–40. Hélène Dechamps-Adams telephone interview with author, June 14, 1997. In author's files.

31. "Letters From American Airmen," Folder H, National Archives. In his Archive file, there is a colored pencil interior drawing of the Angulo house drawn by Hage to illustrate the layout of the home.

32. Ibid.

33. Claude Hélias, correspondence with author, November 15, 1997. In author's files.

34. Summary of Wilf Gorman experience written and provided by Michael Leblanc. In author's files.

35. Ibid.

36. David Goldberg, correspondence with author, April 16, 1998. In author's files.

37. Hines, unpublished manuscript.

38. "Escape and Evasion Report 832 William Hawkins," H.Q., Air Force Service Command, April 6, 1944 to August 26, 1944, IRIS No. 00116857, in USAF Collection, AFHRA; René Charpentier, "Souvenirs De Jeunesse La Guerre 1939–1945, La Resistance," unpublished memoir. Sent by René Charpentier. In author's files; "E and E Report 239 Peter Seniawsky," AFHRA.

39. Keith Patrick, correspondence with author, April 26, 1998. In author's files; Harold Brennan, correspondence with author, April 30, 1998. In author's files.

40. [Black Book], AFHRA. Bailing out was usually an emergency situation, but if the plane was not in imminent danger of crashing, the men jumped at intervals. Often, bailing at intervals occurred even if there was an emergency situation, since the plane was large and the intercom system that allowed the crew to communicate was commonly knocked out of commission by enemy fire. Without an intercom, the men needed extra time to pass the "bail out" order by word of mouth.

41. [Black Book], AFHRA.

42. [Black Book], AFHRA; "Escape and Evasion Report 484 Willis Spellman," Folder Willis Spellman #484, Box 14, Entry ETO MIS-X, Record Group 338, National Archives, Washington, D.C.; "Escape and Evasion Report 1030 Richard Reid," Folder Richard Reid #1030, Box 32, Entry ETO MIS-X, Record Group 338, National Archives, Washington, D.C.; "Escape and Evasion Report 12 Marc McDermott," Rossiter papers; "Escape and Evasion Report 1411 Merrill Caldwell," Folder Merrill Caldwell #1411, Box 39, Entry ETO MIS-X, Record Group 338, National Archives, Washington, D.C.

43. Richard M. Smith, *Hide And Seek With the German Army*, Part I, ed. Clarke M. Brandt (Aurora, Colo.: Army Education Center, 1997), 13.

44. "Escape and Evasion Report 556 Richard Faulkner," Rossiter papers.

45. Marco, *A Little Bit of History,* 2; "Simon Crew," Operational Chronology of the Carpetbaggers, 801st Bomber Group, Maxwell Air Force Base, Montgomery, Alabama; Tom Emsinger, correspondence with author, 1998.

46. Emerson Lavender and Norman Sheffe, *The Evaders* (Montreal: McGraw-Hill Ryerson, 1992), 202; Edmund Cosgrove, *The Evaders* (Markham: Simon and Schuster of Canada, 1976), 13; Joe Walters, correspondence with author, September 13, 1997. In author's files; Gus Bubenzer, "Shot Down In Occupied France: Memories of World War II," *Laurels,* fall 1988, 81; Eveland, "Memories and Reflections."

47. Langley, *Fight Another Day,* 154.

48. Robert Horsley, "Maximum Effort," unpublished manuscript. Sent by Robert Horsley. In author's files; "Pre-Capture Training Lecture," National Archives; [Black Book,] AFHRA.

49. Brennan correspondence.

50. Stead, unpublished manuscript.

51. Ibid.

52. "Escape and Evasion Report 833 Joseph Lilly," Rossiter papers.

53. "Escape and Evasion Report 679 Travis Ross," Folder Travis Ross #679, Box 22, Entry ETO MIS-X, Record Group 338, National Archives, Washington, D.C.

54. "Escape and Evasion Report 679 Travis Ross," National Archives.

55. "Escape and Evasion Report 448 William Olsen," Folder William Olsen #448, Box 13, Entry ETO MIS-X, Record Group 338, National Archives, Washington, D.C.

56. [Black Book,] AFHRA.

57. "Getting Away From the Krauts Was Tough Stuff But With Able Hands to Help, It Could Be Done," Box 1: Newspaper Articles, Entry ETO MIS–X, Record Group 338, National Archives, Washington, D.C.

58. Foot and Langley, *MI9 Escape and Evasion,* 200; Darling, *Secret Sunday,* 136; "Escape and Evasion Report 833 Joseph Lilly," Rossiter papers; Thomas Yankus, correspondence with author, October 10, 1997. In author's files. Some of the farmers' wives saved the parachute fabric to make underclothes and dresses. Evader Thomas Yankus was able to save a piece of his chute, which was later used to make part of his fiancée's wedding dress.

59. "Escape and Evasion Report 536 Keith Sutor," Folder Keith Sutor #536, Box 17, Entry ETO MIS-X, Record Group 338, National Archives, Washington, D.C.

60. "Escape and Evasion Report 2157 John Dutka," Rossiter papers.

61. Foot and Langley, *MI9 Escape and Evasion,* 200.

62. "Escape and Evasion Report 658 Webber Mason," H.Q., Air Force Service Command, April 6, 1944 to August 26, 1944, IRIS No. 00116857, in USAF Collection, AFHRA.

63. Kenney, unpublished manuscript; "Escape and Evasion Report 1761 Leo Arlin," Rossiter papers.

64. David Chapple, correspondence with author, September 1998, In author's files; Charles Kroschel, correspondence with author, September 1998, In author's files.

65. [Black Book,] AFHRA.

66. Kenney, unpublished manuscript.

67. Neil Roggenkamp, "Evasion in Normandy," *Against The Odds,* ed. Bob Lindsey (Queensland, Aus.: Royal Air Forces Escaping Society–Australian Branch Newsletter, 1995), 131;

68. Bubenzer, "Shot Down In Occupied France," 85; Stan Lawrence, correspondence with author, April 7, 1998. In author's files.

69. Neave, *Saturday at MI9,* 103.

70. George Bennett, *Shot Down! Escape and Evasion* (Morgantown, W.Va.: Mediaworks, 1992), 75; Merrill Caldwell, taped correspondence with author, undated. In author's files.

71. Keith Sutor, unpublished manuscript. Sent by Keith Sutor. In author's files; Buckner, "Down and Out in Forty-Four Days," unpublished manuscript.

72. *Prix spécial à la mémoire de Madame Rosine Witton, Madame Berthe Fraser, Madame Zoe Evans,* (Departement du Pas-De-Calais: Concours National De La Resistance Et De La Deportation); Pierre Moreau, correspondence with author, 1998. In author's files.

73. "Visit of Mme Paul Beau and Mlle Jacqueline Beau," Folder B, Box 4, Captain Tucker's Correspondence Regarding French Aid to American Airmen, Entry ETO MIS-X, Record Group 338, National Archives, Washington, D.C.

74. Gordon Young, *In Trust and Treason* (London: Studio Vista, 1959), 66–67.

75. Milton Mills, "One Hundred Fourteen Days in German-Occupied France," unpublished manuscript. Sent by Clarke M. Brandt. In author's files.

76. Neave, *Saturday at MI9,* 22. According to Neave, 90 percent of escapers and evaders were repatriated through Spain.

77. Barlow, unpublished manuscript, 36; "Escape and Evasion Report 687 Archie Barlow," Folder Archie Barlow #687, Box 22, Entry ETO MIS-X, Record Group 338, National Archives, Washington, D.C.

78. Ralph McKee, "The Winged Boot," unpublished manuscript. Sent by Ralph McKee. In author's files; Angus MacLean lost 36 pounds while evading, weighing only 129 pounds by the time he reached Spain. Angus MacLean, "Escape From Europe," *The Canadian Aviation Historical Society,* fall 1997, 117.

79. Stead, unpublished manuscript.

80. Barlow, unpublished manuscript, 41; Wilf Gorman summary. There is an interesting connection between Gorman and Barlow. They were together on their second evasion attempts, and when the Germans raided their cabin, each ran in a different direction. The vast majority of their group was captured immediately, and Gorman was captured the next day, as stated earlier. Barlow and three other Americans managed to get to Spain together without the help of a guide and, toward the end, with the Germans on their trail—yet another example of the part luck played in a successful evasion experience.

81. Eveland, "Memories and Reflections."

82. Ibid., 73.

83. "Escape and Evasion Report 686 Fred Glover," Folder Fred Glover #686, Box 22, Entry ETO MIS-X, Record Group 338, National Archives, Washington, D.C. An additional note on Glover: he was shot down on his fiftieth mission—an accomplishment that few shared with him.

84. Angus MacLean, "Escape From Europe," 117.

3. My Brother's Keeper: The Helpers

1. Alan Cooper, *Free to Fight Again* (Shrewsbury, Eng.: Airlife, 1988), 48.

2. "German Poster," copy provided by Alain Sibiril. In author's files.

3. John McGlynn, correspondence with author, October 19, 1997. In author's files. McGlynn died January 30, 1999.

4. Neave, *Saturday at MI9,* 17.

5. Former American, Canadian, Australian, and British evaders established organizations that hold reunions between evaders and helpers and provide assistance to former

helpers who are in need. Escape line workers also formed groups called *amicales,* which organize annual reunions for their members to renew their wartime friendships and keep in touch.

6. Reine Mocaer, unpublished memoir. Sent by Reine Mocaer. In author's files.

7. Neave, *Saturday at MI9,* 315.

8. "Escape and Evasion 449 Charles Adcock," Folder Charles Adcock #449, Box 13, Entry ETO MIS-X, Record Group 338, National Archives, Washington, D.C.

9. Langley, *Fight Another Day,* 251.

10. Stan Jolly, correspondence with author, September 18, 1998. In author's files.

11. Alain Camard, correspondence with author, May 1998. In author's files.

12. Long, *Safe Houses are Dangerous,* 37, 56.

13. Mocaer, unpublished memoir.

14. Maurice Leech, correspondence with author, August 1997. In author's files. The cemetery at Serre Road No. 2 contains over seven thousand graves, including two that hold German soldiers. The tool shed is still in use today.

15. Neave, *Saturday at MI9,* 96.

16. Ibid., 96, 106.

17. Peggy van Lier Langley, interview with Margaret Rossiter, October 12, 1976, Rossiter papers. After the war, Peggy married Jim Langley of MI9.

18. Georges Broussine, interview with Margaret Rossiter, undated, Rossiter papers.

19. Denise Bacchi, letter to Paul Clark, July 14, 1944. Sent by Betty Clark. In author's files.

20. Betty Clark, letter to author, June 1998. In author's files.

21. Langley, *Fight Another Day,* Introduction, n.p.; Bertranne Auvert, "Memoirs 1940–1945," unpublished memoir. Sent by George Buckner. In author's files.

22. Auvert, "Memoirs 1940—1945," 11–12.

23. Van Lier Langley–Rossiter interview, undated.

24. Richard M. Smith, *Hide and Seek with the German Army,* Part II, ed. Clarke M. Brandt (Aurora, Colo.: Army Education Center, 1997), 25; Horsley, "Maximum Effort."

25. "Rapport de Andrée de Jongh," National Archives.

26. Denise Bacchi, letter to Paul Clark, July 14, 1944.

27. "Letter From Valeria and Esther Fosset," Folder M, Box 1, Letters From American Airmen, Entry ETO MIS-X, Record Group 338, National Archives, Washington, D.C.

28. Darling, *Secret Sunday,* 94.

29. Kenney, unpublished manuscript.

30. Hélène Deschamps-Adams, telephone interview.

31. Rossiter, *Women in the Resistance,* 18.

32. Jean François Nothomb, interview with Margaret Rossiter, undated, Rossiter papers.

33. Langley, *Fight Another Day,* Introduction, n.p.; "Escape and Evasion Reports," Boxes 1–70, Entry ETO MIS-X, Record Group 338, National Archives, Washington, D.C. The E and E reports identify the occupations of many of the helpers. Some, such as farmers and café workers, appear numerous times.

34. "Report on the Activities of Agent Legrelle," History of the French Evasion Networks, Folder Comet, Box 1, Entry ETO MIS-X, Record Group 338, National Archives, Washington, D.C.

35. Escape and Evasion Report 667 Philip Warner, Folder Philip Warner #667, Box 22, Entry ETO MIS-X, National Archives, Washington, D.C.; Alfred Martin, unpublished memoir. Sent by Alfred Martin. In author's files.

36. Darling, *Secret Sunday,* 94–95; "Obituary: Air Marshal Sir John Whitley," *The Daily Telegraph,* (London), February 1998.

37. Langley, *Fight Another Day,* 192; Rossiter, *Women in the Resistance,* 56; Foot and Langley, *MI9 Escape and Evasion,* 16.

38. Leslie Atkinson, correspondence with author, February 16, 1998. In author's files; Jean Jacques Piot, correspondence with author, November 20, 1998. In author's files.

39. Atkinson correspondence.

40. Darling, *Secret Sunday,* 131. After the war, "The Fair Charmer" received an award by the British Government for her services to the RAF.

41. Atkinson correspondence.

42. Darling, *Secret Sunday,* 74; Rossiter, *Women in the Resistance,* 65.

43. "Escape and Evasion Report 534 Robert Rujawitz," Folder Robert Rujawitz #534, Box 17, Entry ETO MIS-X, Record Group 338, National Archives, Washington, D.C.

44. Maurice Bidaud, correspondence with author, July 1998. In author's files. Mr. Leger received the Medal of Freedom from the American government for his contribution to downed American airmen.

45. Maryse de la Marnierre McKeon, correspondence with author, March 13, 1998. In author's files.

46. Auvert, "Memoirs 1940–1945"; Cooper, *Free to Fight Again,* 62; Bubenzer, "Shot Down In Occupied France," 84;

47. Jean Crouet, letter to Warren Tarkington, December 30, 1945. Sent by Clarke M. Brandt. Copy in author's files.

48. Donald Cheney, *Adventure In France 1944,* unpublished manuscript. Sent by Donald Cheney. In author's files.

49. René Le Cren, correspondence with author, March 1998. In author's files.

50. Lavender and Sheffe, *The Evaders,* 205.

51. Claude Bacchi, correspondence with author, August 25, 1998. In author's files; Felix Bacchi, journal entry, June 30, 1966. Sent by Betty Clark. In author's files.

52. Bidaud correspondence.

53. Long, *Safe Houses Are Dangerous,* 48.

54. Darling, *Secret Sunday,* 159; Broussine—Rossiter interview, Rossiter papers; Maryse McKeon correspondence; Tony D'Arcey, unpublished manuscript. Sent by Tony D'Arcey. In author's files.

55. Rossiter, *Women in the Resistance,* 69; "E and E Report 478 Wayne Eveland," Folder Wayne Eveland #478, Box 14, Entry ETO MIS-X, Record Group 338, National Archives, Washington, D.C.; "Escape and Evasion Report 461 Neelan Parker," Folder Neelan Parker #461, Box 14, Entry ETO MIS-X, Record Group 338, National Archives, Washington, D.C.; Kenney, unpublished manuscript; Caldwell, taped correspondence.

56. Smith, *Hide and Seek With the German Army,* 27; "E and E Report 489 Robert Lorenzi," Folder Robert Lorenzi #489, Box 15, Entry ETO MIS-X, Record Group 338, National Archives, Washington, D.C.

57. Lavender and Sheffe, *The Evaders,* 204.

58. Ibid., 204.

59. "Escape and Evasion Report 455 Manuel Rogoff," Folder Manuel Rogoff #455, Box 13, Entry ETO MIS-X, Record Group 338, National Archives, Washington, D.C.

60. "Escape and Evasion Report 1671 Charles Davis," Folder Charles Davis #1671, Box 39, Entry ETO MIS-X, Record Group 338, National Archives, Washington, D.C.

61. Alan Monaghan, taped correspondence with author, spring 1998. In author's files.

62. Darling, *Secret Sunday,* 77; Desiré Le Cren, correspondence with author, March

18, 1998. In author's files; Reine Mocaer, correspondence with author, March 25, 1998; Kenney, unpublished manuscript; McKeon correspondence; Tony D'Arcey, unpublished manuscript; Moreau correspondence. Moreau claimed that food was their biggest problem.

63. René Le Cren correspondence; Marguerite Pierre, correspondence with author, April 8, 1998. In author's files; Bacchi correspondence; Caldwell, taped correspondence; Marco, *A Little Bit of History.*

64. Yvonne Kervarec, correspondence with author, June 16, 1998. In author's files; Moreau correspondence; "Escape and Evasion Report 535 Robert Sweatt," Folder Robert Sweatt #535, Box 17, Entry ETO MIS-X, Record Group 338, National Archives, Washington, D.C.

65. René Le Cren correspondence.

66. Langley, *Fight Another Day,* 191; Buckner, "Down and Out in Forty-Four Days"; Barlow, unpublished manuscript, 18.

67. Stead, unpublished manuscript.

68. "Escape and Evasion Report 547 Leon Blythe," Folder Leon Blythe #547, Box 17, Entry ETO MIS-X, Record Group 338, National Archives, Washington, D.C.

69. Vincent Brome, *The Way Back* (New York: W.W. Norton, 1958), 45, 90.

70. "Report on the Activities of Agent Legrelle," National Archives; "Obituary: Elvire de Greef," *Daily Telegraph,* September 3, 1991; Camard correspondence.

71. Buckner, "Down and Out in Forty-Four Days;" Barlow, unpublished manuscript.

72. "Report on the Activities of Agent Legrelle," National Archives; "Liberation Vengeance," Folder Liberation Vengeance, Box 2, Entry ETO MIS-X, Record Group 332, National Archives, Washington, D.C.; "Report of Jean Jacques," Folder Comet, Box 1, Entry ETO MIS-X, Record Group 338, National Archives, Washington, D.C.

73. "Burgundy," Folder Burgundy, Box 1, Entry ETO MIS-X, Record Group 338, National Archives, Washington, D.C.; Horsley, "Maximum Effort."

74. Buckner, "Down and Out in Forty-Four Days"; Rossiter, *Women in the Resistance,* 64.

75. Micheline Dumon, interview with Margaret Rossiter, undated, Rossiter papers; Murphy, *Turncoat,* 68–70. The guide, Paul Cole, was an agent for the Pat line and later became a double agent for the Germans. He was responsible for the arrest of about one hundred workers on the Pat line. See also Chapter 4.

76. Dumon–Rossiter interview; Rossiter, *Women in the Resistance,* 64.

77. Brome, *The Way Back,* 58–59.

78. "Burgundy," National Archives.

79. Raymond Itterbeek, correspondence with author, October 20, 1998. In author's files.

80. Moreau correspondence.

81. Charpentier, "Souvenirs de Jeunesse La Guerre"; Maurice Leech, correspondence, March 25, 1998. In author's files; "Benjamin Leech," Folder Benjamin Leech, Box 245, Entry ETO MIS-X, Record Group 338, National Archives, Washington, D.C. In military intelligence documents, Benjamin gives credit to Maurice, claiming he did most of the work.

82. Moreau correspondence.

83. Leech correspondence.

84. McKeon correspondence.

85. Georges Jouanjean, "The War and Its Bitterness," unpublished memoir. Sent by Georges Jouanjean. In author's files.

86. Bidaud correspondence.

87. Stead, unpublished manuscript.

88. Cooper, *Free To Fight Again*, 63–64; Darling, *Secret Sunday*, 76; Cheney, "Adventure In France;" Sutor, unpublished manuscript.

89. Olympe St. Leger, correspondence with author, May 1998. In author's files; Long, *Safe Houses Are Dangerous*, 127. Rodocanachi helped airmen, servicemen, and Jews to escape. He died February 10, 1944, at Büchenwald concentration camp for his humanitarian efforts.

90. René Le Cren correspondence; Jean and Jeanne Tréhiou, correspondence with author, May 1998. In author's files; Hélène Jeanson Arnould, correspondence with author, fall 1998. In author's files.

91. François Moal, correspondence with author, March 3, 1998. In author's files.

92. George Buckner, correspondence with author, March 1997. In author's files.

93. Bacchi correspondence.

94. "Fils de passeur sur France 3: l'histoire d'un réseau d'évasion," *Le Télégramme*, March 7, 1998.

95. Ibid.

96. Drue Tartiere, *The House Near Paris* (New York: Simon and Schuster, 1946), 201; "There Were Many Unsung Heroes in the Global Conflict, And Not the Least of These the Belgians, French and Dutch, Who Aided Allied Fliers to Avoid Enemy Capture," *Stars and Stripes Magazine*, November 10, 1945, Folder Newspaper Articles, Box 1, Entry ETO MIS-X, Record Group 338, National Archives, Washington, D.C.

97. Bayliss, *No Flying Without Wings*, 132.

98. "There Were Many Unsung Heroes . . . ," National Archives.

99. "Raymond Lefevre," Folder Raymond Lefevre, Box 246, Entry ETO MIS-X, Record Group 338, National Archives, Washington, D.C.

100. Pat Cheramy, "The Quiet Heroine," *The Weekly News*, London, May 26, 1973.

101. Jouanjean, "The War and Its Bitterness." Jouanjean passed away July 1, 1998, only two months after writing this memoir.

102. "Pierre Robert," Folder Pierre Robert, Box 352, French Helper Files, Entry ETO MIS-X, Record Group 338, National Archives, Washington, D.C. Mme Leroy was deported and shot a few days before the liberation.

103. "Lily Dumon," Folder Comet, Box 1, Entry ETO MIS-X, Record Group 338, National Archives, Washington, D.C. The agent was Jacques Cartier.

104. Gabrielle Buffet Picabia, interview with Constance Greenbaum, March 6, 1979, Rossiter papers.

4. Adolph Should Stay: The Pat O'Leary Line, 1940–1941

1. Robert A. Doughty and Ira D. Guber, *World War II: Total Warfare Around the Globe* (Lexington, Mass.: D.C. Heath, 1996), 27. There were also some Dutch and Belgian forces evacuated in this operation.

2. Neave, *Saturday at MI9*, 78.

3. Murphy, *Turncoat*, 56.

4. Helen Long, *Safe Houses Are Dangerous*, 23.

5. Murphy, *Turncoat*, 99.

6. Langley, *Fight Another Day*, 104.

7. Ibid., 104.

8. For a description of U.S. policy toward Vichy, France, refer to William Langer's book *Our Vichy Gamble,* published 1947 by A.A. Knopf.

9. Murphy, *Turncoat,* 57.

10. Darling, *Secret Sunday,* 26; Foot and Langley, *MI9 Escape and Evasion,* 65; Long, *Safe Houses Are Dangerous,* 63.

11. Russell Braddon, *Nancy Wake,* (London: Cassell, 1956), 65.

12. Darling, *Secret Sunday,* 25; Foot and Langley, *MI9 Escape and Evasion,* 65.

13. Long, *Safe Houses Are Dangerous,* 22–23.

14. Darling, *Secret Sunday,* 28; "Rapport du Pat O'Leary," Folder Pat O'Leary, Box 1, Entry ETO MIS-X, Record Group 338, National Archives, Washington, D.C.

15. Long, *Safe Houses Are Dangerous,* 57–58; Brome, *The Way Back,* 32. André Vagliano gave Nouveau about fifty thousand francs to help fund the line's activity. After the war, Pat O'Leary returned the money, but Vagliano refused to accept it and turned it over to a charity. Louis Nouveau, *Des Capitaines Par Milliers* (Paris, France: Calman-Lévy, 1958), Chapter 12. Translation provided by Michael Leblanc, a Canadian historian.

16. Albert Leslie Wright, correspondence with author, January 8, 1999. In author's files. *Reseau* is the French term for network.

17. Murphy, *Turncoat,* 60–61; Long, *Safe Houses Are Dangerous,* 204–11. In their correspondence, several helpers from Brittany have recounted Nouveau's visits to Brittany while establishing the line there. His code name was Saint Jean.

18. Rodocanachi was highly decorated for his efforts during World War I. Murphy, *Turncoat,* 61.

19. Murphy, *Turncoat,* 61; Long, *Safe Houses Are Dangerous,* 29, 36; Darling, *Secret Sunday,* 20.

20. "Rapport du Pat O'Leary," National Archives; Long, *Safe Houses Are Dangerous,* 31–33; Murphy, *Turncoat,* 61. Only a handful of people knew the location of the line's headquarters.

21. Fanny Rodocanachi, *Memoir: Dr. George Rodocanachi* (London: The Estate of Fanny Rodocanachi, 1946), n.p.

22. Donald Caskie, *The Tartan Pimpernel* (London: Oldbourne, 1957), 32, 34.

23. Ibid., 40–41.

24. Ibid., 55.

25. Ibid., 44.

26. Long, *Safe Houses Are Dangerous,* 43; Murphy, *Turncoat,* 58–59; Caskie, *The Tartan Pimpernel,* 65.

27. Long, *Safe Houses Are Dangerous,* 30, 44. Caskie later said he was unaware at that time that Rodocanachi was also sheltering evaders.

28. Murphy, *Turncoat,* 59.

29. Long, *Safe Houses Are Dangerous,* 135.

30. Caskie, *The Tartan Pimpernel,* 85.

31. Ibid., 86.

32. Long, *Safe Houses Are Dangerous,* 69. Some accounts say O'Leary was a member of SOE and as such received a commission in the Royal Navy to disguise his real role.

33. "Rapport du Pat O'Leary," National Archives; Brome, *The Way Back,* 24.

34. Brome, *The Way Back,* 27–28.

35. "Rapport du Pat O'Leary," National Archives; Long, *Safe Houses Are Dangerous,* 78–79.

36. Caskie, *The Tartan Pimpernel,* 71.

37. Alex Wattebled, personal interview with author, July 20, 1999. Pontorson, France.

38. Georges Zarifi, correspondence with author, summer 1998. In author's files. Zarifi died December 1998.

39. Langley, *Fight Another Day,* 163.

40. Murphy, *Turncoat,* 98; Albert Leslie Wright, correspondence with author, May 31, 1998. In author's files.

41. Translation: "Adolphe should stay." Pat had two code names. Joseph Cartier, the name in which his false papers were made, and Adolphe. According to Darling's account, the BBC message stated "Joseph doit reste."

At Claude Dansey's orders, MI9 made an effort to keep the Belgian government in exile from knowing that Pat was working for British military intelligence. They feared Belgian officials would try to find him and in so doing compromise his work. As a result of this, all agents in the field were given code names different from those they used in the field. Langley, *Fight Another Day,* 152–53.

42. Darling, *Secret Sunday,* 24.

43. Ibid., 25. "Rapport du Pat O'Leary," National Archives.

44. "Rapport du Pat O'Leary," National Archives.

45. The RAF was extremely anxious to have Higginson back in the RAF as an active fighting member. They requested that the Pat line do whatever it could to help him escape.

46. Pat Hicton, correspondence with author, July, 1999; Brome, *The Way Back,* 100–103.

47. Brome, *The Way Back,* 104.

48. Neave, *Saturday at MI9,* 87,89. Straight told Neave and Langley about passing time away in Rouen, France, while waiting for his train to arrive. He wandered through the streets dropping British pennies in the mailboxes of houses that had been requisitioned by Germans.

49. Ibid., 92; Long, *Safe Houses Are Dangerous,* 139.

50. "Reseau Burgundy," Folder Reseau Burgundy, Box 1, Entry ETO MIS-X, Record Group 338, National Archives; "Possum," Folder Possum, Box 2, Entry ETO MIS-X, Record Group 332, National Archives; Neave, *Saturday at MI9,* 222–25. Possum is also commonly referred to as "Martin Marathon."

51. BCRA was an agency set up by de Gaulle's Free French Forces that practiced espionage and sabotage, placing it in direct conflict with England's SOE. David Schoenbrun, *Soldiers of the Night* (New York: New American Library, 1980), 82.

52. Georges Broussine, correspondence with author, January 1999. In author's files; "Reseau Broussine," Folder Reseau Burgundy, Box 1, Entry ETO MIS-X, Record Group 338, National Archives.

53. Neave, *Saturday at MI9,* 95.

54. Ibid., 311.

55. Long, *Safe Houses Are Dangerous,* 86; Murphy, *Turncoat,* 57.

56. Gordon Young, *In Trust and Treason,* 59.

57. Ibid., 59.

58. Long, *Safe Houses Are Dangerous,* 94; Neave, *Saturday at MI9,* 100; Cooper, *Free to Fight Again,* 20.

59. Murphy, *Turncoat,* 52–53.

60. Langley, *Fight Another Day,* 105.

61. Zarifi correspondence.

62. Caskie, *The Tartan Pimpernel,* 90.

63. Murphy, *Turncoat,* 108.

64. Brome, *The Way Back,* 38; Long, *Safe Houses Are Dangerous,* 87.

65. After delivering the men to the rendezvous—usually a café, bar, restaurant, or public park bench—Cole left, after which the next link in the line picked the men up. This kept the two sections of the line separate, neither knowing anything about the other. It was probably this precaution that limited Cole's betrayal to the northern section of the line. Long, *Safe Houses Are Dangerous,* 85.

66. Brome, *The Way Back,* 39–40.

67. Accounts differ with regard to Cole's reaction to Garrow's appearance at the party. As a result, it is unclear whether Garrow and O'Leary both attended, or Garrow alone. There is also a slightly different cast given to Cole's response in each account.

68. Murphy, *Turncoat,* 129; Brome, *The Way Back,* 40; Long, *Safe Houses Are Dangerous,* 98.

69. Spelling of the name Duprez varies. This spelling was taken from Pat O'Leary's personal intelligence report filed in the National Archives. "Rapport du Pat O'Leary," National Archives.

70. Brome, *The Way Back,* 42–43; Long, *Safe Houses Are Dangerous,* 100–101; Murphy, *Turncoat,* 130.

71. Murphy, *Turncoat,* 120, 123.

72. Long, *Safe Houses Are Dangerous,* 106–7.

73. "Rapport du Pat O'Leary," National Archives; Long, *Safe Houses Are Dangerous,* 124.

74. Murphy, *Turncoat,* 121.

75. Rodocanachi, *Memoir,* n.p. Most accounts state that four men were in the main room with Cole, while Duprez, the fifth, hid in the bathroom. Only three men are identified in any of the published works. Fanny Rodocanachi's memoir is the only work that identifies the fifth man. André Postel-Vinay, another worker on the escape line, waited in another room to meet with Dr. Rodocanachi.

76. Brome, *The Way Back,* 44. The meeting occurred on November 1, 1941.

77. Ibid., 44.

78. Brome, *The Way Back,* 45; Long, *Safe Houses Are Dangerous,* 112. O'Leary broke his hand when he hit Cole, and it remained misshapen for the rest of his life. Fearing he might reveal his true identity as a medical doctor, he chose not to ask Dr. Rodocanachi to set it for him.

79. Brome, *The Way Back,* 45.

80. Murphy, *Turncoat,* 154.

81. "Rapport du Mademoiselle Genevieve Fillerin," Folder Jean de la Olla, Box 110, Entry ETO MIS-X, Record Group 338, National Archives, Washington, D.C.; Long, *Safe Houses Are Dangerous,* 118.

82. Ross Christensen, "Papa's Tour de France," unpublished manuscript. Sent by Ross Christensen. In author's files. Dowding's Australian accent gave quite a shock to two of his fellow countrymen who were evading with the help of the Pat line. While following their guide, the two evaders were shocked when Dowding passed them on the street, winked, smiled, and whispered loudly, "Good day mate, how'd you like to be on Bondi Beach today?" They continued following their guide in some confusion and a few minutes later, found themselves given into Dowding's care.

83. Murphy, *Turncoat,* 137–51. There is disagreement as to whether this was the point at which Cole became a double agent. Some claim he had been a German agent for months previous to his arrest and present evidence to this end; however, it is inconclu-

sive as a result of the continued classified status of pertinent files. Verloop claims that he had no contact with Cole before his arrest on December 6.

84. Ibid., 153.

85. Brome, *The Way Back,* 49–50; Long, *Safe Houses Are Dangerous,* 119. Though Carpentier states that there were five men with Cole and that the German who arrested him entered later, other accounts claim there were only three men. Neave stated that the arrest of Carpentier was the first in which "fake" airmen were used, though it was not the last. Neave, *Saturday at MI9,* 84.

86. Ibid.; Anton Steinhoff, letter to Mr. Dowding, January 27, 1949. Provided by Peter Dowding. In author's files.

87. Brome, *The Way Back,* 97–99.

5. In the Wake of Betrayal: The Pat O'Leary Line, 1942–1943

1. "Pat O'Leary," French Helper Files, Folder Pat O'Leary, Box 309, Entry ETO MIS-X, Record Group 338, National Archives, Washington, D.C.

2. Darling, *Secret Sunday,* 54.

3. Brome, *The Way Back,* 79.

4. Ibid., 80. In reference to O'Leary's first radio operator, Brome wrote, "who will be referred to as Feriere...." Other accounts have used the same name. O'Leary called him Drouet in his military intelligence report. "Rapport du Pat O'Leary," National Archives.

5. Brome, *The Way Back,* 80, 87; "Rapport du Pat O'Leary," National Archives.

6. "Rapport du Mademoiselle Genevieve Fillerin," National Archives; Folder Jean de la Olla, Box 110, Entry ETO MIS-X, Record Group 338, National Archives, Washington, D.C.

7. Langley, *Fight Another Day,* 172; "Pat O'Leary," National Archives. Lysanders used open fields as landing spaces and depended on aid from Resistance workers on the ground to land. They usually remained on the ground only a few minutes and then returned to England.

8. Long, *Safe Houses Are Dangerous,* 156–58; "Pat O'Leary," National Archives.

9. Long, *Safe Houses Are Dangerous,* 154.

10. Darling, *Secret Sunday,* 60; Jack Misseldine, unpublished memoir. Sent by Jack Misseldine. In author's files.

11. "Rapport du Pat O'Leary," National Archives. Accounts by Brome, Neave, and Long state that there were six evacuations; however, only two are described in any detail. Langley writes that there were only three evacuations. O'Leary's report suggests that there were only five evacuations, identifying one from Pont Miou in June, two from St. Pierre Plage in July and August, and two from Canet Plage in September and October. Alex Wattebled confirms that there were five operations. Alex Wattebled, correspondence with author, February 1999. In author's files.

12. Dumais, *The Man Who Went Back* (London: Leo Cooper, 1975), 91; Brome, *The Way Back,* 111; "Rapport du Pat O'Leary," National Archives; Brome refers to Mme LeBreton as Mme Chouquette.

13. "Rapport du Alex Wattebled," Folder Pat O'Leary, Box 1, Entry ETO MIS-X, Record Group 338, National Archives, Washington, D.C.

14. Brome, *The Way Back,* 111–12.

15. Brome, *The Way Back,* 112–13.

16. Wattebled correspondence; Brome, *The Way Back,* 114.

17. Brome, *The Way Back,* 115.

18. Ibid., 116.

19. Ibid., 116.

20. The turnover rate of radio operators was quite high, and none of O'Leary's operators lasted more than two to three months before being arrested. Jean Nitelet was arrested in late August, and Roger Gaston in early September. Both of the evacuations from Canet Plage were arranged with the help of Vallat, an operator from another organization, who was himself arrested in October. "Rapport du Pat O'Leary," National Archives; Langley, *Fight Another Day,* 177.

21. "Rapport du Pat O'Leary," National Archives; Brome, *The Way Back,* 116.

22. Langley, *Fight Another Day,* 176; Brome, *The Way Back,* 119.

23. Brome, *The Way Back,* 120.

24. Dumais, *The Man Who Went Back,* 93; Brome, *The Way Back,* 121.

25. Neave, *Saturday at MI9,* 107.

26. Rodocanachi, *Memoir;* Long, *Safe Houses Are Dangerous,* 174, 183, 189.

27. "Rapport du Pat O'Leary," National Archives.

28. Neave, *Saturday at MI9,* 111; Langley, *Fight Another Day,* 184.

29. Brome, *The Way Back,* 130; "Rapport du Pat O'Leary," National Archives; Braddon, *Nancy Wake,* 51. Braddon's account differs considerably from Brome's; however, both establish that Wake and O'Leary did work together on this operation. This is further substantiated in O'Leary's report.

30. Brome, *The Way Back,* 130.

31. Ibid., 132.

32. Berthet died at Mauthausen concentration camp in January 1944 after being arrested in a subsequent operation for the Pat line. "Rapport du Pat O'Leary," National Archives.

33. Barry Wynne, *No Drums . . . No Trumpets* (London: Arthur Baker, 1961), 148. Groome had originally been assigned as radio operator for Mary Lindell's escape line. Repeated efforts to air drop Groome and Lindell had aggravated incompatible feelings between the two of them because Groome got hopelessly airsick every time he flew. Besides the fact that she simply did not like him, Lindell was convinced that he would be incapable of serving her in France and asked that he be released from her service. Instead, he was assigned to O'Leary, with whom he got along admirably, and played a significant role in Garrow's escape.

34. Some accounts claim the operation was carried out at the end of the night shift. Brome's account identifies it as the end of the day shift. Though he comments on the operation, O'Leary's report does not identify the time of day. He does, however, set the date as December 8, 1942, while other accounts give the date as December 6, 1942. Ironically, December 6 was exactly one year to the day after Cole's arrest.

35. Brome, *The Way Back,* 132–33.

36. Ibid., 133–34.

37. Ibid., 134.

38. Ibid., 135; Neave, *Saturday at MI9,* 115.

39. Brome, *The Way Back,* 136.

40. "Rapport du Pat O'Leary," National Archives; Brome, *The Way Back,* 136.

41. Brome, *The Way Back,* 135; Neave, *Saturday at MI9,* 115–16.

42. The Hotel Du Paris was run by M. and Mme Mongelard, who were associated with the escape line. Georges Broussine and other airmen had hidden there while await-

ing passage to Spain. Both were later arrested and deported. M. Mongelard died, but Mme Mongelard, though brutally tortured, survived Ravensbrük concentration camp.

43. See Chapter Two for information on Mme Cheramy's experience at the hands of the Gestapo.

44. Brome, *The Way Back,* 146.

45. "Rapport du Pat O'Leary," National Archives; Brome, *The Way Back,* 147–48; Neave, *Saturday at MI9,* 118–19.

46. "Rapport du Pat O'Leary," National Archives; Brome, *The Way Back,* 148.

47. "Rapport du Pat O'Leary," National Archives. Groome and O'Leary were reunited in late summer 1943 at Fresnes prison in Paris. They were deported to Germany, where they managed to stay together despite transfers to several concentration camps. Both survived and were liberated from Dachau together in 1945.

48. "Rapport du Pat O'Leary," National Archives; "Rapport du Alex Wattebled," National Archives; "Rapport du Mademoiselle Genevieve Fillerin," National Archives.

49. "Rapport du Pat O'Leary," National Archives; Brome, *The Way Back,* 150.

50. Bayliss, *No Flying Without Wings,* 144.

51. Colin Bayliss was the evader. Bayliss was unaware that he had been betrayed by his guide. Ironically, he spent the next fifty years feeling guilty about the likelihood that Le Neveu had been shot or deported for helping him. In 1992, he learned that Le Neveu had betrayed him.

52. Nouveau, *Des Capitaines Par Milliers,* Chapter 12.

53. Nouveau, *Des Capitaines Par Milliers,* Chapter 12; Brome *The Way Back,* 151; Neave, *Saturday at MI9,* 120.

54. Nouveau, *Des Capitaines Par Milliers,* Chapter 12.

55. "Rapport du Pat O'Leary," National Archives; Brome, *The Way Back,* 162; Neave, *Saturday at MI9,* 120; Long, *Safe Houses Are Dangerous,* 185.

56. "Rapport du Pat O'Leary," National Archives; Brome *The Way Back,* 163–64; Long, *Safe Houses Are Dangerous,* 186.

57. "Rapport du Alex Wattebled," National Archives; Brome, *The Way Back,* 155–56.

58. "Rapport du Alex Wattebled," National Archives; Brome *The Way Back,* 157.

59. "Rapport du Mademoiselle Genevieve Fillerin," National Archives.

60. Brome, *The Way Back,* 160.

61. Ibid., 173. "Rapport du Pat O'Leary," National Archives. O'Leary stated in his intelligence report that he was "tortured a little," but in fact, he was brutally beaten. He met Paul Ulmann in a prison cell the first night, but never saw him again. Ulmann was Jewish and was probably deported and killed.

62. "Rapport du Pat O'Leary," National Archives; Brome, *The Way Back,* 183. Fabien de Cortes survived the war and remained close to Pat throughout his life.

63. "Pat O'Leary," National Archives. See chapter 8 for information concerning Pat's post-war life.

6. Riding the Tail of a Comet: The Comet Line, 1941–1944

1. First names will be used in some instances throughout this chapter to avoid confusion, due to the fact that many of Comet's workers came from the same family and shared the same last name.

2. "Cométe: Historique de la Ligne," History of the French Evasion Networks, Folder Comet, Box 1, Entry ETO MIS-X, Record Group 338, National Archives, Washington, D.C.

3. "Cométe: Historique de la Ligne," National Archives.

4. Jean Rafferty, "The Last of the Line," *Sunday Times Magazine,* 11, June 1989, 21–27.

5. "Rapport de Andrée de Jongh," History of the French Evasion Networks, Folder Comet, Box 1, Entry ETO MIS-X, Record Group 338, National Archives, Washington, D.C.; "Reseau History," Folder Comet, Box 1, Entry ETO MIS-X, Record Group 338, National Archives, Washington, D.C. "GoGo" was the name of the de Greefs' deceased pet bulldog.

6. "Albert Edward Johnson," *Royal Air Forces Escaping Society–Australian Branch Newsletter,* February 10, 1998, No. 1, p. 1.

7. "Rapport de Andrée de Jongh," National Archives; Rossiter, *Women in the Resistance,* 26–27; Rafferty, "Last of the Line," 24.

8. "Reseau History," National Archives.

9. Cecile Jouan, *Cométe: Histoire d'une Ligne d'Evasion,* Furnes, Belgium: Editions du Belfroi, 1948, 11; "Cométe: Historique de la Ligne," National Archives; Juan Carlos Jiménez de Aberasturi, *En Passant La Bidassoa* (Biarritz, France: Société Atlantique d'Impression, 1996), 29.

10. Nothomb–Rossiter interview.

11. "Rapport de Andrée de Jongh," National Archives.

12. The amount that is given in several of the intelligence reports is thirty-two hundred pesetas.

13. Langley, *Fight Another Day,* 166–67.

14. "Rapport de Andrée de Jongh," National Archives.

15. Langley, *Fight Another Day,* 169.

16. "Rapport de Andrée de Jongh," National Archives; "Tante Go," History of French Evasion Networks, Folder Comet, Box 1, Entry ETO MIS-X, Record Group 338, National Archives, Washington, D.C.

17. Darling, *Secret Sunday,* 57; Long, *Safe Houses Are Dangerous,* 92; Neave, *Saturday at MI9,* 79.

18. The Basque territory runs along the edge of the Pyrenees on both the French and Spanish side. The inhabitants speak neither French nor Spanish, but Basque.

19. Neave, *Saturday at MI9,* 138–39; Cosgrove, *The Evaders,* 34. Florentino had little use for the money given to him by MI9 in payment for his services. Not knowing what else to do with it, he stuffed the money in a kitchen cabinet, where it was found after the war. Nothomb–Rossiter interview.

20. Cosgrove, *The Evaders,* 35.

21. Neave, *Saturday at MI9,* 141; John Dix, "Come Walk With Me," unpublished manuscript. Sent by John Dix. In author's files.

22. Cosgrove, *The Evaders,* 35.

23. "Reseau History," National Archives; Darling, *Secret Sunday,* 55–56.

24. "Tante Go," National Archives. The number of times the helpers crossed the mountains refers to round trips.

25. Jouan, *Cométe,* 26; "Rapport de Andrée de Jongh," National Archives.

26. "Rapport de Andrée de Jongh," National Archives. Morelle was later executed. The line intended to evacuate his wife, Renée, and children to England, but Renée wanted to see her mother a last time before she left. While in Belgium for this purpose, she was killed during an air raid. After the war, Charlie's sister Elvire raised the children. "Tante Go," National Archives; Nothomb–Rossiter interview.

27. "Rapport de Andrée de Jongh," National Archives; Jouan, *Cométe,* 31.

28. Neave, *Saturday at MI9,* 135.

29. "Rapport de Raymonde Coache," French Helper Files, Folder Raymonde Coache, Box 83, Entry ETO MIS-X, Record Group 338, National Archives, Washington, D.C.; "Rapport de Andrée de Jongh," National Archives; Neave, *Saturday at MI9,* 136. Aylé was a member of the Free French Forces, so had numerous contacts with other Resistance organizations.

30. Using the name Cecile Jouan, Suzanne de Wittek wrote the book *Cométe,* which has been cited in this work. Written in 1948, its purpose was to let the many helpers know more about the organization with which they had worked throughout the war.

31. "Rapport de Andrée de Jongh," National Archives; "Tante Go," National Archives. Efforts were also being made at this time to help Charles and Michelli escape. Greindl negotiated with a German official through a mediating lawyer, "Y." The effort proved unsuccessful and "Y" was later arrested and executed.

32. Little is known of the exact activities of these centers since Greindl, Ingels, and others associated with their organization were executed or died during the war. "Report of Albert Greindl on Activities of Jean
Greindl," Folder: Jean Greindl. Reference No. AA1333. Bestand snlichtings—en octiendiensten van de Veiligheid van de staat. Belgian State Security. CEGES. Brussels, Belgium; Andrée de Jongh, correspondence with author, September 2000.

33. Rafferty, "The Last of the Line," 25.

34. "Rapport de Andrée de Jongh," National Archives; Neave, *Saturday at MI9,* 147.

35. "Rapport de Andrée de Jongh," National Archives.

36. Jouan, *Cométe,* 52–53.

37. Ibid., 53.

38. Ibid., 53.

39. "Rapport de Andrée de Jongh," National Archives; Jouan, *Cométe,* 67.

40. "Rapport de Andrée de Jongh," National Archives; Jouan, *Cométe,* 53; Neave, *Saturday at MI9,* 149.

41. Jouan, *Cométe,* 54; "Rapport de Andrée de Jongh," National Archives; Neave, *Saturday at MI9,* 149.

42. "Tante Go," National Archives; "Rapport de Andrée de Jongh," National Archives; Neave, *Saturday at MI9,* 154. Because the apartment used by Dédée and Frederic was rented in Elvire's name, they moved as soon as they received word of her arrest.

43. Van Lier Langley–Rossiter interview, October 17, 1976; Jouan, *Cométe,* 55; Neave, *Saturday at MI9,* Neave states that van Lier spoke German fluently, but in an interview with Rossiter, van Lier Langley said that her German speaking ability was very weak. The officers in the photographs were old family friends.

44. Van Lier Langley–Rossiter interview. Van Lier Langley said she was always helped by a "jolly good prayer." Before convoying evaders, she always prayed, "Grace of God descend on you."

45. Neave, *Saturday at MI9,* 164.

46. Neave, *Saturday at MI9,* 144; Langley, *Fight Another Day,* 169; Nothomb–Rossiter interview.

47. Jouan, *Cométe,* 56.

48. Neave, *Saturday at MI9,* 157.

49. "Tante Go," National Archives; "Rapport de Andrée de Jongh," National Archives.

50. "Rapport de Andrée de Jongh," National Archives; "Tante Go," National Archives.

51. "Cométe: Historique de la Ligne," National Archives; "Rapport de Andrée de Jongh," National Archives; "Tante Go," National Archives; Jouan, *Cométe,* 59; "Note on my Arrest" (Jan. 15, 1943), Folder: Andrée de Jongh, CEGES, Brussels, Belgium.

52. Jouan, *Comête*, 63; Neave, *Saturday at MI9*, 157.

53. "Rapport de Andrée de Jongh," National Archives; "Tante Go," National Archives; Jouan, *Comête*, 71. Dassié was a veteran of World War I. He died shortly after being released from a concentration camp. Neither he nor any of his family betrayed the line.

54. "Tante Go," National Archives; Jouan, *Comête*, 71; Neave, *Saturday at MI9*, 165; "Rapport de Andrée de Jongh," National Archives. Johnson went to work for MI9 and returned to France after the liberation of Paris to work with the Awards Bureau, established to care for the needs of helpers who were suffering.

55. Neave, *Saturday at MI9*, 163.

56. "Jean Greindl." Centre d'Etudes et de Documentation Guerre et Sociétés Contemporaines, Brussels, Belgium; Jouan, *Comête*, 67; Neave, *Saturday at MI9*, 164; "Report of Suzanne de Wittek," Folder: Elsie Maréchal, CEGES, Brussels, Belgium; "Report of the Interrogation of Otto Weil," Folder: Jean Greindl, CEGES, Brussels, Belgium.

57. "Report of Dr. Pfaw," Folder: Jean Greindl, CEGES, Brussels, Belgium.

58. "Report of Werner Theiss," Folder: Jean Greindl, CEGES, Brussels, Belgium.

59. Neave, *Saturday at MI9*, 151–52.

60. Jouan, *Comête*, 189–90.

61. "Reseau Burgundy," National Archives; "Reseau Brandy," History of French Evasion Networks, Folder Evasion Reseau Brandy, Box 1, Entry ETO MIS-X, Record Group 338, National Archives, Washington, D.C.; "Rapport de Andrée de Jongh," National Archives. None of the helpers was aware of Masson's real name until after the war.

62. "Raymonde Coache," National Archives. Coache passed through eleven prisons before finally being sent to Ravensbrük, then Mauthausen, where the inmates suffered from hunger and physical mistreatment. At Cottbus prison, she found Elvire Morelle and several other Comet helpers.

63. "Personalities of SD Counter-Evasion Service (Paris), Summer of 1944," Folder DDE Personal Investigations and Actions on SD Counter-Evasion Service, Box 3, Entry ETO MIS-X, Record Group 332, National Archives, Washington, D.C. Bouteloupt died shortly after returning to France as a result of mistreatment during her imprisonment in a concentration camp.

64. Jouan, *Comête*, 89; Neave, *Saturday at MI9*, 169; "Personalities of SD Counter-Evasion Service," National Archives; "Interview with Michou," Rossiter papers; History of French Evasion Networks, Folder Comet, Box 1, Entry ETO MIS-X, Record Group 338, National Archives, Washington, D.C.

65. "Personalities of SD Counter-Evasion Service," National Archives; "Interview with Michou," Rossiter papers.

66. Georges Broussine, correspondence with author, February 13, 1999. In author's files.

67. "Personalities of SD Counter-Evasion Service," National Archives; "Evasion Reseau Brandy," National Archives. Jean Masson's real name was Jacques Desoubrie, and he was one of the most callous traitors of World War II. He began his efforts against the escape lines in 1941 and continued working for the German Gestapo throughout the war. In 1944, he renewed his efforts against the newly restored Comet line, penetrating it a second time after disguising his looks and taking the name Pierre Boulain.

68. Jean François Nothomb, correspondence with author, March 12, 1999, in author's files; Neave, *Saturday at MI9*, 170.

69. "Report on the Activities of Agent Legrelle," National Archives; "Rapport de Andrée de Jongh," National Archives; Neave, *Saturday at MI9*, 173. Legrelle broke his back while parachute training in England and spent several months recuperating. As a result, he

could not be parachuted into France. He flew to Gibraltar, then sailed to Madrid and crossed the Pyrenees on foot.

70. "Cométe: The Agent Jean Jacques' Report," Folder Comet, Box 1, Entry ETO MIS-X, Record Group 338, National Archives, Washington, D.C.; "Rapport de Andrée de Jongh," National Archives.

71. "Cométe: The Agent Jean Jacques' Report;""Report on the Activities of Agent Legrelle," National Archives.

72."Report on the Activities of Agent Legrelle," National Archives.

73. Two other men traveled with them also—a Belgian by the name of Daniel Mouton and an unidentified Frenchman.

74. Jean François Nothomb, "Excerpt from Memoirs of Jean François Nothomb," *Communications,* vol. 6, no. 2, summer 1992, 5. The remaining three airmen crossed into Spain, where they were arrested by Spanish patrols and later released to Allied personnel. USAAF Robert Grimes was one of these. A memorial marks the place where the two men drowned.

75. "Report on the Activities of Agent Legrelle," National Archives; "Cométe: Jean Jacques," National Archives.

76. "Report on the Activities of Agent Legrelle," National Archives.

77. "Report on the Activities of Agent Legrelle," National Archives; Neave, *Saturday at MI9,* 180.

78. Nothomb correspondence.

79. "Interview with Michou," Rossiter papers.

80. Nothomb correspondence; Nothomb–Rossiter interview;"Report on the Activities of Agent Legrelle," National Archives.

81. Jouan, *Cométe,* 193; "Report of Philippe d'Albert Lake," Rossiter papers, Folder Virginia d'Albert Lake. The five men were Thomas H. Hubbard, Donald K. Willis, and Jack D. Cornett, of the USAAF, and Leonard A. Barnes and Ronald T. Emeny of the RAF.

82. Rossiter, *Women in the Resistance,* 31.

7. Out of the Ashes: The Shelburne Line, 1944

1. Moreau correspondence.

2. Bouryschkine was born in Russia, but reared in the United States. At the outbreak of the war, he was in France working for the American Red Cross. Donald Caskie convinced him to remain in France to help evaders. Labrosse was a member of the Canadian Signal Corps.

3. Langley, *Fight Another Day,* 193.

4. Langley wrote that the effort to keep Bouryschkine happily occupied during the interval between drop attempts "drove me nearly mad." Langley, *Fight Another Day,* 193.

5. Roger Huguen, *Par Les Nuits Les Plus Longues* (Spézet, France: Coop Breizh, 1993), 250–51.

6. Raymond Labrosse, taped interview with Margaret Rossiter, undated, Rossiter papers.

7. Eventually the Comet line's Jean François Nothomb carried a radio over the Pyrenees and left it in a locker at the train station, where Labrosse later collected it. Unfortunately, the line collapsed soon afterwards, so it was probably not used more than once or twice, if at all.

8. Alain Le Nédélec, *Les Nuits de la Liberté* (St. Brieuc, France: Presses Bretonnes, 1993), 36; Huguen, *Par Les Nuits Les Plus Longues,* 259; Moreau correspondence.

9. The Chateau de Bourblanc where Countess de Mauduit lived was located near Paimpol, about nine miles from Plouha. She spent two years in Ravensbrük as a result of her Resistance activity sheltering airmen.

10. Jouanjean, "The War and its Bitterness."

11. Huguen, *Par Les Nuits Les Plus Longues,* 262. The Françoise network was organized by Françoise Dissart, one of the chief agents in Toulouse for the former Pat line.

12. Neave, *Saturday at MI9,* 223; Huguen, *Par Les Nuits Les Plus Longues,* 263. Jouanjean, de Mauduit, and a number of others were arrested as a result of Le Neveu's activities. Many of those helpers who were not arrested were forced to flee the area, hiding from the Gestapo and relying on the aid of others in order to survive. Val Williams was known to the Gestapo for his work on the Pat line, but they were unaware of his association with Oaktree, which stopped them from making further inquiries into his Brittany connections.

13. "Burgundy," National Archives; Georges Broussine, correspondence with author, March 9, 1999. In author's files; Labrosse–Rossiter interview. With permission from MI9, Broussine asked Labrosse to remain in France in the service of the Burgundy line, but Labrosse chose to return to England instead.

14. Neave, *Saturday at MI9,* 109.

15. Hugeun, *Par Les Nuits Plus Les Longues,* 285. Neave and Rossiter both date the landing as October 1943, but according to Raymond Labrosse, the date was in November.

16. Dumais, *The Man Who Went Back,* 127.

17. Le Nédélec, *Les Nuits de la Liberté,* 42; Labrosse–Rossiter interview.

18. Shelburne was not the only line to evacuate airmen across the channel. Several French people organized small evasion lines from France to England during the war years, including Ernest Sibiril, Yves Le Henaff ("FanFan"), and numerous others.

19. See Appendix B for a list of the men who were transferred from Burgundy to Shelburne. "Burgundy," National Archives. Broussine, correspondence, March 9, 1999.

20. "The Case of Zerling, Marie Rose, 'Claudette,'" Correspondence Regarding French Aid to American Airmen, Folder XYZ, Box 7, Entry ETO MIS-X, Record Group 338, National Archives, Washington, D.C.

21. "Escape and Evasion Report 460 Edward Donaldson," Folder Edward Donaldson #460, Box 14, Entry ETO MIS-X, Record Group 332, National Archives, Washington, D.C.

22. Dumais, *The Man Who Went Back,* 157–58; "The Case of Zerling, Marie Rose 'Claudette,'" National Archives.

23. Huguen, *Par Les Nuits Les Plus Longues,* 340.

24. "Escape and Evasion Report 461 Neelan Parker," Folder Neelan Parker #461, Box 14, Entry ETO MIS-X, Record Group 332, National Archives, Washington, D.C.

25. Auvert, "Memoirs 1940–1945," 9.

26. Richard Smith, *Hide and Seek With the German Army,* 25.

27. Rossiter, *Women in the Resistance,* 79–80; Dumais, *The Man Who Went Back,* 163.

28. Neave, *Saturday at MI9,* 236.

29. Buckner, "Down and Out In Forty-Four Days,"

30. Marie Thérése was courageous and well respected among those whom she helped and with whom she worked. Shortly after the war, she suffered a nervous breakdown from which she never recovered. Lloyd Bott, *The Secret War From the River Dart* (Dartmouth, Eng.: Dartmouth History Research Group, 1997), 35; Labrosse–Rossiter interview.

31. Buckner, "Down and Out In Forty-Four Days."

32. Dumais, *The Man Who Went Back,* 147; Neave, *Saturday at MI9,* 229; Lavender and Sheffe, *The Evaders,* 95. The code messages were later changed to protect against penetration.

33. Dumais, *The Man Who Went Back,* 148.

34. Bott, *The Secret War From the River Dart,* 1. The Shelburne operations were conducted by each of three motor gunboats: MGB 502, MGB 503, and MGB 718. MGB 502 hit a floating mine off the Norwegian coast on May 12, 1945. All but three of the twenty-six-member crew were killed immediately, as were four passengers. Three crewmen—Tom Sheehan, Norman Hine, and Fred Bristow—climbed on a floating device, but Bristow later slipped off and Sheehan and Hine were too weak to help him. The two survivors were finally rescued three days later, barely alive. Due to damage from exposure, Sheehan had to have both legs amputated below the knee, though Hine only lost his toes. The greatest tragedy of the loss of the courageous crew was that it happened after the war was over.

35. Dumais, *The Man Who Went Back,* 149. Though Dumais's book specifies that the men were to hold on to coattails, the personal accounts of the airmen claim they were told to hold onto shoulders.

36. Huguen, *Par Les Nuits Les Plus Longues,* 208; Rossiter, *Women in the Resistance,* 83.

37. Sutor, unpublished manuscript.

38. Dumais, *The Man Who Went Back,* 151; Rossiter, *Women in the Resistance,* 80.

39. On at least one occasion, the crew manning the rowboat was unable to find its way back to the boat as a result of heavy fog and had to be left behind. Anne Roper recalled that the three men stayed at her parents' house while waiting for the next evacuation operation. Anne Roper, correspondence with author, February 18, 1998. In author's files; Keith Sutor recalled being deathly afraid that he would be washed overboard as the waves were washing over the edge of the rowboat, and he did not know how to swim. Sutor, unpublished manuscript.

40. The motor gunboats disembarked the men at Dartmouth, England.

41. Lavender and Sheffe, *The Evaders,* 111.

42. "Report of Ralph Patton about his escape from France," Folder Ralph Patton, Rossiter papers.

43. The dates for the operations were as follows: January 28, February 26, March 16, March 19, and March 23. Bott, *The Secret War From the River Dart,* 37.

44. Dumais, *The Man Who Went Back,* 161.

45. Albert Speer, *Inside the Third Reich.* Translated by Richard and Clara Winston (New York: Galahad Books, 1970), 253; Huguen, *Par Les Nuits Les Plus Longues,* 348. After the war, German prisoners were assigned the job of digging up the mines, and to the surprise of Huet and Mainguy, they dug up eighteen instead of the seventeen that had been detected and marked. Luckily, no one had stepped on the mine during the four evacuations that were conducted after April 1944. Jean Tréhiou stated that one area designated by the Germans as a minefield revealed no mines when the war ended. He claimed there was more propaganda involved with the minefields than actual mines. Jean Tréhiou, personal interview with author, July 18, 1999. In author's files.

46. The dates for these operations were June 15, July 12, and July 23. Bott, *The Secret War From the River Dart,* 37–38.

47. Marie Gicquel, "My Story," unpublished manuscript. Sent by Marie Gicquel. In author's files; Huguen, *Par Les Nuits Les Plus Longues,* 358–61.

48. Gicquel, "My Story." Jean left France that night on the motor gunboat that had

come to collect the British officers. He returned to France five months later.

49. Though Airey Neave claims 365 airmen were rescued, the more common number cited by M.R.D. Foot, Dumais, and the Air Forces Escape and Evasion Society is 307.

50. Roger Le Neveu did attempt to penetrate the line, but was unsuccessful.

51. William Spinning, *Operation Bonaparte* (Birmingham, Eng.: William H. Spinning, 1965), 24.

8. We Will Never Forget: The Aftermath

1. Cooper, *Free To Fight Again,* 30.

2. Gordon Carter, correspondence with author, January 15, 1998. In author's files.

3. Carter correspondence. Raymond Labrosse also married a French helper, Ginette Dorré, the daughter of the man who housed him. Ginette helped him carry out radio transmissions during the war.

4. "Jean de la Olla," National Archives.

5. Gabriel Nahas, conversation with author, May 9, 1998.

6. Cheramy, "The Quiet Heroine," June 9, 1973.

7. Brome, *The Way Back,* 246–47; Neave, *Saturday at MI9,* 314; Obituary for "Major General Albert Marie Guerisse," *London Times* March 29, 1989.

8. Darling, *Secret Sunday,* 101, 177.

9. "Letter of Andrée de Jongh to Evasion Services Administrator," Jan. 15, 1948, Folder: Jean Greindl, CEGES, Brussels, Belgium.

10. Jean François Nothomb, correspondence with author, March 12, 1999. In author's files.

11. Braddon, *Nancy Wake,* 142.

12. "Jacques Desoubrie," MIS-X Miscellaneous Files, Folder DDE Personal Investigations and Actions on SD Counter-Evasion Service, Box 3, Entry ETO MIS-X, Record Group 332, National Archives, Washington, D.C.; Neave, *Saturday at MI9,* 307.

13. Young, *In Trust and Treason,* 125.

14. "Traitor Dies In Battle," newspaper articles, folder unlabeled, Box 1, Entry ETO MIS-X, Record Group 338, National Archives, Washington, D.C.

15. "Traitor Dies In Battle," National Archives; "British Deserter, Resistance Traitor, Is Killed In Paris," newspaper articles, folder unlabeled, Box 1, Entry ETO MIS-X, Record Group 338, National Archives, Washington, D.C.; Neave, *Saturday at MI9,* 308–10.

16. Brown correspondence.

17. Cooper, *Free To Fight Again,* 235–36. In 1995, RAFES closed the social portion of the organization, but kept up the charitable agency until January 1, 2000, under the able leadership of Elizabeth Harrison.

18. Clayton David, "AFEES History Dates Back to '64," *Communications,* spring 1995, 5.

19. This will be covered in more detail in the conclusion.

20. Jill Nichols, correspondence with author, October 1998.

21. Bubenzer, "Shot Down In Occupied France," 99.

22. Arnould correspondence.

23. Sutor, unpublished manuscript.

24. Kenney, unpublished manuscript.

25. Darling, *Secret Sunday,* 74.

26. Langley, *Fight Another Day,* 252.

27. Langley, *Fight Another Day,* 202, 254.

Bibliography

Few competitive works are available to compete with this study, not because of a lack of interest, but because most of what has been written is out of print. The last twenty years have seen the history of the escape lines sorely neglected, at least in the English-speaking countries. What literature there is has been based largely on interviews or references to earlier works written by former members of British intelligence and lacks documentation of any kind. The books written by intelligence agents Airey Neave, James Langley, and Donald Darling are extremely valuable, since without them, it would be difficult to develop a sense of the way the lines worked in connection with Allied intelligence. But since the early 1980s, valuable military intelligence documents outlining the history of the various escape lines, the work of individual people, and some of the work of American intelligence agencies have been declassified and made available to researchers. These papers and documents—in addition to correspondence, interviews, and earlier literature—enable historians to present a more accurate picture of the work of the evasion networks and provide a framework for future exploration of this important part of the history of the war. This study is the first comprehensive examination to be done on the escape lines in twenty to thirty years and the only one that contains complete documentation to support the author's claims.

Works in the area of escape and evasion can be divided into three categories: intelligence, evaders' and helpers' stories, and escape lines. In the area of intelligence, Donald Darling (1975), Airey Neave (1969), M.R.D. Foot and J.M. Langley (1980), and Lloyd Shoemaker (1990) have done works related to the lines, but all of them are out of print. In addition, some were published only in England and have never been available in the United States. Of these, only Shoemaker's book uses documentation of sources. Foot and Langley provided a good bibliography but did not document the material used in the text.

There are three fairly recent books available that present escape and evasion using personal accounts from evaders or helpers, but none of them provide any documentation of sources. Philip Caine (USA 1997), Ian Dear (England 1997), and Emerson Lavender and Norman Sheffe (Canada 1992) have all published works of this kind. While these are easily attainable for purchase, they are lacking when one considers the vast amount of material currently available in the National Archives. Dear's work could have been far more beneficial if he had provided references to his original sources and if he had contacted participants of the escape lines—either evaders or helpers—both of whom could have provided him with valuable material and possibly corrected some of his misstatements.

Like the works dealing with intelligence, all of those related to the escape lines are also out of print. These include works by Margaret Rossiter (1986), Helen Long (England 1985), Vincent Brome (1958), Barry Wynne (England 1961), and Lucien Dumais (England 1975). Of these, only Rossiter documented her material. She was also the only author to use the valuable archival papers available. However, Rossiter's book focused on women involved with the Resistance and as such, only touched on the evasion networks. While Long provided a small bibliography, the other works are based completely on the personal remembrance of the participants.

All of these books have great value in this field of study, but the research done for this book is of much wider scope and has incorporated numerous elements that have allowed a more accurate and complete view of the escape lines of World War II and the people involved with operating them.

There is much study yet to be done on the escape lines. Escape and evasion took place throughout Europe during the war, almost always with the help of civilian people. The lines through Holland, Belgium, and Italy are all waiting to be explored and their histories recounted for a new group of readers largely ignorant about the work of the helpers.

Unpublished Primary Sources

Centre de Documents Historiques, Military Archives. Brussels, Belgium.

H.Q., Air Force Service Command, in USAF Collection. Air Force Historical Research Agency (AFHRA), Maxwell Air Force Base, Montgomery, Alabama.

Margaret Rossiter Papers. Harlan Hatcher Graduate Library, University of Michigan, Ann Arbor.

Operational Chronology of the Carpetbaggers. 801st Bomber Group. Maxwell Air Force Base, Montgomery, Alabama.

Records of Belgian State Security, Evasion Service. Centre d'Etudes et de Documentation Guerre et Sociétés, Brussels, Belgium.

Records of European Theater of Operations U.S. Army (ETOUSA)/U.S. Forces European Theater (USFET). Record Group 338. National Archives, Washington, D.C.

Records of Headquarters MIS-X (Military Intelligence Service, Escape and Evasion Section) Detachment. Record Group 332. National Archives, Washington, D.C.

Communications with Participants

Note: Correspondence Unless Otherwise Noted

Hélène Deschamps Adams   Hélène Arnould   Leslie Atkinson
Claude Bacchi   Maurice Bidaud   Harold Brennan   Georges Broussine
John Brown   George Buckner   Merrill Caldwell (audiotape)
Alain Camard   Gordon Carter   David Chapple   Paul and Betty Clark
Andrée de Jongh   Nadine Dumon   David Goldberg   Pat Hicton
Raymond Itterbeek   Stan Jolly   Yvonne Kervarec   Charles Kroschel
Stan Lawrence   Desiré Le Cren   René Le Cren   Maurice Leech
John McGlynn   Maryse de la Marnierre McKeon   François Moal
Reine Mocaer   Alan Monaghan (audiotape)   Pierre Moreau
Gabrielle Nahas (personal interview)   Jean François Nothomb
Keith Patrick   Ralph Patton   Marguerite Pierre   Jean Jacques Piot
Anne Roper   Alain Sibiril   Olympe St. Leger   Jean and Jeanne Tréhiou
David Turner   Joe Walters   Alex Wattebled   Albert Leslie Wright
Thomas Yankus   Georges Zarifi

Communications with Non-Participants

Clarke Brandt   Peter Dowding   Claude Hélias   Randy Johnson
Michael Leblanc   Jill Nichols

Unpublished Memoirs

Note: All of the following may be found in author's files:
Auvert, Bertranne. "Memoirs 1940–1945." [Typescript]
Barlow, Roland. Untitled. [Typescript]
Buckner, George. "Down and Out In Forty-Four Days." [Typescript]
Charpentier, René. "Souvenirs De Jeunesse La Guerre 1939–1945, La Resistance."
    [Typescript]
Cheney, Donald. "Adventure in France 1944." [Typescript]
Christensen, Ross. "Papa's Tour De France." [Typescript]
D'Arcey, Tony. Untitled. [Typescript]
Dix, John. "Come Walk With Me." [Typescript]
Eveland, Wayne. "Memories and Reflections." [Typescript]
Gicquel, Marie. "My Story." [Typescript]
Hines, Frank. Untitled. [Typescript]
Horsley, Robert. "Maximum Effort." [Typescript]
Jouanjean, Georges. "The War and Its Bitterness." [Typescript]
Kenney, Paul. Untitled. [Manuscript]
Marco, Virgil. "A Little Bit of History." [Typescript]

Martin, Alfred. Untitled. [Typescript]
McKee, Ralph. "The Winged Boot." [Typescript]
Mead, John. Untitled. [Typescript]
Mills, Milton. "One Hundred Fourteen Days in German-Occupied France."
      [Typescript]
Misseldine, Jack. Untitled. [Typescript]
Mocaer, Reine. Untitled. [Typescript]
Rodocanachi, Fanny. "Memoir: Dr. Georges Rodocanachi." [Typescript]
Stead, Jack. Untitled. [Typescript]
Sutor, Keith. Untitled. [Typescript]

Sources Consulted but Not Cited

Note: All of the following people provided useful information that, though not cited in the study, contributed greatly to my knowledge and understanding of the topic.

Correspondents

AFEES   J.W. Bradbury   René Defourneaux   Tom Emsminger
Pierre Demalvillain   Elizabeth Harrison   Eric Goodman
Dr. Patrick Guérisse   Emmanuel Huille   Dany Lemoine
Christopher Long   Tom Morgan   RAFES–Australian Branch
RAFES–Canadian Branch   RAFES–England   Mrs. H.P. Rouillard
Roger Stanton

Helpers

Marcel Closset   Paulette Declerq   Odile De Vaselot
Raymond and Jeanne Gaborit   Gervais Gorge   Jean Pena
Jean and Jeanne Tréhiou

Royal Air Force

Terry Bolter   Alan Day   Bert Dowty   Norman MacKenzie
Harry Simister   George Woods

Royal Australian Air Force

C.A. Campbell   R.G. Collins   Jack Down   Don Dyson   Noel Elliot
Edwin Greatz   Stan Hawkins   Mrs. Bob Hunter   Mr. and Mrs. Ian Innes
Stan Jolly   Arthur Levy   Bob Lindsey   Neil Roggenkamp
Phil Smith   Dudley Ubbotson

Royal Canadian Air Force

Douglas Cox   T.J. Kanakos   Tom Lynch   Angus MacLean   John Neal
Keith Patrick   Raymond Sherk   Maurice Smith   Thomas Wilby

United States Army Air Force

James Armstrong   Clare Blair   Bill Davis   Fred Gleason
Larry Grauerholz   Ashley Ivey   Ernst Lindell   Frank MacDonald
Roy Martin   Karl Miller   E.T. "Mo" Moriarty   James O'Brien
Joseph Peloquin   Fred Reain   Richard Reid William Rendall
Charles Screws   Robert Starzynski   Bob Titus   Donald Toye
Robert and Jenny Vandergriff   Audrey Vitkus   Cliff Williams
James Williams   Verne Woods

Published Sources

Adams, Murray, ed. *Against the Odds.* Australia: Royal Air Forces Escaping Society—Australian Branch, 1995.

Adamson, Iain. *The Great Detective.* London: Frederick Muller, 1987.

"Albert Edward Johnson." *Royal Air Forces Escaping Society–Australian Branch Newsletter,* February 10, 1998, 1.

Astor, Gerald. *The Mighty Eighth.* New York: Donald I. Fine Books, 1997.

Aubrac, Lucie. *Outwitting the Gestapo.* Lincoln: Univ. of Nebraska Press, 1993.

Bayliss, Colin. *No Flying Without Wings.* Perth, Australia: Colin Bayliss, 1994.

Bennett, Col. George Floyd. *Shot Down! Escape and Evasion.* Morgantown, W.Va.: Mediaworks 1992.

Blyth, Kenneth K. *Cradle Crew: Royal Canadian Airforce World War II.* Manhattan, Kans.: Sunflower Univ. Press, 1997.

Bodson, Herman. *Agent for the Resistance.* College Station, Texas: Texas A&M University, 1994.

Bott, Lloyd. *The Secret War From the River Dart.* Dartmouth, Eng.: Dartmouth History Research Group, 1997.

Bowman, Martin W. *Home By Christmas.* Wellingborough, Eng.: Patrick Stephens, Ltd., 1987.

Braddon, Russell, *Nancy Wake.* London: Cassell and Co., Ltd., 1956.

Brome, Vincent. *The Way Back.* New York: W.W. Norton and Co., 1958.

Brooks, Sir Richards. *Secret Flotillas.* London: HMSO, 1995.

Broussine, Georges. *L'Evade de la France Libre.* Paris: Tallandier, 2000.

Brusselmans-Daley, Yvonne. *Anne Brusselmans: Mission Accomplished.* Yvonne Brusselmans-Daley, n.d.

Bubenzer, Gus. "Shot Down In Occupied France: Memories of World War II." *Laurels,* fall 1988, 72–100.

Burkett, Molly. *Once Upon a Wartime V.* Hough-On-The-Hill, England: Barny Books, n.d.

Caine, Philip D. *Aircraft Down: Evading Capture in WW II Europe.* Washington, D.C.: Brassey's, 1997.

Carey, Brian Todd. "Operation Pointblank: Evolution of Allied Air Doctrine." *World War II,* November 1998, 50.

Caskie, Donald C. *The Tartan Pimpernel.* London: Oldbourne Book Co., Ltd., 1957.

Cheramy, Pat. "The Quiet Heroine." *The Weekly News,* London, May 19, 1973; May 26, 1973; June 2, 1973; June 9, 1973.

Concours Nationale de la Resistance et de la Deportation. *Prix Spécial à la Mémoire de: Madame Rosine Witton, Madame Berthe Fraser, Madame Zoe Evans.* Department du Pas de Calais: Concours Nationale de la Resistance et de la Deportation, n.d.

Cooper, Alan. *Free To Fight Again.* Shrewsbury, Eng.: Airlife Publishing Ltd., 1997.

Cosgrove, Edmund. *The Evaders.* Markham: Simon and Schuster of Canada, Ltd., 1976.

The Daily Telegraph (London), 1991, 1998.

Darling, Donald. *Secret Sunday.* London: William Kimber and Co., 1975.

David, Clayton. "AFEES History Dates Back to '64." *Air Forces Escape and Evasion Society Communications,* 8, spring 1995, 5.

Dear, Ian. *Escape and Evasion: Prisoner of War Breakouts and the Routes to Safety in World War II.* London: Arms and Armour Press, 1997.

De Champlain, Hélène. *The Secret War of Hélène De Champlain.* London: W.H. Allen and Co., Ltd., 1980.

De Vasselot de Régné, Odile. *Tombés Du Ciel: Histoire d'une Ligne D'évasion.* Paris: Odile De Vasselot de Régné, n.d.

Doughty, Robert A. and Ira D. Guber. *World War II: Total Warfare Around the Globe.* Lexington, Mass.: D.C. Heath and Co., 1996.

Dumais, Lucien. *The Man Who Went Back.* London: Leo Cooper, Ltd., 1975.

Foot, M.R.D. and J.M. Langley. *MI 9–Escape and Evasion.* Boston: Little, Brown and Co., 1980.

Ford, Herbert. *Flee the Captor.* Nashville: Southern Publishing Association, 1966.

Hawken, Stanley A. *Missing Presumed Dead.* Melbourne, Australia: Hill of Content, 1989.

Hawkins, Ian L., ed. *B-17s over Berlin.* Washington, D.C.: Brassey's, 1990.

Horning, Art. *In the Footsteps of a Winged Boot.* New York: Hearthstone, 1994.

Huguen, Roger. *Par Les Nuits Les Plus Longues.* Spézet, France: Coop Breizh, 1993.

Jiménez de Aberasturi, Jean Carlos. *En Passant La Bidassoa.* Biarritz, France: Société Atlantique d'Impression, 1996.

Jouan, Cecile. *Cométe: Histoire d'une Ligne d'Évasion.* Furnes, Belgium: Editions Du Belfroi, 1948.

Langley, J.M. *Fight Another Day.* London: William Collins Sons and Co., Ltd., 1974.

Lavender, Emerson, and Norman Sheffe. *The Evaders.* Toronto: McGraw-Hill Ryerson, 1992.

Lay, Beirne, Jr. *Presumed Dead.* New York, N.Y.: Dodd, Mead, 1980.

Le Nédélec, Alain. *Les Nuits de la Liberté.* St. Brieuc, France: Presses Bretonnes, 1993.

Le Telegramme (Ouest France), 1998.

Long, Helen, *Safe Houses Are Dangerous.* London: William Kimber and Co., 1985.

MacLean, Angus. "Escape From Europe." *The Canadian Aviation Historical Society,* fall 1997, 84–93, 116–18.

McBride, Charles C. *Mission Failure and Survival.* Manhattan, Kans.: Sunflower Univ. Press, 1989

Miller, Russell. *The Resistance.* World War II–Time-Life Books Series. Alexandria, Va.: Time-Life Books, Inc., 1979.

Moriarty, E.T. "Mo." *One Day Into Twenty Three.* E.T. Moriarty, 1987.

Murphy, Brendan. *Turncoat.* San Diego: Harcourt Brace Jovanovich, Publishers, 1987.

Murray, James. *A Faint Recollection.* Ed. Clarke M. Brandt. Aurora, Colo: Army Education Center, 1997.

Nahas, Gabriel. *Network to Freedom.* Paris: F.X. de Guibert, 1998.

Neal, John. *The Lucky Pigeon.* Paducah, Ky.: Turner Publishing, 1997.

Neave, Airey. *Little Cyclone.* London: Hamilton, 1957.

———. *Saturday at MI 9.* London: Hodder and Stoughton, 1969.

———. *They Have Their Exits.* Boston: Little, Brown and Co., 1953.

Nothomb, Jean François. "Excerpt from Memoirs of Jean François Nothomb." *Air Forces Escape and Evasion Society Communications,* 6, summer 1992, 5.

Nouveau, Louis. *Des Capitaines Par Milliers.* Paris, France: Calman-Lévy, 1958.

O'Hara, Kelly, ed. *Air Forces Escape and Evasion Society.* Paducah, Ky.: Turner Publishing, 1992.

Rafferty, Jean. "The Last of the Line." *Sunday Times Magazine,* London, June 11, 1989, 20–27.

Rawlings, Barney. *Off We Went Into the Wild Blue Yonder.* Washington, North Carolina: Morgan Printers, Inc., 1994.

Rings, Werner. *Life with the Enemy.* Garden City: Doubleday, 1982.

Rossiter, Margaret. *Women in the Resistance.* New York: Praeger Publishers, 1986.

Rougeyron, André. *Agents for Escape.* Translated by Marie Antoinette McConnell. Baton Rouge: Louisiana State Press, 1996

Rynhout, Bart M. *In Dienst Van Hun Naaste.* Rotterdam: Wyt Uitgevers, n.d.

Schoenbrun, David. *Soldiers of the Night.* New York: New American Library, Inc., 1980.

Shoemaker, Lloyd. *The Escape Factory: The Story of MIS-X.* New York: St. Martin's Press, 1990.

Shiber, Etta. *Paris Underground.* New York, N.Y.: Scribner's, 1943.

Skidmore, Kenneth. *Follow the Man With the Pitcher.* Merseyside, England: Countyvise, Ltd., 1996.

Smith, Richard M. *Hide and Seek With the German Army.* Parts I and II. Ed. Clarke M. Brandt. Aurora, Colo.: Army Education Center, 1995.

Speer, Albert. *Inside the Third Reich.* Trans. Richard and Clara Winston. New York: Galahad Books, 1970.

Spinning, William. *Operation Bonaparte.* Birmingham, Eng.: William H. Spinning, 1965.

Strong, Russel. *First over Germany.* Winston-Salem, N.C.: Russel Strong, 1990.

Tabor, Gail and Kathleen Ingley. "Leslie Says It Rained Aviators." *The Air Forces Escape and Evasion Society Communications,* 11, September 8, 1997, 5.

Tartiere, Drue. *The House Near Paris.* New York: Simon and Schuster, 1946.

Times (London), 1989.

Titus, Robert. *European Adventures.* Ed. Clarke M. Brandt. Aurora, Colo: Army Education Center, 1997.

Toye, Donald. *Flight from Munich.* Salt Lake City: Northwest Publishing, 1993.

Watts, George. *The Comet Connection: Escape from Hitler's Europe.* Lexington: Univ. Press of Kentucky, 1990.

Williams, James E. *One Soldier's Story.* Huntsville, Ala.: Hicklin Printing, 1984.

Wynne, Barry. *No Drums . . . No Trumpets.* London: Arthur Barker, Ltd., 1961.

Young, Gordon. *In Trust and Treason.* London: Studio Vista, Ltd., 1959.

Acknowledgments

It has been my good fortune to study the history of escape and evasion at a time when there is much renewed interest in the people who took part in World War II. However, the passing of time will soon take from us all of those who participated in the events that are recounted in this study. Many have already passed away, taking their stories with them. Among those who remain, I found a group of people gladly willing to share their experiences as evaders and helpers. The U.S. Air Forces Escape and Evasion Society (AFEES) was a valuable source for finding American evaders; it also supplied contacts with the Royal Air Force Escaping Society (RAFES) and its branches in Canada and Australia. These organizations embraced my project, providing contacts with former evaders from their countries' air forces. Many of those I contacted contributed memoirs, books, pictures, manuscripts, and correspondence detailing their experiences.

It was more difficult to locate the French helpers, but once I found them, they too were very generous with their stories, pictures, and precious mementos. I was touched by the many things they entrusted to me and by their offers of friendship. It was obvious that many had taken a great deal of time to answer my questions and ensure that I had all the information I needed. In light of the assistance they gave, I often felt my expressions of appreciation, however heartfelt, were inadequate. Without the cooperation of both the helpers and the evaders this work could not have been written.

The staffs at both the National Archives and the Alfred F. Simpson Historical Research Agency patiently provided guidance and assistance during the days I spent researching in their facilities. I am also very grateful to Bryan Skib of the Harlan Hatcher Graduate Library at University of Michigan–Ann Arbor, who arranged for me to have access to the Margaret Rossiter papers through Interlibrary Loan. Mississippi College reference librarian Susan Newman was a great help in finding books and other sources as well as helping to arrange the loan of the Rossiter papers. I am most appreciative for her interest and enthusiasm at every stage of this project.

Many people throughout the United States, England, France, Canada, Australia, Belgium, New Zealand, and Italy provided information, contacts, and support. In many instances, people I first contacted for research purposes became good friends. I knew I could always count on them to provide an answer to any problem that arose, whether finding an elusive address or simply providing encouragement. I am grateful to Tom Morgan, Jenny Johnston, Christopher Long, Georges Broussine, Tom Emsminger, Roger Stanton, and Michael Leblanc for all of their help and friendship. I am also deeply indebted to Ralph Patton, who answered countless questions and wrote numerous letters on my behalf, and to Lt. Col. Clarke Brandt, who supplied several accounts of evaders' experiences. Claude Hélias, whose translations of questionnaires and excerpts from French works were very helpful, provided additional assistance by facilitating contact with other French researchers. Belgian Air Force pilot Johan Samyn was also very helpful, taking several days of personal time to search through the Belgian archives, track down books, translate Dutch works, and contact people for me. He made it possible for me to access a group of files that I would otherwise have been unable to use and was kind enough to chauffeur me back and forth from the archives in Brussels. I greatly appreciate his efforts and those of his co-worker Maj. Eddy Lievrouw, who arranged for me to spend an afternoon visiting Dedée de Jongh in her home, as well as facillitated my participation in the ceremonies celebrating the sixtieth anniversary of Comet's organization in September 2000. Were it not for the supplies and support provided by Johan, Sgt. Jean-Luc Gilot, Sgt. Daisy Albrecht, and 1SM Bob Croes, I would have been unable to attempt the second crossing. I am grateful to them for allowing me the pleasure of the experience.

I also wish to thank Gordon and Janine Carter and Jean and Jeanne Tréhiou for the work they did to organize a reunion of former helpers in Plouha when they learned I would be visiting. They helped to make it an unforgettable visit.

Without the hours of translation done by my mother, Claudette Naggs, and Mississippi College student Adam Murray, much of the archival material and correspondence from the French helpers would have been useless to me. I deeply appreciate their taking time out of their already busy schedules to translate hundreds of pages of letters and documents. Karen Johannson put a great deal of time and effort into cleaning up and reprinting old photos as well as new ones. It was a great relief to know that my old photographs were safe in her hands. I appreciate all she has done, including venturing out on a Sunday morning at short notice and no cost to take a photograph for the book jacket.

As with any major project, the expenses involved with researching and writing were considerable. My mother provided a great deal of financial assistance, enabling me to travel to France and Belgium to experience firsthand what I had been studying. In the true spirit of a mother she even attempted to cross the Pyrenees Mountains with the intention of seeing me safely to the other side. I am also sincerely thankful for the efforts of Dr. Edward McMillan of Mississippi College, who instituted the Graduate Research Assistance program, which helped to defray expenses associated with translating documents and travel.

My husband, Steve, was helpful in many ways, from sorting out the complexities of the computer to cooking dinner when my single-track mind could not leave the 1940s long enough to do it myself. I also appreciate his patience as he followed me to conventions and presentations, endured my constant discussion of matters pertaining to escape and evasion, and played the roles of both Mom and Dad while I spent several weeks wandering around France. Though not a fascinated student of history himself, he bore my preoccupation with escape and evasion with great tolerance. It would have been difficult to engage in such a time-consuming and all-encompassing activity without his support.

My children, Brian and Catherine, have been wonderfully tolerant over being forced to share my attention with my studies. They have made sacrifices not usually required of children their age, and I am very proud of their mature understanding and acceptance of the lengthy hours I spent reading and writing. They will be happy to have more of my attention given to them, and I will be happy to give it, but I hope they have learned something from watching me work that will serve them well in the future.

It is difficult to express my gratitude to Dr. Kirk Ford for all he has done to contribute to the success of this project. As a friend and mentor, he has encouraged, supported, and guided me each step of the way, always willing to make suggestions, but allowing me the freedom to disagree. I could rely on his enthusiasm when I found a new contact or received new material, and he never seemed to tire of our endless conversations concerning the evasion networks. Each time I encountered difficulties, I could depend on him to graciously take time to look at the problem. Perhaps I am most thankful for Dr. Ford's belief in my ability to write the story of the evaders and helpers and to do it well. His unwavering confidence made me believe in myself and greatly influenced the final outcome of this study.

Index